SERBIA: THE HISTORY BEHIND THE NAME

STEVAN K. PAVLOWITCH

Serbia

The History behind the Name

HURST & COMPANY, LONDON

First published in the United Kingdom by
C. Hurst & Co. (Publishers) Ltd.,
38 King Street, London WC2E 8JZ
© 2002 by Stevan K. Pavlowitch
All rights reserved.
Printed in Malaysia

The right of Stevan K. Pavlowitch to be identified as the
author of this work has been asserted by him in accordance
with the Copyright, Designs and Patents Act, 1988

A British Library Cataloguing-in-Publication
Data Record is available for this book.

ISBNs
1-85065-477-8 casebound
1-85065-476-X paperback

CONTENTS

Foreword   *page* vii

Chapters

1. Shifting Serbias – Kings, Tsars, Despots and Patriarchs: from the beginning to the eighteenth century   1

2. Serbia Takes Root – The Liberators, Karageorge and Prince Miloš: 1804–1839   26

3. Serbia Becomes a State – From Autonomy to Independence: 1839–1878   41

4. Independent Serbia – Rival Dynasties and Political Parties: 1878–1914   65

5. Serbia at War – Between Destruction and Yugoslavia: 1914–1918   93

6. Serbia into Yugoslavia – Between the Two World Wars: 1918–1941   111

7. Fragments of Serbia – Victims, Resisters and Collaborators: 1941–1945   139

8. Serbia under Tito – Part of a Wider Communist Plan: 1945–1980   156

Contents

9. Serbia after Broz – From Tito's Apotheosis to Milošević's Consecration: 1980–1989	184
10. Serbia in Darkness – The Milošević Years: the 1990s	199
Conclusion: A Plea for Saint Guy	227
Bibliography	237
Index	243

MAPS

The medieval Serbian realm	6
The territorial expansion of Serbia and Montenegro in modern times	27
Serbia and the other Yugoslav lands on the eve of unification, 1918	112
The partition of Yugoslavia during the Second World War	140
The federated units of Yugoslavia, 1945–91	157

FOREWORD

This is not a history of Serbia; I would not know how to define Serbia through the ages. There has been no continuous polity or territory with that name. Serbias have come and gone, and they have moved about.

Nor is this a history of the Serbs; I would not know how to find them before the time when they stated what they believed they were in the 'nationality' box of their identity cards. And since they ebbed and flowed, I would be like Professor Bartleboom, the character of Alessandro Baricco's *Oceano mare* (Milan, 1993), who was trying to study where the sea ended. He wanted to write something precise, something 'that could go in an encyclopedia, so that people, when they read it, could understand that the sea ends, and how, independently of all that can happen around it ...'

Indipendentemente da tutto quello che può succedergli attorno, indipendentemente da ... That is precisely the problem. I had just written *A History of the Balkans*, because I felt the various territories and populations of the region could only be understood in that wider context of intertwined geography and history that encompasses them all. I could not isolate a dispersed group of people called 'Serbs', who lived with other people, who were rarely united even when they were all in one state, and place them under the microscope, without totally distorting their history. History is difficult enough to write without going through the tunnel vision and the fabulation of national history.

I have thus written an historical *essay* on the subject of 'Serbia', knowing that I could not attempt what is erroneously called an 'exhaustive' or 'definitive' *history*—not even a 'short' one. This is no more than a personal sketch. I have tried to look at the institutional forces, at the historical actors, and at the time-gaps that separate them, which have moulded entities that go by the name of 'Serbia'—the Nemanjić rulers, the church, the principality and the kingdom of modern times, unification within Yugoslavia, the nation and the republic of Tito's era, the disintegration of Communism and the collapse of Yugoslavia. I have tried to understand how groups of people were influenced by these forces through feudal, tribal or family links, church commemoration, folklore, imported ideologies, competing imperial policies, citizenship, education, military service, brainwashing, and by positive and negative discrimination, into feeling identified with the name.

These people rarely had one centre. There were discontinuities in their area of settlement. In 1918, when they all found themselves united in the kingdom of the Serbs, Croats and Slovenes, they differed as much among themselves as they did from the other Southern Slavs, and they were still as different in 1991 when the Socialist Federal Republic of Yugoslavia broke up. What is it that unites them? Is it the fact that they are Eastern Orthodox Serbo-Croat speakers or Serbo-Croat-speaking Eastern Orthodox Christians? the aspiration to unite into one state? the cult of common memories? mythical acts of heroism or mythical retreats?

It is often said (after a quotation attributed to Winston Churchill that I have never traced to a source) that the peoples of the Balkans—more recently, the Serbs—suffer from a surfeit of history. This is to confuse History, critical and controllable knowledge; Memory, the affective mythological construction of identity; and what J.H. Plumb called the Past (*The Death of the Past*, London, 1969), the manipulated History-and-Memory that is 'designed to control individuals, or motivate societies, or inspire classes'.

History has been read backwards, so as to give 'Serbian national history' a unique significance. This has been done by Serbian historiographers as by Western observers, within the usual framework of national reductionism. It is the sort of reductionism that leaves one with the feeling that Serbs (or, for that matter, Croats, English, French, and all the others at one time or another according to needs) had been created by God in His image on the sixth day, as related in some apocryphal national footnote to Genesis 1:27. It has also been done in the light of a changing present, which picks up certain episodes while ignoring others, and isolates them from developments elsewhere. National history thus becomes unique, and its outcome in our time is seen as inevitable.

Foreword

Outside chroniclers and commentators notice something called 'Serbia' when it makes the headlines, when its rebellions, its coups, its assassinations or its wars are such that they can fill the distant viewer with admiration or revulsion. If the outside viewer wants to know more, he looks for precedents.

In modern times, Serbia and the Serbs have been noticed during the Eastern Crisis of 1875–8, when the insurgents of Herzegovina and Bosnia had a good press; in 1903, when the gruesome murder of King Alexander Obrenović and Queen Draga shocked the courts and foreign ministries of the more conservative powers; in 1914–16, when gallant little Serbia stood up to, and was crushed by, the Central Powers, and when its cause was a good one, to be explained in schools and prayed for in churches; in 1941, when the Serbs were said to have done the same again by standing up to Hitler; and after Yugoslavia collapsed in 1991, when they were collectively seen as faceless war criminals, lookalikes of mispronounced President Milošević, Dr Karadžić and General Mladić.

Serbia has had its ups and downs. There were times, now forgotten, when the 'Spirit of Kosovo' was a good thing, exploited by British and French propagandists more than by Serbian ones. There were times when Serbian warriors were lauded, supported, armed and trained by Western governments, consultancies, agencies and non-governmental organizations. Even in the 1990s there were oscillations in Western attitudes, from integration at all costs to absolute disintegration, and to re-integration; from Milošević 'butcher of the Balkans' to Milošević 'guarantor of the peace in the Balkans'; from the older posture of achieving territorial compromise in order to preserve agreement between the Great Powers, to the newer feeling of pride at being both right and strong.

In difficult times, Serbian leaders and intellectuals have been prone to see the powers as pursuing clearly-devised and consistent aims, rather than as reacting to events 'in the Balkans'—a part of Europe that is still 'far away' even though it is 'in our backyard'. Likewise, politicians and experts in the West often see these Serbian leaders as following long-term strategies, rather than reacting to their perception of the policies of the powers.

In the chapters that follow I try to work out what are the elements that contribute to a Serbian strand in the history of the Balkans, to understand, not an alleged surfeit of history, but the history of a past that has not always been overcome. I have been confirmed in my opinion that 'Serbian history' cannot be studied in separation from its wider context, and that it is not unique. However, this is not the place to repeat what I have tried to do for the period 1804–1945 in my earlier book—to place specifically Serbian institutions, rulers, territories and population groups within the wider context of the history of the Balkans. To the extent that the period of the last ten years has indeed been unique, it is because most of the problems of unfinished historical business of the twentieth century, including most of the problems of the disintegration of Communism, have come together in what used to be Yugoslavia, especially in those parts of it inhabited by Serbs.

Serbs will have to come to terms with the truth of what happened during that decade, and live with plain History rather than with the Past. This is, in the first instance, the task of historians—to question, rather than provide answers. Needless to say, I have not come up with any answers, except that lies and illusions cause long-term damage, whereas knowledge and acceptance of the truth, however much it may hurt, makes easier the matter of choosing between the different possibilities offered by reality.

Writing this book has been a challenging and most difficult task, and at the end of it I say after my hero Alessandro Barrico's fictional scholar, Professor Ismael Bartleboom, who wrote to his non-existent future beloved: '*Mia adorata* [...] *il lavoro mi stanca e il mare si ribella ai miei ostinati tentativi di capirlo. Non avevo pensato che potesse essere così difficile stargli davanti.*'

Besides my publishers, C. Hurst & Co., three Serbian friends were insistent in pressing me to undertake the task. I shall not compromise them by naming them. I am, however, grateful to them for having forced me into yet another period of intensive study from which I have learnt much, even though I have grave doubts about the result. They are in no way responsible for it, and I do not even know whether they will like it.

Be it as it may, many other people have helped me during the two years it has taken me to write this book. I would particularly like to thank the following, in alphabetical order:

Dr Wendy Bracewell located references to written traces of various instances of what it was to be a Serb in eighteenth-century Habsburg marches. Professor Sima Ćirković, the foremost scholar of Serbia's medieval history, has been good enough to set me right over several aspects of the early history in chapter 1. Mr Dejan Djokić has been generous with his time and his green ink, in going over chapters 6 and 8–10. Dr Jasna Dragović-Soso provided some detailed information, and pointed out some howlers, in chapter 8. Dr Petre Guran enlightened me on the rôle of princely saints in medieval Europe. Mr Nenad Petrović's piercing eye and clear spectacles alerted me to the globe in Hans Holbein the Younger's 'Ambassadors'. Professor Tim Reuter told me what to read on Norse sagas. Father Paul Spellman helped me to find all that there is to be known on St Guy. Mr Bob Smith of the Cartographic Unit, University of Southampton, drew the maps. Mr Desimir Tošić, diligent and critical as ever, has scribbled over most of the initial draft.

Serbia: The History behind the Name is offered to my Serbian cousins, my Serbian friends and my Serbian colleagues.

Strasbourg, April 2001   ST. K. PAVLOWITCH

1

SHIFTING SERBIAS – KINGS, TSARS, DESPOTS AND PATRIARCHS

FROM THE BEGINNING TO THE EIGHTEENTH CENTURY

Much to the chagrin of protogenetic nationalists, little is known of the origins of the present-day populations of the Balkans, of those who were there 'at the beginning' and those who arrived during the struggle of the Barbarian peoples against the Roman empire. The Southern Slavs came from an area beyond the Carpathians, vaguely located as being between Warsaw and Kiev. Caught up in the movements of other tribes, they swept across the Danube from the beginning of the sixth century in search of new land, dispersing and dividing into many groups. After a century or so they gradually turned into settlers, and completely modified the ethnic structure of the peninsula. They carried with them the names of leading tribes such as Croats and Serbs; the latter spread to those who set themselves up in the valleys and basins south of the Danube between the rivers Bosna and Ibar. The story of their settlement as neighbours of Byzantium was recorded early in the tenth century, from the traditions that they themselves had kept, by the historian emperor Constantine Porphyrogenitus.

They were not drawn together until permanently converted to Christianity, and thus opened up to civilization, by Byzantine missionaries in the ninth century. The link to the Eastern church through the archbishopric of Ohrid in the eleventh century did not prevent Western influences coming into the Serbian lands from the coastal towns and the contemporary Latin archbishopric of Bar (Antivari).

Embryonic polities linked to the ancestral tribal Serbian name had begun to emerge from the seventh century, in eastern Bosnia and in the southern Dinaric uplands. Little is known of them until the ninth century when more permanent names appear, in Zeta (around Scutari, the present-day Shköder in Albania, and towards the southern Adriatic coast) and especially in Raška (Rascia in Western sources, around Ras, near the present-day Novi Pazar). Venice and the Magyars had diverted their rulers' ambitions from the Adriatic and the plains to the nominally Byzantine lands of the Morava-Vardar corridor running through the central Balkans. By the eleventh century the emperor linked them to his authority through titles and marriages.

The turning point came at the end of the twelfth century with Nemanja (c.1113–99), the ruler of Raška. As a result of the wars waged between Hungary and Byzantium for predominance in the region, he managed to wriggle out of Byzantine authority and avoid being subordinated to the king of Hungary like his counterparts of Croatia and Bosnia.

From his base in the Ibar valley he incorporated Zeta, took over the plain of Kosovo where his predecessors had made incursions, and expanded eastwards to the Morava valley and up the coast from the mouth of the river Drin to beyond Dubrovnik (Ragusa), which always retained its political identity. However, a certain duality was retained between the 'Serbian' or 'Rascian' lands and the 'maritime' lands. A few years before his death in 1199, Nemanja retired to his monastic foundation of Studenica before withdrawing to Mount Athos as the monk Simeon. There he joined his youngest son, the monk Sava (1176–1236), and together they founded the monastery of Hilandar.[1]

Nemanja had entrusted various regions to brothers and sons. There followed a power contest which was won by his younger son Stephen (1196–1228), who fully exploited the fascination of the West with Byzantium and the Holy Land which had hardened the religious differences between Rome and Constantinople. When the Fourth Crusade carved up the empire and plundered its capital in 1204, he played off Latin, Greek, Bulgarian and Hungarian rivals. Divine will expressed through the emperor in Constantinople or the pope in Rome was a necessary condition for kingship. A contemporary of Henry III of England and of Philip Augustus of France, Stephen Nemanjić had been married to a daughter of Alexius III Angel, and had a Byzantine title, but had not neglected his links with the papacy and with Venice.

---

[1] Rastko Nemanjić had adopted the name of the sixth-century Saint Sabbas, one of the great figures of Eastern monasticism, and the founder of a monastery in the Jordan valley that can claim an unbroken history to the present day.

In 1217 (by then remarried to a doge's granddaughter) he obtained a royal crown from Rome, which emphasized his independence from Byzantium, and enabled him to take the title of 'king of all Serbia',[2] and to be known to posterity as Stephen the First-Crowned. He then proceeded to obtain ecclesiastical independence from the ecumenical patriarch.

Serbia was under the archbishop of Ohrid, in the despotate of Epirus—a Byzantine survivor in Europe and a rival to the emperor's remaining power in Asia Minor. Sava, who had been acting as Stephen's political adviser, went to Nicaea in 1219, where the exiled emperor and patriarch had taken up residence. In exchange for the moral support given to the Nicaeans, he obtained the establishment of an archbishopric for the dominions of the Serbian king. This was an independent archbishopric under its own head—an autocephalous church, according to the canons and the practice of the Eastern church—and Sava was consecrated as its first archbishop.

In ecclesiastical matters Sava was a staunch 'Easterner'. His action counterbalanced his royal brother's flirtation with the 'West'. As archbishop he essentially took up again the spirit of the Byzantine missionaries who had brought Christianity closer to the Balkan Slavs. With his Athonite training he set up new dioceses based on monasteries, and relied on monks for the formation of his clergy. Though now clearly anchored in the Eastern church, Serbia kept a moderate stance towards the Catholic world. Relations with the papacy were not broken; the Latin faithful in the king's dominions and the work of their clergy were not interfered with.

The connexion between dynasty and church contributed to binding the Nemanjić lands. Originally military chieftains, and whatever their way of life otherwise, Balkan rulers looked up to a model imbued with the monastic spirit that implied a link between heaven and earth. The cult of local dynastic saints was an innovation willed by the princes. Serbia's patrons were soon Saint Simeon—Nemanja, already venerated as a saint on Athos the year after his death, and translated to Serbia—followed by Saint (once Archbishop) Sava. Rulers founded and made donations to churches and monasteries

---

[2] The Southern Slavs used the word *kralj* (Carolus). Sources disagree as to whether Stephen was crowned by a papal legate in 1217 or by his brother, the then Archbishop Sava, in 1220. Could he have been crowned twice, to satisfy both East and West? Serbia's medieval kings after him took the additional royal name Stephen—from the Greek 'Stephanos' (crowned).

both in and outside their dominions, from Rome and Bari to Jerusalem and Mount Sinai.

The Serbian realm continued to develop under Stephen's successors, in spite of power struggles between royal kinsmen, the reaction of great feudatories, and the intervention of neighbouring rulers. Its borders moved to the Save and Danube, along with the first wave of northward colonization, even if some of these territories (with Belgrade) tended to be held separately and under the suzerainty of the king of Hungary. They expanded down the Morava-Vardar corridor into northern Macedonia, interrupting there the process of Hellenization.

Such development both favoured and was favoured by the increase in royal revenues. Initially hampered by its location away from fertile lowlands, the sea and important rivers, Serbia's economy had been essentially pastoral. Mines were now exploited, trading centres set up, roads and bridges built. The main rôle in the development of non-agrarian activities was played by foreigners, traders from Dubrovnik and German miners from Transylvania. Mines, crafts, trade, customs and coinage came to contribute more to the king's revenues than his personal domain. The adoption of the Byzantine practice of life grants of land specifically for service provided military support less subject to the whims of vassals, and increased means allowed the king to hire mercenary troops.

The accession of King Stephen Dušan in 1331 followed on the defeat of Bulgaria in the battle for power in the Balkans. Byzantium was collapsing in civil strife, with Venetians, Genoese and Ottomans intervening as allies to its factions. The new Serbian monarch joined in. His Serbian and Albanian barons were eager for spoils. Between 1334 and 1348 a series of expeditions doubled the extent of his dominions: they now stretched from the Danube to the Gulf of Corinth, from the Adriatic to the Aegean. As the strongest ruler in the Balkans, and with most of Byzantium's European territories in his hands, Dušan aimed to replace the worn-out empire with a powerful Serbian-Hellenic state. He used Byzantine ceremonial and titles, styled himself 'king of Serbia and Romania' (the land of the Romans) and 'lord of almost all the empire of Romania'. At the turn of 1345/6 he proclaimed himself 'emperor of the Serbs and the Greeks'.

He knew that this called for consecration by the church, and coronation by a patriarch. He thus raised the Serbian archbishop to the rank of patriarch of the Serbs and the Greeks, with the consent of the Bulgarian patriarch of Turnovo and of the archbishop of

Shifting Serbias – kings, tsars, despots and patriarchs

Ohrid, but not of the ecumenical patriarch in Constantinople, who excommunicated them all. On Easter Sunday 1346, he had himself crowned emperor at Skopje, which had been the Serbian ruler's main residence since the days of Dušan's grandfather. In 1349 he issued a code of laws that drew heavily on the Byzantine model in matters of state and church, blended with Serbian practice. At this time Edward III reigned in England, Philip VI of Valois in France, and the Hundred Years' War had started.

The Nemanjić dynasty had pursued a quest for Balkan power, using the rivalry between Rome and Constantinople, the eclipse of Byzantium by the Latin Crusaders in the thirteenth century, and the subsequent contests both within the empire and between its Western rivals. Their Serbia was steeped in Byzantine civilization. Its church liturgy and canons were derived from the Greek models; Greek was much used by the royal chancery and by leading churchmen. Yet Dušan's code was in Serbian, the generally hagiographic literature remained written in Church Slavonic, and the use of the Cyrillic script spread to his Greek dominions. Athos was more than the spiritual centre of the Eastern Orthodox world: it was the spiritual cradle of the Nemanjić realm, and Serbia's Athos-moulded ecclesiastics were not reconciled to the break with Constantinople.

All the same, Nemanjić Serbia was never turned exclusively to the East. Its rulers had looked to both centres of Christendom until they realized the potent force of integration provided by the Byzantine concept in its local adaptation. Not having experienced at first hand the devastations wrought by the crusades, they had no great feeling of schism. For them the division was still essentially a political one. Indeed, they participated with Catholic clergy in joint efforts to combat the Bogomil heresy. Dušan, like his predecessors, made donations to churches in Italy as he did to Athonite monasteries,[3] but he did not become a saint.

Constant links with both sides of the Adriatic had brought in Western influences. There were Western merchants, mercenaries and adventurers in Serbia who affected the life-style of nobles and of native townsfolk, mostly merchants and craftsmen. More important, builders, craftsmen and artists formed in Western ways came up from

---

[3]In particular to the basilica in Bari that enshrines the remains of Saint Nicholas, to perpetuate prayers for his forefathers, for himself and for his family (see Gerardo Cioffari, OP, *Gli zar di Serbia, la Puglia e San Nicola*, Bari: Centro Studi Nicolaiani, 1989).

6　　　　　　　　　　　　　　Serbia

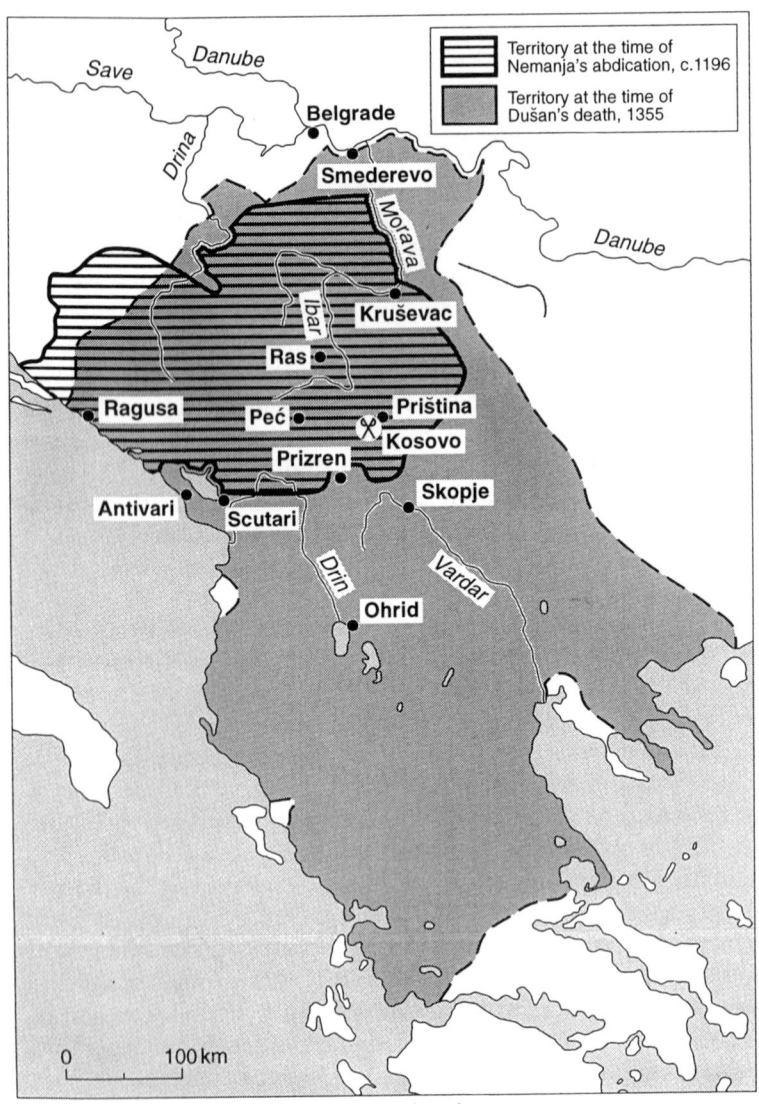

The medieval Serbian realm.

the coast. The monuments of the Serbian schools of architecture, with their original blend of Byzantine and Romanesque, their sculptural decorations and their frescoes (which have also immortalized the royal saints), somehow survive to this day in the great churches of Studenica, Žiča, Mileševo, Sopoćani, Dečani, Gračanica, Prizren ...

By the time Tsar Dušan had reached his apex, the Ottoman threat gave an added dimension to his links with the West. Turkish mercenaries had been used by Byzantium's rival claimants. Dušan himself had maintained links with Sultan Orhan. When the Turks took Gallipoli in 1354, he realized that they threatened his own objectives. Preparing his expedition against Constantinople, he opened negotiations with Venice for naval help, and with Pope Innocent IV at Avignon to be appointed 'captain' of a crusading coalition against the Infidel Turks. For that he was ready to recognize the pope as Christ's vicar. The West, however, was generally reluctant to go along, and Hungary was opposed to the venture, which was stopped in its tracks by Dušan's sudden death in December 1355, at the age of forty-seven, during his last campaign against Byzantium.

In spite of the church, of the dynasty and of Dušan's personality, his dominions were not integrated. The centre of gravity had shifted to the Greek lands, while the tsar's son Uroš formally and symbolically administered the Serbian lands with the title of king. Dušan kept the existing order in the newly-conquered Byzantine territories so as to legitimize his usurpation, and they were never really part of Serbia. The great lords held on to their territories. There were old Serbian fiefs and new Greek military benefits. The nobles never turned into a closely-knit estate, for they were too heterogeneous.

Monasteries received extensive lands and immunities, but there were divisions in the clergy too, with displaced Greek clergy, and Serbian clergy saddened by the anathema. Ethnic communities were also granted immunities—Vlach shepherds, German miners, Latin merchants. The tsar's relatives and the most powerful lords behaved in the manner of small rulers. Dušan's power was dependent on the loyalty of his grandees. His conquests had come about too quickly for him to be able to weld the disparate elements of his dominions; they had undermined the slow development of the Nemanjić state.

The authority of Dušan's nineteen-year-old son Uroš was immediately ruined by the powerful feudatories. Dušan's half-brother Simeon in Epirus laid claim to the succession in the Greek lands, stressing his mother's Paleologus inheritance, as 'emperor of the Greeks, of the Serbs and of the whole of Albania'. The Mrnjavčević brothers, Uglješa and Vukašin, held enormous territories in Macedonia. While Uroš remained in the northern, Serbian, lands, it was Vukašin in the south who called himself 'king of Serbia', as co-ruler with the tsar. In the north-west Nikola Altomanović extended his domain from Rudnik to the sea, with most of the Drina valley and Kosovo.

Uglješa was the first of the magnates to face the Ottoman threat. He teamed up with his brother, and turned to Byzantium, for a reconciliation with the mother church, and for military help. In 1371, the year of Uroš's death, which also marked the end of the Nemanjić dynasty, he finally obtained reconciliation with the patriarchate of Constantinople, for his territories only. No other help was forthcoming, however, as the Byzantines were divided between those who sought Western aid and those who were ready to give in to the Ottomans. It was thus on their own that the Mrnjavčević brothers set off against the Turks, only to be defeated and killed in battle on the river Maritsa.

So decisive was the defeat, which changed the map of Macedonia, that the pope tried and failed to form a league for the defence of Christendom. The Byzantine emperor had to become a vassal of the Ottoman sultan, and one by one the magnates of Macedonia followed. Vukašin's son Marko (the legendary hero of later folk narratives throughout the South Slav world) took up the title of 'king of Serbia', but as a Turkish vassal and on a much reduced territory in western Macedonia, until his death in battle in 1395. With the loss of the Vardar valley and the struggle for power among the disunited Serbian lords, the line of defence moved up to the more central regions of the former Nemanjić empire, where the most prominent were Lazar Hrebeljanović and Nikola Altomanović.

Freed from the overbearing shadow of Serbia, and once removed from the Turkish advance, Bosnia reached its peak, and remained there for half a century before it too slid into feudal anarchy and was taken over. Set between Croatia and Serbia, its religious identity ill-defined, it had started on an independent development which reached its high point under Tvrtko I Kotromanić (1353–91).

Having extended his dominions to Serbian territories, he used his kinship with the Nemanjić dynasty in order to claim its inheritance. In 1377 he was crowned king at Mileševo monastery, the burial site of Saint Sava and the centre of his cult, in newly-acquired Serbian territory, with the ceremonial and titles used by Nemanjić rulers. He styled himself 'king of Serbia, of Bosnia and of the Coast'. He ruled over a disjointed region, with Orthodox and Catholic populations, its nobility increasingly prone to the Bogomil heresy.

Tvrtko was a friend and ally of Lazar Hrebeljanović (1329–89), with whom he had eliminated the power, and shared the lands, of Nikola Altomanović in 1373. From his original holdings south-east of Priština, Lazar consolidated his authority over the central region of Serbia and built his fortified court city at Kruševac. Djurdje Balšić was lord of Zeta, and Vuk Branković, Lazar's son-in-law, was lord of Kosovo. Everything south and east of Kosovo was already under Ottoman rule.

Unlike his contemporaries Tvrtko and Marko, Prince (*knez*) Lazar never claimed to be 'king of Serbia', even though he was married to a Nemanjić relative. However, he did consciously take up something of the Nemanjić inheritance, hence the appellation of 'Tsar Lazar' by which popular tradition remembers him. The support of the church was essential, and he too worked for reconciliation with Constantinople, as his lands, along with the Branković and Balšić lands, were still under anathema. In 1375, thanks to Lazar's efforts and the mediation of several important monastic figures, the patriarch of Constantinople agreed to rescind the excommunication and recognize a Serbian patriarchate. All the important territorial lords had agreed on an elderly hermit who had come from Athos, and who was duly elected as the new patriarch of Serbia by a local council at Peć.

Lazar was now acknowledged as successor to the Nemanjić tradition, if not to the title. The territory over which he ruled was less than a quarter of Dušan's one-time empire, but he was the most powerful of the Serbian lords who were not yet subjects of the Ottoman sultan. Stabilized, bolstered by the support of the church and by important mineral resources, Lazar's principality acted as a magnet for refugees from south and east, clerics, writers, artists, architects, Greeks and Bulgars as well as Serbs. It became a thriving cultural centre.

It was natural that Lazar should co-ordinate resistance to increased Turkish incursions, in alliance with Tvrtko and with neighbouring lords. Lazar and Tvrtko were caught between the sultan and his vassals on one side, and King Sigismund of Hungary and his supporters on the other. In 1389, Sultan Murad moved to attack the strategic area of Kosovo, an important crossroads and the richest source of mineral wealth in the Balkans.

There, on the narrower field of Kosovo near Priština, on 15 June (St Guy's day, or Vidovdan), he confronted a coalition of Serbian lords under Lazar, with contingents sent by King Tvrtko of Bosnia, and a diverse collection of knights and other warriors that included Albanians, Vlachs, Bulgars and sundry opponents of Sigismund of Luxemburg who had sought refuge in Tvrtko's realm. The battle was not as catastrophic as the later legend would suggest. Closer to a draw, it was nevertheless a great massacre in which both Lazar and Murad died, and which impressed contemporaries as a portentous event.

Ottoman expansion was stopped for a while by Tamerlane's victories in Asia, which allowed the survival of a belt of vassal principalities in Europe. Protected from further plundering, paying tribute, and providing military help in Asia, they continued to live by their own tradition for as long as the Ottomans were not able to launch the final onslaught. Serbia recovered under Lazar's son Stephen, whose youngest sister was given in marriage to the new sultan.

The battle of Kosovo gave rise to legends so soon after the event that its basic facts were quickly obscured. Sources stress the martyrdom of the Serbian prince (and of the Ottoman sultan), but they were not intended to provide objective accounts of the encounter. The first Serbian references to it are to be found in panegyrics in memory of Lazar. The church had supported him as God's chosen successor to the Nemanjić dynasty who had restored stability in troubled times. The cult of the fallen prince, quickly elevated to sainthood, was meant to combat a deep feeling of pessimism.

The aftermath of the battle was a period of crisis for those who had survived it, and the monastic authors of the panegyrics sought to interpret the events in as positive a light as possible. Lazar's death was thus seen as a martyr's sacrifice for the Christian faith, and one that established a new link with Heaven. Eventually, to make it bearable, physical defeat was turned into spiritual victory. The defeat on the battlefield was then attributed to the alleged treachery of Lazar's ally Vuk Branković, who had survived, and held out into the 1390s.[4]

The cult of the Holy Prince encouraged a sense of hope and served the interests of his successor. Stephen Lazarević managed to reunify lands; he received most of the Branković territory from the Turks, and then inherited Zeta in 1421 on the death of the last Balšić. Along with other Christian tributaries, he fulfilled his obligations to Sultan Bayezid, in Europe as well as in Asia. Freed by Tamerlane's

---

[4] As the popular legend evolved from the religious cult, events and personalities became so distorted that it was not before the end of the nineteenth century that critical historians began to see the real contours of the period. On the history and legend of the battle of Kosovo see Thomas A. Emmert, *Serbian Golgotha: Kosovo 1389*, New York: Columbia University Press, 1990.

Shifting Serbias – kings, tsars, despots and patriarchs

crushing victory over Bayezid at Angora (Ankara) in 1402, Stephen returned home by way of Constantinople, where he received from the emperor the title of despot.

Having started as the sultan's vassal, and obtained the despotate from the Byzantine emperor, Stephen Lazarević turned to the king of Hungary, Sigismund of Luxemburg, whose suzerainty he accepted along with extensive land. This included Belgrade, which he adopted as his capital, and the Bosnian silver mine of Srebrnica. Reconciled to his surviving Branković relative Djuradj, he returned to Ottoman vassalage to help Bayezid's son Mehmed I set himself up on the throne in 1413, and enjoyed twelve years of peace.

Trade thrived again. New monasteries and churches were built in the northern lands that had become the core of Serbia. In Despot Stephen's great fortified foundation of Manasija manuscripts were copied and illuminated, liturgical chants composed, chronicles and genealogies written which linked the Nemanjić kings to Rome and recorded their worldly activities. The last rays of Serbia's medieval culture glowed in those first decades of the fifteenth century, just as the Renaissance was starting in Florence.

The childless Despot Stephen was succeeded in 1421 by his Branković kinsman Djuradj (c. 1375–1456), Lazar's grandson. Confirmed by Sigismund, Djuradj set up court in his new fortress of Smederevo on the Danube. He also had to accept increased commitments to the sultan, who had taken Niš and Kruševac. The patriarch, whose seat had moved between Žiča and Peć, joined the despot at Smederevo[5] as intermittent Turkish-Hungarian warfare started up again in the 1430s, increasingly over Serbia. For a few years Djuradj was actually in exile, until a truce with Hungary restored him, but as a full tributary of the sultan, helping in the conquest of Constantinople.

The last Balkan principalities had survived wedged between Hungary and Turkey. Despot Djuradj's final years were but a temporary pause in the Ottoman advance, which resumed as soon as Constantinople had fallen in 1453. When he died three years later,

---

[5]The Serbian archbishop, or archbishop of all the Serbian lands, had originally resided at Žiča, but since the monastery there had suffered from troubles in the area in the thirteenth century, the building of a new monastic complex on land belonging to Žiča at Peć had been started. Serbian primates had since then moved between the two, and the patriarchate was no less fixed to a see than the earlier archbishopric. Miodrag Al. Purković's *Srpski patrijarsi srednjega veka* (Düsseldorf: Srpska pravoslavna eparhija zapadnoevropska, 1976) has analysed the question on the basis of a thorough reading of all available sources.

most of his despotate was already controlled by the Turks. Infighting over what remained between his heirs and vassals, divided between pro-Hungarians and pro-Ottomans, led to the fall of Smederevo in 1459. Bosnia went down in 1463. Under native lords there remained only the mountainous area of Zeta north of the Bay of Kotor, soon to be known as Montenegro (Crna Gora), which kept up the struggle until the end of the century.

The Serbian realm had been a shifting one, moving from eastern Bosnia in the west to Macedonia and further southeast, and then again from south to north, as the power of Byzantium oscillated, as its Bulgarian rival rose and fell, and as the Ottoman Turks advanced. It had never covered all that territory in any one time. The Nemanjić kingdom had come into being and expanded at a time when the Balkans as a whole were becoming ever more linked to the economy of Western Europe, but it was not able to take over from the dying Byzantine empire. Its fragmentation created a power vacuum which drew the Turks up through Macedonia into Europe.

It had maintained itself longer and better than the other South Slav polities. And yet, even though it faced far less religious division than they did, and even though it enjoyed the support of its own autocephalous Orthodox church, it was never as politically centralized as some of its rulers might have desired, or as ethnically homogeneous as later romantic perceptions would presume.

The medieval kingdoms bore names linked to their rulers' affiliations—remembered, supposed or desired. The names were to a certain extent passed on to the vassals longest under them, and to the cultured clerics who wrote about them. But below them who had any conception of belonging to a 'nation'? To the extent that some did, it was of belonging to a medieval community linked to lineage or territory, not to a later-modern romantic or revolutionary 'nation'.

The model for political integration was never based on an ethnic identity. All these realms sought to reproduce if not actually to replace other more established and more divinely or historically ordained polities. Ethnic groups, where they intermingled, coexisted, with scant evidence of long-standing hostility. Rulers did not think in terms of ethnic consolidation. The rulers of medieval Serbia simply pursued a policy of imperial expansion; they both won and lost territories.

They never had the apparatus to exercise central control. The Nemanjić kings; Lazar as bearer of their heritage; and the despots who came after him did, however, produce the framework for a culture that can be called Serbian because it was linked to the Serbian realm and its rulers. That culture was both received from Byzantium and widely open to the achievements of the Western world. It accompanied the pursuance of a systematic dynastic policy, carried out by relying on the twin spiritual and material pillars of the church and of natural resources, on monasteries, mines and fairs. That policy, however, remained without long-term political consequences. The material pillar did not have the time to develop, but the spiritual pillar survived. Only to the extent that the dynastic policy blended into church tradition did it somehow pass into the faithful's collective memory.

What was forgotten thereafter for a long time, however, was that between the twelfth and fifteenth centuries the whole Balkan peninsula, and Serbia in particular, had been a bridge between East and West. This was forgotten as Serbian feudal society gradually dissolved, partly eliminated in warfare, rebellion and repression, partly included for a time in the new Ottoman order, partly taking refuge in the mountains of Zeta, in the towns of Dalmatia, and across the rivers in the devastated frontier zone of Hungary. The Ottoman invasion had been resisted; it had also been accepted as inevitable. It had even been welcomed as bringing in its wake the restoration of order after a long period of instability.

The new order came about gradually. It rested on the right of the sultan to exploit and defend all sources of wealth, and on his duty to maintain harmony between social estates and religious-ethnic groups. The office-holders shared in the revenues of the imperial possessions in return for service; they were the 'Ottomans'. The *sipahi* landlord was an officer who supplied a number of horsemen, in proportion to the size of his *timar*—the holding which provided him with an income. The whole economic potential was placed in the service of the empire and of its military enterprise, thus interrupting the trend to general European lines. The new order disrupted the grain-growing lowlands, favoured animal husbandry, and caused the decline of mining.

The conquest was at first characterized by accommodation. The greater part of the population continued to live according to its old ways. Numerous native Christian nobles were included among the *timar* holders, but the process of removing them—starting from the south and with the best lands—accelerated in the sixteenth century as the Turks completed their conquest.

After the fall of Bosnia the Hungarian King Mathias Corvinus had set up defensive frontier areas manned by refugees from Serbia, as the nobility crossed into his dominions. To ensure their loyalty he even restored the title of despot, with grants of extensive estates, for a descendant of Despot Djuradj. For about a century until 1537 there were Serbian despots who helped in the defence of Hungary. The fiction of a Serbian polity thus survived, along with the name 'Serbia' on European maps.[6]

Ottoman expansion brought about the greatest demographic changes since the settlement of the Slavs. The wars were accompanied by devastation; newly-conquered territories were depopulated and thus ready to take a subsequent overspill from the mountainous south. People moved out of Macedonia with the remnants of the Serbian realm. They moved out of the way of armies, and were also resettled for strategic and political reasons. They withdrew into the uplands. They went north and west, to southern Hungary, Bosnia, Croatia, Slavonia and Dalmatia. They were welcomed to till and defend ravaged border areas. The Turks too brought in settlers from the more mobile but poorer pastoral populations of their earlier conquests; they used Serbian soldiers on the Hungarian border.

There were local migrations to avoid hunger, disease, retaliation for outbreaks, or periodic conscription of Christian boys for conversion and slave service in the sultan's administration and in his élite janissary infantry. Mountains became refuges at times of danger, and population reserves at other times. Conditions in the Dinaric uplands had favoured a semi-nomadic and patriarchal way of life which had been hardly touched by feudalism. Each successive wave of migrants in and out of them rekindled historical memories and at the same time carried forward the process of mixing populations. Traditions and dialects were combined, but never integrated because of the division between dominant powers and religions. While those who converted to Islam were tied to the Ottoman order, Orthodox and Catholics would in time become identified with Serbs and Croats respectively.

Belgrade had fallen to the Turks in 1521, five years before Hungary's defeat at Mohács in 1526, and eight years before they were stopped

---

[6]As, for instance, in a detail of Hans Holbein the Younger's painting 'The Ambassadors' in the National Gallery, London; on the ambassadors' globe 'Servia' appears as the area south of the middle Danube.

Shifting Serbias – kings, tsars, despots and patriarchs

in front of the Habsburgs' capital Vienna, in 1529. The greater part of the medieval kingdom of Hungary—including its Croatian-Slavonian adjunct—was then incorporated into the Ottoman empire, and the Habsburg succession was acknowledged over what remained of it.

As more and more refugees were incorporated into the Habsburg defence system, they left behind the best of the lowland clearings. The forested interior of Serbia proper discouraged settlement by Turks, but the depressions of Kosovo attracted the pastoral population from the mountains of Albania, especially as the latter became converted to Islam. Because it is not easy to distinguish between Serbs and Albanians among departing or remaining Christians, the emphasis of later scholarship has been placed on outgoing Christians and incoming Muslims.

Towns became 'Turkish'. There was a break in the urban culture in so far as towns became military and administrative centres in which the Muslim Ottoman element predominated, even if mostly of native origin, with non-Muslim but non-native traders and craftsmen—Greeks, Armenians, Jews and Gypsies. The urban environment was one of garrison and government, of army-geared crafts and of transit trade, and one that attracted those who wanted to gain money or status. Belgrade had some 40,000 inhabitants by 1632.

Christians were tolerated, as were Jews, and organized as *millets*—communities that were self-governing as far as anything outside the sphere of government was concerned. The vast majority formed a world apart from the ruling Ottomans. Catholics, linked to the Western enemies of the Turks, were at a disadvantage compared to the Orthodox, who were no great threat until Russia became a powerful factor in international relations. The Ottoman rulers allowed the Orthodox church to get on with its own business, and even put it to good use, for as long as it loyally performed its task. Yet all those who wanted personal advancement or simply to retain their status took up the religion of the new masters, particularly in towns.

Converts were seen as having 'become Turks'. They could serve in the army and administration. Many made their way up. The most famous was Mehmet Pasha Sokollu, or Sokolović (*c.*1505–79), an Orthodox Christian from Višegrad in Bosnia who became all-powerful grand vizier and son-in-law of Sultan Suleyman II, at a time when there were so many Serbs in the corridors of power that the business of state at the Porte—as the sultan's government was known—was often conducted in their language. This was even more the case in cross-border correspondence and talks between Habsburg and Ottoman governors and generals.[7]

The archbishopric of Ohrid had been the first Orthodox jurisdiction to come under the Turks at the end of the fourteenth century. As they advanced, they extended it at the expense of the declining Serbian patriarchate, which was eventually reunited with Ohrid sometime before 1540. Yet in 1557 the patriarchate was restored with its see at Peć. Not only had all the lands of the one-time Serbian realm been reunited under Turkish rule, but most of Hungary had been conquered as well. Serbs had taken a large part in the wars on both sides, and the sultan was persuaded by the Serbian lobby around Mehmet Pasha to place them under a spiritual authority which he could control.

A kinsman of Mehmet Pasha, the Athonite monk Makarije, was made archbishop of Peć, patriarch and ethnarch of the Serbs. His church was again autocephalous, with its largest area ever, stretching from present-day eastern Bulgaria and northern Macedonia across Serbia, Montenegro, Bosnia and Herzegovina, with some forty dioceses. With almost all of the sultan's Orthodox Slavs under its wing, this sole surviving institution of the Nemanjić monarchy continued the development and the extension of a Serbian consciousness.

It soon provided a well-organized framework for its faithful over all the European lands controlled by the Turks, and remained across Hungarian and Venetian borders even after the tide had receded. It acted on behalf of the 'Serbian nation', and spread the name 'Serb'. It fact, one could say that it was only then that something approaching a Serbian ethnic consciousness appeared. The patriarchate took up again its cultural activities, albeit in much reduced form, with several printing presses, copying workshops, and the compilation of chronicles and lives. Even the building, restoration and painting of churches revived.

It was in this context that the battle of Kosovo became the most important event in the historical memory of Serbs. The cult of Lazar the Martyr had actually lost much of its strength with the death of

---

[7]Another Ottomanized Sokolović, Ferhad Pasha, was governor of Bosnia and of Turkish Hungary. In the early 1580s he built in Banjaluka (today the seat of government of the Serbian Republic in Bosnia and Herzegovina) the beautiful mosque named after him. It more or less survived world wars and earthquakes, only to be destroyed by Serbs in 1993. Many other places of worship, Christian and Muslim, were destroyed in the wars of the Yugoslav succession after 1991.

Shifting Serbias – kings, tsars, despots and patriarchs

Stephen Lazarević, followed by the collapse of the despotate, as Ohrid with its mostly Greek prelates took over. However, grass-roots culture had added to religious rituals to produce a tradition of folk poetry which invented its own version of history, and became as famous as Icelandic and Norse sagas. Poems transmitted anonymously and orally, from village to village and from generation to generation, sang of love and death and of past events and figures. Facts and chronology were confused over time and through exposure to new environments, until they were recorded in the nineteenth century.

The early religious cult of Saint Lazar the Prince was lost in the legend as, in the most important of the epic cycles, the battle of Kosovo came to symbolize the end of a golden past and, eventually, the hope of a new future. It was in the central mountainous regions that it became the watershed between freedom and servitude, with its images of heroism and treachery.

Evolved from the end of the fifteenth century, this version of the legend came to be related throughout the Balkans, by Muslims and Christians alike. The Dubrovnik historian Mavro Orbini established a permanent record of it in his *Il regno dei Slavi*, printed in 1601 at Pesaro, across the Adriatic. Thereafter copied, translated and echoed throughout the seventeenth century, it helped to open the eyes of the Southern Slavs to their own past. The battle of 1389 thus came to be generally accepted as one of those fateful encounters which changed the course of history.[8] Through its celebration of Serbia's royal saints, which was a way of commemorating the history of medieval Serbia, the church provided a major ingredient for the elaboration of a common ethnic identity. Church and popular traditions would eventually and much later provide a political inspiration when they came to be combined with other elements.

When Ottoman expansion stopped in the latter half of the sixteenth century, the crisis that set in explains the seeming contradiction between a deterioration in the condition of the population of Serbia, and the restoration of the Serbian patriarchate at Peć. The latter fitted in with the general tendency to stabilize the borderlands with special arrangements. A struggle for rights over land went with increased demands on peasants. There was growing unrest among both the remains of Serbia's one time nobility and the lower classes. A tradition of outlawry

---

[8]See Richard Knolles's *Generall Historie of the Turkes*, London, 1603, and subsequent editions, which remained a standard reference in English to the nineteenth century.

and resistance developed which was open to foreign influences.

The first of such movements, incited by the Habsburgs and supported by the church, occurred during the Austro-Turkish war of 1593—1606; links ranged as far as Herzegovina. Millenarianism was then widespread among the populations of the Ottoman empire, and Serbs looked forwards to the return of their Saint Sava. To stem the spread of rebellion, an infuriated grand vizier resorted to taking the bones of Saint Sava from Mileševo monastery to Belgrade, where they were publicly burnt.

Risings and migrations nevertheless went on throughout the seventeenth century. From the close of the sixteenth, Habsburg dignitaries and commanders called on Serbs from across the border to come over to the abandoned areas of Slavonia and Croatia. They first attracted frontiersmen whom the Turkish authorities had previously settled on their side. All sorts of refugees and renegades were established on lands granted to farm communally, with religious freedom and no feudal obligations, in return for military service. This was to bolster defences against further Turkish encroachments, but also to increase direct Habsburg ascendancy. Thus what was to be the Military Border was gradually institutionalized and organized.

Villages ran their own affairs in return for building fortifications and fighting for the emperor. In time, however, the privileges were whittled down as direct imperial authority took over; the Orthodox clergy faced pressure to become 'Uniates'—to acknowledge union with Rome, under the terms of the Union of Florence of 1439, under which the supremacy of the pope was accepted in exchange for the maintenance of Eastern practices.

The majority of the settlers were Orthodox, but the Military Border also attracted Catholic peasants, eager to escape the obligations to the church and nobility of Hungary and Croatia. During the Thirty Years War (1618–48), many South Slav subjects of the Habsburgs fought in battles all over Europe. Brave and undisciplined, they were often left to pillage, in order to frighten people with their 'Turkish' aspect. Thus 'Croat' (which represented as many Serbs as Croats) became a household world all over Europe, leaving us with the characteristic 'cravat' worn by these soldiers.

If there was relative peace thereafter on the Habsburg frontier between 1606 and 1683, it was more like warfare as usual on the Venetian border. Agents of pope, emperor and Italian states incited Orthodox bishops to involve Serbian and Albanian clansmen. The price for real help was again union with Rome, for Catholics, devoid of clergy, were becoming Orthodox by default, and Peć was trying to extend its tithes over them. This was not pleasing to the lower clergy and faithful, or to the Turks, who hanged a patriarch. Montenegro profited from its buffer position along Venetian territory. It was one of those areas where the Ottoman conquest was never completed. As in the neighbouring uplands of Herzegovina and Albania, a clan structure had developed out of communities of cattle breeders who were also cattle rustlers and warriors. Their bishop had emerged as a factor of cohesion; chosen locally, he remained nominally dependent on Peć, and a line of succession was established in the Njegoš clan from the turn of the seventeenth century. The bishops sought external support in turn from Venice, Russia and the Habsburg emperor, but relied on their own forces to repel attempts by pashas from Herzegovina and Albania to chastise the clans' plundering activities. In their humble way they set up the first Serbian polity in modern times.

The failure of the Turks' last thrust into central Europe in 1683, again in front of Vienna, definitively turned the tide. More Southern Slavs than ever before partook in the war. The sultan's armies and landholders had to withdraw from most of Hungary and Croatia. In 1688 Belgrade fell to the Austrians, who marched deep into the Balkans until they captured Niš, and were in Macedonia and Kosovo. Poland and Venice had joined in the war, but Venice was a rival to Austria, with its own sphere of interest. With Louis XIV supporting Turkey, the emperor had to fight on two fronts, and needed more and more Serbian combatants.

Patriarch Arsenije III (1633–1706), who had helped to incite the risings and who feared for his safety, had sought refuge in Montenegro which was then under Venetian influence. The Austrians threatened to have him replaced if he did not return. He did return, and with Serbian and Albanian notables agreed to provide help for the emperor, but the Turks recovered, put down the rebellion, and pushed back the Austrians. Patriarch Arsenije and other Christian leaders withdrew to Belgrade, and with them went the monks of Lazar's foundation of Ravanica, and his relics. They were joined on their way by all those who feared Turkish reprisals—the richer layer, most of the Christian urban population, and all those who had collaborated with the invaders. By March 1690 there were tens of thousands of them gathered in front of Belgrade, appealing to the emperor for protection.

The returning Turks tried to keep them, promising an amnesty and temporary tax exemptions. The departing Austrians enjoined them to resist, Emperor Leopold recognizing the patriarch's continued authority over the Orthodox in his territories. By the time Belgrade was abandoned in October, the refugees had crossed the rivers, and they moved on further into southern Hungary as the Turks continued to advance.

The emperor had earlier talked of recognizing one of them as their military leader or *voivod*; the patriarch requested him to do so.[9] All that the Vienna court did was to appoint a Serbian 'deputy *voivod*', and to grant the patriarch civil powers over his flock in addition to his spiritual jurisdiction. Arsenije III did not return to Peć. The name Voivodina stuck to where the Serbs had settled in Hungary. Serbian historical memory would fasten on what came to be called the Great Migration of 1690—a string of events that saw the departure of the patriarch from Peć, the emigration of at least 30,000, of whom some all the way from Kosovo, and the hardships linked to such a move.

Venice had also had to withdraw from the coast and hinterland, as the Turks entered Cetinje in 1692, setting fire to its monastery. The war was eventually ended by the peace of Karlowitz in 1699 (Sremski Karlovci, on the Danube): each party retained what it had when the fighting stopped. The emperor had most of Hungary with Croatia.

The peace of Karlowitz provided barely a breathing space, for the wars against Turkey were resumed by Peter the Great in 1710. The Orthodox tsar's call to arms was an even greater stimulus than that of the Catholic emperor. The Montenegrins eagerly responded, Venice was dragged in, and Austria returned to the fray. The peace of Passarowitz (Požarevac in Serbia) in 1718 completed the Habsburg control of Hungary, with northern Serbia and western Wallachia added for good measure.

Russia went to war again in 1735, followed by Austria. Once again Orthodox church leaders, Patriarch Arsenije IV of Peć (1698–1748) and the archbishop of Ohrid, with the heads of Montenegrin and Albanian clans, were in the forefront of the extensive local support that

---

[9]This would have been Djordje Branković (1645–1711), a claimant to the despotate. His brother was bishop of Transylvania, and he himself had been in the service of the princes of Transylvania and Wallachia. Acknowledged as despot by Patriarch Arsenije, he planned a kingdom of Illyria under the emperor, managed to convince the court in Vienna of his influence in Serbia, was made a count of the Holy Roman Empire ... but was kept in Vienna.

was forthcoming everywhere. Once again Austrian troops advanced to and captured Niš, Serbian insurgents took Novi Pazar, the Turks recovered themselves and passed on to the counter-offensive. The peace of Belgrade in 1739 returned Belgrade and Serbia to the sultan. The border between the two empires would thereafter remain unchanged on the Save and Danube, and the Serbian population divided between the two.

The twenty-year Austrian administration of Serbia introduced a totally new system, under the central government, with native headmen at local level. The emperor as king of Hungary had long been titular 'king of Serbia', the Austrian-held territory was now officially called the 'kingdom of Serbia', and a Serbian militia was organized. Because of the ravages of war, Serbs from both north and south were resettled there. Germans also came to towns, mainly Belgrade. There were attempts to start up the mines with foreign technicians. The population benefited from ordered rule, but found the taxes heavy.

Ottoman sovereignty was fully restored in 1739. *Sipahis*, garrisons and a major part of the Muslim urban population returned. The Porte's good intentions of moderation, to maintain stability in a border province, were impeded by the janissaries, who controlled the fortresses and would not accept orders that went against their interests. There was renewed emigration, as Patriarch Arsenije IV and the remaining élite of Christians left with Austrian troops. This was the beginning of the end of the patriarchate. Peć and Ohrid had been conspicuously disloyal and in crisis since the 1690s. Arsenije IV was deemed to have abandoned his post and committed treachery, and died in Vienna. The Porte interfered with appointments, which succeeded one another in rapid succession, leading to indebtedness, disputed authority and paralysis.

While the Porte distrusted those debilitated Orthodox jurisdictions that flirted with its enemies, the ecumenical patriarchate was worried by Uniatization and Islamization. As more and more prelates were appointed from Constantinople, the local synods appealed for help. The patriarch of Constantinople took them back under his fold— with reluctance because of the antiquity of their primatial sees, and because of their debts. He was careful to lay down the canonical basis of the decision to relinquish their autocephaly (they did not correspond to separate political units), and to confirm the right of the imperial sovereign to legislate in the matter. The patriarchate of Peć was abolished in 1766 and the archbishopric of Ohrid in 1767.

A more specifically Serbian Orthodox hierarchy found a new base north of the border that separated the two empires, in the territory that provided a sanctuary for those who wished to leave Ottoman territory. It was centred on the archbishopric of Karlovci, whose metropolitan formally acted as exarch of the patriarch of Peć, but who was in fact, within the framework of imperial privileges, head of the Orthodox in the Habsburg monarchy.

Originally set up on the Croatian side of Ottoman Bosnia, the Habsburg border régime was gradually extended until, at its fullest by the late eighteenth century, the Military Border (*Militärgrenze* or *Vojna Krajina*) extended from the Adriatic to the Carpathians. Its populations were tied to the emperor, through his military commanders, by land granted to extended family communities, freedom from manorial obligations, freedom of religious practice, and the obligation to fight against his enemies.

Orthodox Serbs were not their only inhabitants. Catholic Croats came there in order to escape feudal dues. Serbs and Croats served in the same regiments, and the solidarity between them became a characteristic of the farmer-soldier society of the Military Border.[10] Some parts of the rich plains of southern Hungary were initially so deserted that Vienna had to resort to a sustained policy of colonization to attract settlers from further afield, particularly those with farming skills. Germans, Hungarians, Ruthenes, Romanians, even French-speakers from Lorraine joined the Serbs and Croats.

Serbs formed an overall majority, and they stamped the new Danubian settlement with their imprint. All over the monarchy they enjoyed the improved Austrian version of a Turkish *millet*, a personal status and religious freedom, with a *sabor* or assembly of representatives of the three categories of clergy, military, and others to discuss financial matters and elect the metropolitan. Their bishops were admitted to the Hungarian diet.

The archbishopric, with jurisdiction over all the Orthodox in the monarchy, served as the focus for Serbian feelings, and set about further defining Serbian identity. The church played an important rôle in moulding and adapting traditions. One catechism published in 1772

---

[10]On the altar screen of the Orthodox church in the village of Plašinci, in northern Croatia, there is a 1770 painting of the Serbs and the Croats receiving from the Byzantine emperor permission to settle on his lands. It actually depicts a Serb and a Croat in contemporary military dress, identified by their respective escutcheons, pledging themselves to the emperor, and symbolizes their cohabitation on the same territory in the service of the Habsburgs.

Shifting Serbias – kings, tsars, despots and patriarchs

defined Serbian identity in the following way. *Question*: Who are you? *Answer*: I am a human being, a Serb, a Christian ... Q: Why do you call yourself a Serb? *A*: I call myself a Serb because of my birth and of my language, which is that of the people from whom I originate and who call themselves Serbs.[11] The cult of Lazar, with his relics translated to their new northern home, was given fresh emphasis, and blended with the Kosovo legend in its most elaborate version as brought there by immigrants from the uplands, but also in its most 'Western' and most pan-Slav version as brought in print by the works of Orbini and his successors.

The emotional attachment of those who had left, and thus lost, Kosovo fed in to the epic legend. At the same time, cut off from Peć and other Orthodox centres in the Balkans, the church faced other directions. Russia provided religious books and education, influencing the development of the literary language into 'Slavo-Serbian'. Central Europe unwittingly provided more and more Baroque elements in the building and decoration of the places of worship. Conditions for trade were favourable in southern Hungary, and there developed a class of Serbian merchants who entered the kingdom's legal and political system through the cities. Along with their *Grenzer* officers and their higher clergy, they had access to the Enlightenment. However, that represented only a thin layer.

South of the border the situation was very different. Whatever the actual numbers and whatever their ethnicity, both of which are difficult to establish, many Christian settlements and their upper layer in particular were literally uprooted from Kosovo, which expatriates would call 'Old Serbia', from northern Macedonia and from 'new' Serbia.

Those who remained were the poorest and the most vulnerable to war and plague. The population declined. The prospect of future ventures by foreign powers that could make use of Christian grievances prompted the Porte to back conversions to Islam in particularly sensitive areas, such as the mountains of Albania and adjoining Serbian and Greek territory. Vigorous campaigns by supposedly loyal Albanian and other Muslim chieftains and grandees were successful, but they were counterproductive because they exacerbated Christian-Muslim relations in territories over which the Porte anyway found it difficult

---

[11] It was printed in Venice in 1772 under the title *Nauk hristijanska*, and written by Stojan Sobat, a parish priest in the southern part of the Border area.

to exercise control. Whereas the Albanian Christians who emigrated with the Slavs became Serbs, the majority of Slavs who stayed behind in these areas were Islamized and even Albanianized.

In Macedonia, where collective identities were still more fluid and essentially religious, but also elsewhere, a general Orthodox community was maintained after the withdrawal of a specifically Serbian church. This was nurtured not so much by the higher Greek clergy sent from Constantinople, and increasingly seen as linked to the Ottoman order, as by the great monastic foundations which were a constant attraction to benefactors and pilgrims great and small, and a source of itinerant monks who travelled bearing objects of veneration.

The Ottoman conquerors—those who had come from the south and east and those who had returned from the north and west—had settled along the main lines of advance and retreat. They had also encouraged the movement of Islamized populations in more difficult but nevertheless strategic areas. However, in Serbia proper there were hardly any outside the towns.

Even though the Ottomans considered Montenegro part of the empire, the barren territory was another centre of the Serbian inheritance, with a particularly strong attachment to the Kosovo cult. In their constant fight against their Muslim neighbours, it helped its flock-tending and predatory clansmen to make up for the lack of material goods, to link Christendom and heroism in a spirit of symbolic justice that extolled vengeance over forgiveness.

Bosnia went through a disturbed period in the seventeenth century. In the towns and particularly in Sarajevo Orthodox Serbs, Catholic Croats and Sephardic Jews lived alongside Muslims from the late sixteenth century, but there was no such accommodation in the rural areas, particularly in the uplands. The Turks had resettled Serb frontiersmen along the borders of western Bosnia—once Croatian but depopulated as a result of the conquest—and the patriarchate of Peć had promoted the spread of a more distinctly Serbian identity. Warfare and the practical imposition of serfdom by Muslim lords had worsened the lot of peasants, many of whom, particularly the Catholics, continued to leave for Habsburg or Venetian territory, while others converted.

The war that the Habsburg Emperor Joseph II and Catherine II of Russia waged in 1787–91 with the aim of partitioning European Turkey marked the end of the century. The pattern was repeated of agents inciting and training local partisans, and of non-combatants taking refuge in the heights and woods and across the border. The restoration of peace left the Danubian border as it had been, and most of the many refugees returned. The French Revolution had stopped the partition, and the sultan was left to deal with anarchy in his European provinces.

The periphery of the Ottoman empire was in a state of transition; the division of Serbs between the two empires would be one of the essential ingredients of the movements about to challenge the Ottoman order. Much had happened from the beginning of the sixteenth century to the end of the eighteenth to develop in time and in space a multi-faceted, multi-centred, multi-layered Serbian identity, of which we still know too little, because of the limitations of sources and the limitations of scholars' approaches.

The contacts between the populations in the advanced and strong Austrian monarchy and those in the weak and backward Ottoman empire were about to spark off the spontaneous rebellions that mark the beginning of the modern era.

2

SERBIA TAKES ROOT – THE LIBERATORS, KARAGEORGE AND PRINCE MILOŠ
1804–1839

The Ottoman order began to crumble when the possibility of securing wealth by military means was brought to an end. It had mostly cut off the Balkans from subsequent European developments, but it had not brought down an 'iron curtain' nor had it uprooted the region totally from its earlier European heritage, which survived in memories. A rationale for rebellion was always provided by the Turks' alien faith; the theme of pushing back the Infidel had been a *leitmotiv* of opponents of the Ottoman order ever since the conquest. Memory and rebellion gushed forth at the turn of the nineteenth century, as local governors, Muslim magnates, rebellious janissary commanders and others refused to take orders from the government in Constantinople, and inserted themselves between the sultan's rule and his Christian subjects.

Generally called 'Serbia', the *sanjak*, or province, of Belgrade corresponded roughly to the one-time despotate and to the area that had been occupied by Austria at the beginning and at the end of the eighteenth century (1718–39, 1788–91). The impact of this occupation had been important. There had been a fair amount of autonomy at village level, free circulation of persons and goods across the border, and military service with the Austrian army.

To prevent further mass emigration and trouble, the Turks on returning not only proclaimed a general amnesty, but extended local self-government to tax collection. The changes of the 1790s in Serbia were an attempt to bolster the sultan's authority in a key border province with the help of the natives. They were part of the policy, introduced by Selim III after the wars, of reforms in the spheres of

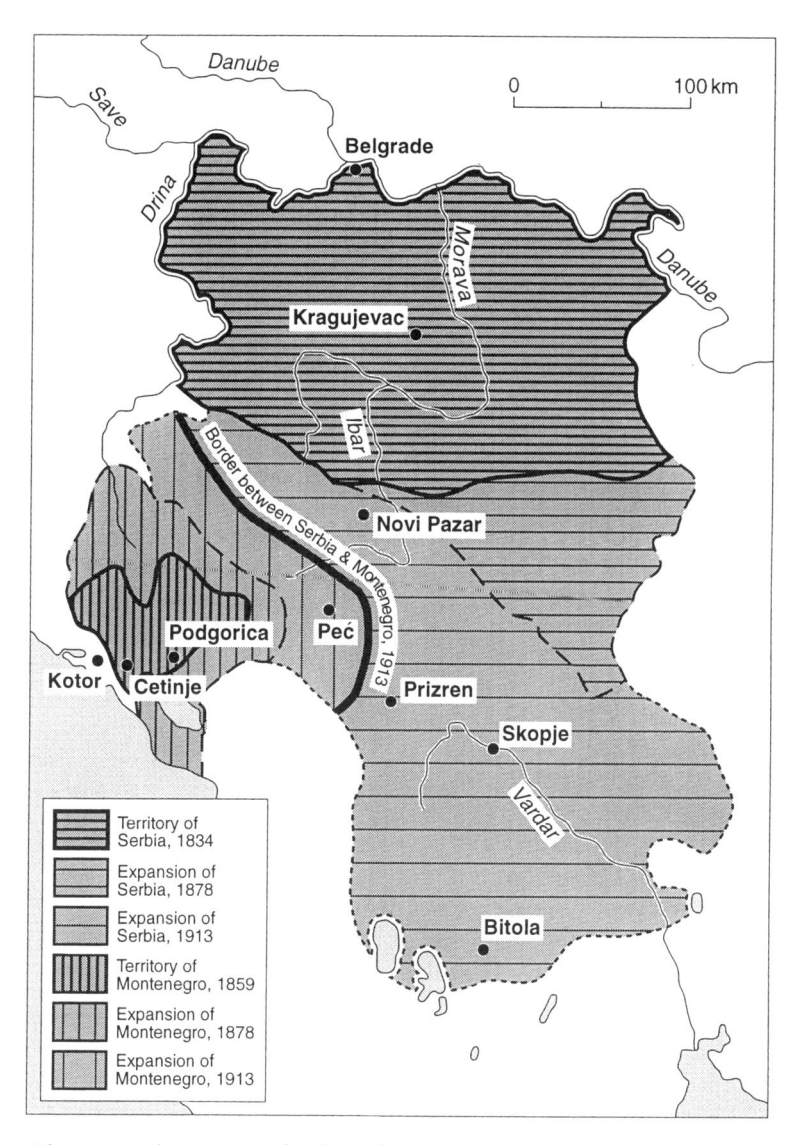

The territorial expansion of Serbia and Montenegro in modern times.

government, finance and the army. The decade that followed 1791 was one of peace in Serbia, when compared to the almost incessant warfare of the preceding century, and the turbulence of the adjoining Ottoman territories.

Far away from the centre of the empire, at a distance of 1,500 kilometres from Constantinople, largely self-administered as a federation of village communities, the province continued to attract immigration from the south, while links over the border were maintained. Tax collecting and the pig trade with the Habsburg lands yielded profits for the local intermediaries between the Ottoman administration and the peasantry. Out of a total population of some 400,000, about 10 per cent were Muslims, who mostly lived in the towns. Relations with the returning *sipahis*—no more than 900, the majority of whom had been settled for generations—were tolerable.

Selim III's reformist zeal did not hold up to Bonaparte's invasion of Egypt in 1798 and to the alliance of the rebellious warlords with the disgruntled janissaries dispersed across the European provinces. Recruiting the dregs of society, the rebels were dreaded by all their potential victims. As their incursions into the Belgrade sanjak grew more frequent, collective fear spread and so did the activity of outlaws. By the beginning of 1804 Serbia had fallen into the hands of the janissaries. In reaction to the massacre of some seventy native elders, there was a spontaneous explosion against the terror felt by everyone. Frightened rural notables organized the resistance of the terrified peasantry with outlaws and former Austrian servicemen and auxiliaries.

Thus unwittingly started the first of the 'national' revolutionary outbreaks against Ottoman rule in the Balkans, each one of which reflected specific conditions prevailing in different parts of the peninsula at the beginning of the nineteenth century, while at the same time being linked by notions of 'revolution'. Traian Stoianovich has noted the millenarianism that reached its peak then, with beliefs in the coming of a liberating saviour from the epic folk tales (such as the fourteenth-century king, or *kraljević*, Marko, who died fighting for the Turks but who seems to have been a larger-than-life character in real life, let alone in posthumous legend) and expectations of a return to a golden age.[1]

At a higher level the notion of revolution spread by Italian political discourse from the seventeenth century onwards, in the sense of changes

---

[1] *Inter alia* in *Balkan Worlds*, Armonk, NY: M.E.Sharpe, 1994, 168–70.

in the fortunes of empires resulting from widespread wars, had fed on the appeals of foreign powers, on the stirrings in the peripheries, on the fears of new oppression. In that world there were distant echoes of the French Revolution.

The First Serbian Rising—as historians would call it—was hardly the outcome of revolutionary ideological thinking or political planning. Its leaders first tended to stick to legitimate Turks, and to look to Austria to restore Selim III's reformed régime, as old-settler *sipahis* clashed with newcomer janissaries, some of the former fighting alongside the insurgents, some of the latter using native fighters. However, in the woodland core of the province the armed men of Karageorge (1752–1817) had sparked off the rising in February 1804 with the typical gesture of outlaws—setting fire to a janissary commander's quarters and killing all the Turks they could lay their hands on.

Nicknamed 'Black George' by the Turks because of his dark hair, looks and reputation, Karageorge Petrović was a better-off pig breeder, an outlaw and a former commander of the native auxiliaries under the Austrians. The captains in the field were nearly all outlaws, who forced hesitant peasants into armed bands and turned ferociously against the janissaries. By the time they had rid the province of them, at the end of 1804, they had practically destroyed the administrative, military and fiscal foundations of Ottoman power in Serbia. To that extent they were the first revolutionaries in the Balkans, carrying out what the German historian Ranke, the father of modern historical scholarship, soon dubbed the 'Serbian Revolution'.[2]

It was difficult for the Porte to react, because of the general breakdown of authority. It could not find enough troops to restore order against both rebellious factions in Serbia. The forces nearest at hand were Muslim irregulars from Bosnia, whose brutality helped to turn the insurgency into an outright bid for independence. The sultan proclaimed a *jihad*—a war waged on behalf of Islam.

Events in the province of Belgrade immediately had wider South Slav, Balkan and European aspects. The rising spilt over into neighbouring sanjaks, as word went round, spread by outlaws, priests, merchants, and agents sent out to seek support. Volunteers were attracted from the Military Border, from Montenegro, Bosnia, Herzegovina and further afield. Money and other forms of support

---

[2]Leopold von Ranke, *Die serbische Revolution. Aus serbischen Papieren und Mittheilungen*, Hamburg, 1829. In subsequent and expanded editions this became a work of reference for European diplomats of the nineteenth century

came from Serbian merchants in Croatia and elsewhere, from Phanariot and diaspora Greeks, from Constantinopolitan ecclesiastical circles, from Danubian princes.

Thinking that only another emperor could deal with the ruler of an empire, the peasant insurgents turned to the Russian, to the Austrian and to the new French emperor. Napoleon had a foot in the Balkans since acquiring the Illyrian Provinces running from Ljubljana to Kotor, with a population of Slovenes, Croats and Serbs. Eventually and however indirectly, the Serbian rising was caught up in the wars against Napoleon. Under Russian pressure, Karageorge rejected Ottoman attempts to reach a settlement, and gambled on winning more in alliance with Russia. Yet anxious not to depend on Russia alone, he also turned to Austria and France, in the belief that one of the emperors would eventually outbid the others to guarantee a new status for Serbia.

However, the emperors merely wanted to use the Serbian insurgents as pawns, or to prevent them from interfering with their own interests. When Napoleon invaded Russia, the tsar hurriedly concluded the treaty of Bucharest with Turkey in 1812—with a clause stipulating the restoration of Serbia's previous régime of local government. Karageorge had not been consulted, and rejected it. The Porte had no intention of giving effect to it, and hurried to crush Serbia in the summer of 1813. Most of the leaders, with their families and many of the fighters, took refuge in Austria; some, including Karageorge, went as far as Russia. Europe, busy getting rid of Napoleon, paid no attention.

The liberated territory had been defended by a local militia, and run by a rudimentary government. Karageorge was acknowledged as the overall leader, the man who provided the military, organizational and revolutionary drive, and who was generally supported by the peasants and the combatants. He was watched jealously by most of the other leaders, all of whom clung to their power over their portion of territory and over their armed followers. In spite of the *jihad*, the insurgents had not fought against enemies seen primarily as Muslims. It was only at the very end, when they realized that the treaty of Bucharest would return them to Turkish rule, that they came to feel that they could not live with 'Turks' again. The Muslim population was then indiscriminately expelled.

Left to its own resources, the rising was ruthlessly suppressed. Serbia was devastated by the mostly Albanian and Bosnian military. Along the roads on which the troops advanced, villages were burnt down, the population who had not taken flight or gone into hiding were massacred or deported, men were impaled, and women and children were taken away as slaves. The collapse of Karageorge's 'bid for freedom' had discredited foreign intervention. The Austrians had come to be associated with heavy taxes and with pressure for union with Rome. The Russians were associated with promises of military assistance that never materialized.

There had been no far-reaching intellectual background or political project behind the rising, it did give new impetus both to the memory of medieval Serbia and to the tradition of defiance and defeat. Karageorge had referred to the need to remove the yoke that Serbia had borne since the battle of Kosovo, and for freedom to extend to Kosovo. He had seen the need to legitimize his authority through symbols such as the relics of the First-Crowned Holy King Stephen, or old heraldic bearings on flags and seals.[3] However, the idea that to restore a Serbian state would be the best way to avoid future suffering was in Karageorge's mind no 'great idea' to restore Dušan's empire.

The price of the transitory period of independence had been high. Although it is not possible to put a number on those who died in battle, in massacres or from disease, the total population remained well under half a million—the mid-eighteenth-century nadir from which the other Balkan areas had recovered by the early nineteenth century—until the 1820s.[4] Serbia's economy was crippled and isolated. The Ottoman-Habsburg transit trade collapsed as a result of the inability to check banditry between Salonica and Belgrade, and of the departure of many of Belgrade's Greek and Hellenized inhabitants.

Disregarding the Bucharest treaty, the Porte restored direct rule. The Turkish population returned. The years 1813–15 were characterized by the exactions of the smaller fry of the Muslim Slav settlers old and new, who now sought justice, compensation and revenge. Yet the

[3]The relics of the sainted King Stephen the First-Crowned, who died as the monk Simon, had been saved by the monks of Studenica monastery, and were authentic enough. The heraldic devices were less so; they were the result of the seventeenth-century heraldic fashion that swept through Dalmatia, when much research and much imagination produced allegedly medieval and splendidly baroque South Slav, or 'Illyrian', coats of arms. They were brought together in the printed collection of Paulo Ritter, *alias* Pavle Vitezović, Croatian polymath and engraver, *Stemmatographia sive armorum Illyricorum delineatio, descriptio et restitutio*, published in Vienna in 1701. Translated into Serbian, the work had provided inspiration for eighteenth-century Serbian church heraldry in the Habsburg lands.

[4]John R.Lampe and Marvin R.Jackson, *Balkan Economic History, 1550–1950: From Imperial Borderlands to Developing Nations*, Bloomington: Indiana University Press, 1982, 110.

formal restoration of the sultan's authority, accompanied though it was by military repression and a return of part of the Turkish population, did not restore the foundations of Ottoman power, which had been destroyed. The revolution had uprooted the landholding system, which precluded the real restoration of pre-revolutionary conditions.

People rose again in the countryside in April 1815, under Miloš Obrenović (1780–1860), who had attained some prominence towards the end of the First Rising, and who had not fled. This was the Second Serbian Rising, another spontaneous rebellion against unbearable local conditions, not directed against the sultan's sovereignty, and not linked to any foreign power. Although the sultan once again took the precaution of proclaiming a *jihad*, both sides were from the outset ready to compromise.

The Porte realized that it would now have to face Russia; it had better control of its troops. The Serbs were exhausted, and their new leader fought only to be in a position to bargain. By November a *de facto* agreement had been reached, with village elders once again collecting taxes, and Miloš Obrenović accepted as 'paramount elder' and sole Serbian representative. Long and arduous negotiations followed, interrupted by the outbreak of the Greek War of Independence and by the Russo-Turkish war of 1828–9. By exploiting the prolonged crisis of the Ottoman state, and by refusing to be drawn into anything more ambitious than local autonomy, Miloš Obrenović achieved more lasting success than Karageorge.

He would have nothing to do with the wider Greek-inspired plan for a general rising of the Christians in the Ottoman empire, which wanted to bring him in. When Karageorge returned secretly to Serbia in 1817 as part of that plan, Miloš had him killed. The rapid growth of livestock exports to the Habsburg lands after 1815 provided him with rising revenues. A Western observer and traveller remarked several years later that the Turks might have been more successful in Serbia if they had killed pigs rather than men, and if they had burnt down the forests, which provided these animals with free acorn feed, rather than the villages in which the people lived.[5] Miloš was thus able to pay and control local headmen, buy off surviving *sipahis*' claims, enrich himself, bribe Ottoman officials in Belgrade

---

[5] Ami Boué, *La Turquie d'Europe*, Paris, 1840, III, 140.

Serbia takes root, 1804–1839

and in Constantinople, and obtain political concessions, formalized by acts issued by the sultan.

In 1830 the political and legal situation of Serbia in relation to the Ottoman empire was defined; it was no longer an insurgent province but an autonomous tributary principality. In 1834 its frontiers were fixed to include all that had been Karageorge's insurgent territory, and they were to remain unchanged until 1878. Miloš was at his zenith. Except for the sultan's ultimate sovereignty, the military presence of garrisons, and limited economic advantages, what remained of the Ottoman régime was largely formal. It was vested in the governor who still resided in the citadel of Belgrade, with direct authority over the garrisons and the remaining 'Turkish' inhabitants, whose eventual departure had been agreed. After all that had happened, they were down to about 15,000, and in a pitiful state, all of them Serb-speakers from Bosnia and Herzegovina, from 'old' Serbia, and from the principality itself; they were to dispose of their property and leave.

The native hierarchy of headmen was formally restored to its functions, capped by Miloš who as hereditary prince of Serbia had supreme authority over the native population. One lump sum was fixed as an annual tribute to the Porte, to include compensation for all Muslim holdings. There were to be no Muslims in Serbia, except for the garrisons, but in spite of provisions to sell and emigrate, and of financial and other encouragements, the question would still take many years to solve.

On a territory of 38,000 square kilometres there lived a population that had reached some 700,000. Within the limits of its exclusively agrarian structure and of its primitive technology, the economy entered a rapid phase of development closely linked to political development, the loosened ties with the Porte and the freeing of the land. Rising prices for pigs on the Habsburg market and the return of security amply made up for the absence of serviceable roads, increased taxes and Miloš's attempts to control exports. Peasants entered trade, and the old extended family community immediately began to fall apart.

Security meant that living together was no longer the only way to survive. Other choices were more appealing to increasing numbers. Land was initially cheap, and many left the restrictive confines of the communities to set up their own smallholdings. They moved down to the lowlands that were now safe enough to clear, inhabit and cultivate. As the country was still largely under-populated and under-cultivated, Miloš attracted settlers with free land and temporary tax exemptions.

A real land rush from neighbouring Ottoman provinces further strengthened the trend to individual ownership. A rising population required wheat and corn to feed itself. With the clearing of woodland, it also needed corn to feed the pigs it reared for export. The individual smallholders who produced cash crops and livestock for export and for towns soon fell into debt. Alarmed by the threat of pauperization of the peasantry, Miloš took what measures he could to try and prevent it.

Most 'towns' were no more than semi-rural townships, with a total population of some 50,000, of whom perhaps as many as half lived in Belgrade, a mixed world of Serbs, Turks, Jews, Greeks, Vlachs and Gypsies who was gradually becoming 'naturalized'. Peace boosted trade with Austria, providing a favourable balance with money for the treasury, the tribute and Miloš's purse. Autonomous Serbia in the 1830s was a rough-and-ready frontier society, with only a very primitive government structure, and hardly the semblance of an educated class. The peasants had traditionally clung to the notion that the land basically belonged to those who tilled it, even when they were paying dues to the *sipahis*. The janissaries' attempt to impose greater obligations and servitudes had been one of the causes of the First Rising.

When the *timars* were abolished, compensation for the *sipahis* was included in the annual tribute to the Porte, so that the peasants never had to pay explicitly for their land. Out of the better-off a thin layer of notables had developed and supplied the local headmen. After 1815 they had taken the best of the vacant and reclaimed lands. They aspired to a restoration on their behalf of the abolished Turkish tenures, for they looked up to the way of life of the Romanian boiars, and bought estates in Wallachia for investment and for status. Miloš was quick to stop such a development, for he did not want intermediaries between him and his people.

Miloš was a new man in more ways than one. His economic policy was radical: in promoting immigration, land clearing and the resettlement of whole villages across Serbia, the embanking of rivers, and in emphasizing the virtues of production. At the same time his mentality remained that of an unreformed Turkish pasha. He ruled with the unlimited authority of the supreme leader who had obtained the rights that Serbia now enjoyed. He had acquired the farming of the sultan's revenues in Serbia, appropriated reclaimed lands, traded, controlled most of the pig export business, and amassed a fortune, which he invested in Wallachian estates and in Viennese banks. His feelings towards the Turks were ambivalent. He understood their mentality and he never used physical brutality against them; he respected the sultan's authority, and cheated it as much as he could get away with.

His only experience of government was that of the Ottoman administration, and he naturally looked to it as a model for both his own way of life and his own administration. He distrusted bureaucrats, and generally tried to rule patriarchally through his household. Government personnel, who numbered a mere twenty-four in 1815, nevertheless multiplied to reach 672 officials in 1839. Habsburg Serbs had to be called to man the new administration. They poured in from Hungary—from a different social environment and a different culture, dissimilar in mentality, dress, outlook, and even speech. They were resented during those first decades when a native educated class of sorts was slowly coming into being in the principality.

The culture of the Habsburg Serbs was challenged by two educational pioneers who turned to the vernacular. Dositej Obradović (*c*.1739– 1811) was a restless monk who had travelled all over Europe from Russia to England before becoming Karageorge's minister of education. He sought to disseminate the ideas of the Enlightenment through didactic writings in the spoken language. His work was continued by Vuk Karadžić (1787–1864), who had also studied and travelled abroad, and acted as secretary to insurgent institutions. Karadžić's research into oral poetry produced published collections in Vienna, which were enthusiastically received by the Romantic intellectuals of Europe to whom Serbia thus came to mean more than to conservative diplomats. Karadćić had been impressed by the purity of the vernacular as spoken in Herzegovina, which he strove to elevate against strong opposition from the Habsburg Serb ecclesiastical and social establishment and its antennae in Serbia.

Miloš's ruthless authoritarianism had been able to halt the trend towards the formation of a land-based privileged estate of the local chieftains, of those who had fought with their own bands of armed followers and then tried to retain control over the areas they had liberated. He had also used it to combat the peasants' anarchical self-centredness, unwilling as they were to assume the obligations of statehood. As long as the Turks had been at the gates, his arbitrary paternalism had been tolerable. However, once the status of Serbia had been settled, with new men beginning to rise from the peasant mass and other more educated people coming with new ideas, he began to appear as outmoded. They all felt the need for legal guarantees of their newly-acquired political, social and economic 'rights'.

Dissatisfaction grew, and he had to face opposition on the issue of the structure of government.

The first symptoms of a politically conscious opposition can indeed be traced to the early 1830s. Its core was made up of men who had risen in Miloš's service and who felt that neither their position nor their wealth was safe. Around them were to be found merchants, local elders and wealthier peasants frustrated in their ambitions, insecure about their property, and antagonized by the prince's arbitrary behaviour. Even the peasants came to feel that they had obtained no legal safeguard for their land, and that they were paying heavier taxes.

The reformists demanded that the prince's powers be limited by a constitution, a word that had come from France; they were known as Constitutionalists. They wanted freedom of trade, security of person and property, and a guaranteed status for state officials. In this contest between the prince and the oligarchy each side tried to satisfy the peasantry at the expense of the other.

The Constitutionalist opposition looked for and found support in Constantinople and St Petersburg. The Porte was the ultimate sovereign authority; Russia was the protecting power according to the treaties that entrenched Serbia's status. Both, fearing Miloš's unpredictable influence, wanted the prince's powers limited, and preferred an oligarchy which they hoped would be more tractable. Striving to impose a friendly quasi-protectorate on the Ottoman empire, Russia was out to limit the power of rulers throughout the Balkans, or to get rid of those who were not subservient to its influence.

In the course of the political struggle that continued from 1834 to 1839, Miloš was invited to come for talks in Constantinople in the summer of 1835. The visit made a deep impression on him. A few months spent in one of the centres of European diplomacy changed his view of international relations. He was received with great honours, and was able to watch at close range the mechanism of great-power diplomacy. As a result, he wished to take Serbia out of the narrow field of relations with the sovereign power and the protecting power, and into the wide field of power politics. The outcome was the paradoxical situation in which Russia backed the Constitutionalist opposition, whereas France and Britain backed the absolutist prince in order to contain the advance of Russian influence, but without sufficient means or even sufficient interests at stake in Serbia.

This diplomatic game coincided with the culmination of the

constitutional crisis that epitomized the outcome of the evolution undergone by Serbia in all fields since 1804. Miloš then began thinking of uniting Slav populations around Serbia in the form of a restored medieval empire, as the only way of escaping from the threat of the impending collapse and partitioning of the Ottoman empire. An increase in territory and in dignity was also seen as a way out of his domestic predicament. It was in order to achieve this that he turned to France and Britain, both of which appointed consuls in Belgrade to watch over the situation, in the wake of similar Austrian and Russian appointments. He obviously made no revelation to them of his long-term aim, and totally misunderstood their show of interest.

Eventually, he came to accept Turkish proposals for a constitutional settlement to be worked out in Constantinople, where he hoped that the other powers would be involved. The talks produced a statute that took the form of an act granted by the sultan at the end of 1838 to his province of Belgrade. This was to underline the authority of the Ottoman sovereign. The statute sanctioned heredity in Miloš's family, but reduced his prerogative to that of a modern constitutional monarch. It was limited not by an assembly, but by a seventeen-member council, appointed for life by the prince from the most important elders. The Porte had been anxious to limit Miloš's powers, to reduce his influence in the European provinces more generally, and to please Russia. The 'Turkish' constitution—as it was called in Serbia—introduced government by prince-in-council. Russia and the notables were the winners; Miloš was the loser. After a few months of increasingly difficult 'constitutional' rule, Prince Miloš abdicated in June 1839 and went into exile.

The rising of the peasants of the border province of Belgrade in 1804 was the first successful movement of a Christian population against Ottoman rule. It had come after a long period of warfare between empires, starting as a reaction to the disintegration of the system of government, but turning into a war of independence. For a few years after 1804 it seemed as if it might become a Balkan revolution, but it attracted little attention in Europe, and the Turks eventually found themselves free to crush the first Serbian rebellion.

Eventually, through negotiation backed by force and cunning, and by keeping out of trouble elsewhere in the Ottoman empire, Miloš Obrenović obtained the status of an autonomous territory, with himself as hereditary prince and direct vassal of the sultan. The struggle then waged against him by a rising oligarchy of local elders, captains and merchants, imposed a constitution with the help of Russia.

'Serbia' had been a dream that had come down from the medieval monarchy, through the despotate and the church, but one with clearer images where Habsburg rule allowed people to benefit from social and cultural promotion, or where Ottoman grip was weaker. By 1839 the notion of Serbia had taken root in a territory whose population consciously perceived itself as being 'Serbia'. Miloš had begun to give shape to the dream of Serbia by consolidating a restricted Serbian territory. He had done so not in the centre of the historical lands of the medieval monarchy but on one of its newer fringes, particularly in terms of population. This was a region affected by a long period of dislocation and turmoil, characterized by extreme mobility of settlement; its inhabitants had come from all sides in the course of the eighteenth century.

Society there had been more communal than patriarchal. Authority rested with the group, delegated to headmen whose authority was conceived as emanating from their respective groups. The sense of identity was no longer being fostered by the church which, locally, was leaderless. It was left floating between the organized Serbian hierarchy of Karlovci, who were oriented towards Russia and even Austria, and the Greek or Hellenized prelates who occupied its two episcopal sees under the jurisdiction of the patriarchate of Constantinople, and were seen as almost belonging to the Ottoman order. Monasteries had been guerrilla centres, and many of them lay in ruins, even though they continued to represent a form of historic continuity and of cultural heritage. Places of worship were few and far between.

Priests were peasants whose function it was to administer the sacraments and celebrate the liturgy—at irregular intervals. The peasants were sincere in their reverence for the church, which was a link with more than one other world, but they were unlikely to take clerics too seriously as individuals. The new élite, backed by popular opinion, wanted to have the local government of the church, along with everything else—political power, land, trade and towns. In fact, no sooner had Miloš established a measure of political autonomy than negotiations were started with the patriarchate for the appointment of native bishops, an autonomous status and financial compensation. By 1832 the grant of autonomy was formalized by the ecumenical patriarch, and the church in Serbia became part of the territory's political structure.

Miloš's authority had been accepted as the delegated authority of Serbia by the population at large. It had even been grudgingly accepted by most of its notables most of the time. The prince was a national hero, the liberator of Serbia and the supreme leader against the Turks, but he was also building something new that could no longer be described as delegated authority. He considered that a permanent all-powerful authority was necessary to maintain the freedom that had been acquired recently.

Once the status of Serbia had been settled, once society in Serbia had acquired a measure of self-control and an even greater one of consciousness of its political existence, the prince's authority came to be regarded as despotic and no longer as delegated. The notables were opposed to its institutionalization, and wanted a return to the group's delegated authority. The revolution ended in a struggle for power between the new oligarchy and the prince. With Russian help, the oligarchs forced a constitution on him, which immediately led to his abdication, and to the imposition of Russia's tutelage. Modern Serbia had been set up. It had freed itself from direct Turkish rule and from its liberator, but it was unable to stand up alone to Ottoman power without turning for support either to Russia or to Austria.

Serbia had acquired a territory and a polity that was to become the national state, offering its peasant population a framework for integration, but it was only one of three very different zones over which the idea of Serbia continued to hover. The other two were the Habsburg monarchy and the Ottoman empire. In the latter both reformers and their conservative opponents sought to safeguard an empire whose equilibrium had been destroyed. The first concern of the reformers had been to establish a new army in place of the janissaries, whose very existence had become a threat. Until that had been achieved, the empire was left exposed to national rebellions and to Russian demands. Although the existence of the state itself was not in danger, the conditions in which its Christian subjects lived continued to fall behind that of their co-religionists in independent Greece or autonomous Serbia.

The Ottomans, whether reformist or conservative, hardly considered Montenegro as being in a practical sense part of the empire—as long as it did not disrupt surrounding territories. Since Napoleon had abolished the republic of Dubrovnik in 1810 (a decade after that other and greater Adriatic republic, Venice) Montenegro was the only South Slav polity, indeed the only Balkan one that had continued to enjoy some sort of *de facto* independence. The Montenegrins had even come to believe that they had never been part of the Ottoman empire (which was their own particular contribution to Balkan political mythology), since they had continued to organize themselves under the two great bishops who ruled over them in the first half of the nineteenth century.

Extremely backward, Montenegro was too poor to support its population, and could only survive through emigration, raiding or expanding across undefined borders, and intermittent subsidies from Russia. Peter I (reigned 1782–1830) had managed to set up an administration with written laws. He had also planned his own imagined restored Serbian empire, extending into Herzegovina, Dalmatia and Bosnia. With Dubrovnik as its capital, it would be ruled by a Russian prince, assisted by the bishop of Montenegro. For all that, he was venerated after his death as Saint Peter of Cetinje, and succeeded by Peter II (reigned 1830–51).

The latter, Europe's last theocratic ruler, was a giant of a man in more ways than one. Two metres tall, one of the great South Slav poets, and the greatest Balkan Romantic, he was regarded as a precursor of the Yugoslav idea for as long as that idea existed. He was also a great interpreter of the Kosovo cult, who extolled the killing of foreign tyrants as the noblest of acts. Whatever the feelings of its inhabitants, Montenegro would emerge as a separate state from Serbia, significantly smaller, weaker and different, and still isolated from both Serbia and the rest of Europe.

In the Habsburg zone too, in spite of all its advantages which explain the lack of revolutionary outbursts, the bulk of the population were brushed aside. The Military Border did not see its productive capacity integrated into the wider imperial economy. Peasant labour was diverted to military duties, and, when the sale of non-transferrable communal holdings was allowed, the way was opened for their purchase by Hungarian estate owners and German colonists, leaving a largely Serbian and Croatian landless peasantry.

3

SERBIA BECOMES A STATE – FROM AUTONOMY TO INDEPENDENCE 1839–1878

Rivalry between Britain and Russia in Serbia ended in 1839 as the Constitutionalists came to power and Miloš went into exile. The threat to the Ottoman empire had moved from the Balkans to Egypt, and Russia compromised with Britain over its influence in Constantinople in order to save Turkey from Mehemet Ali. Miloš's eldest son and heir, Milan (1819–39), died of tuberculosis after twenty-five days in office, and the ruling oligarchy went on with the younger son Michael (1823–68) until 1842, when it replaced him with Karageorge's more pliant son, Alexander Karadjordjević (1806–85). The change of prince had been carried out through two more or less elected assemblies; it was confirmed by the sovereign Porte as well as by Russia, the protecting power.

The Constitutionalists were now fully in the saddle. They were the notables who had obtained the constitution, who had brought down two Obrenović princes, installed a Karadjordjević, and were thereafter the real rulers of the principality of Serbia until 1858 as councillors and ministers. They had social standing, and felt the pressure of the new generation behind them. The importance of their régime was in laying the foundations of a European-type state apparatus. The next generation had no direct experience of Turkish rule; it had known only that of Miloš. It wanted formal guarantees for all that had been acquired in Serbia—essentially, but not exclusively, property. The grabbing phase had come to an end, and that is what 'constitution' and legality meant to most people. The régime provided the guarantees, and it was well accepted at first by a grateful population.

The Constitutionalists saw themselves as the rulers of the state

41

on behalf of a 'people' that was still in its infancy, like tutors to a ward, but they themselves did not have much of an education and they were not sufficiently numerous. They had to recruit officials from the more sophisticated milieu of the Habsburg Serbs to implement their policies. These imported officials were more interested in a state of law on the Austrian model than in representative institutions and political rights. The Constitutionalists' greatest achievement was thus the Civil Code of 1844, based on the Austrian and hence indirectly on the Napoleonic code.

Greater numbers of educated people were needed to run the new administration and the new judiciary. Much was consequently done for education, with a network of primary and some secondary schools, a few professional colleges, and even the embryo of an institution of 'higher' education—the *Lycée*. The emphasis was on training a bureaucracy. Right from the start the government began to finance the higher education abroad, mostly in Paris, of selected students intended for the most technical and, eventually, the highest posts. The Constitutionalists earmarked money to train the best products of their schools in what they saw as the best place in Europe, because they wanted the top posts of their new institutions filled by the best qualified civil servants, and because they did not want to go on depending on Austrian sources.

After two decades, there were about 200 'Parisians', as the French-trained graduates were called. Through them French influence entered Serbia as a rival to the Central European Habsburg influence. That was probably the most important consequence of the Constitutionalists' educational policy: the young men who returned from abroad brought back with them much more than skills; they brought a broader outlook on culture and politics. The influence of the Habsburg Serbs waned.

Not only did Belgrade, from the middle of the century, come to challenge the intellectual accomplishment of the Habsburg Serbs, but it was even able to offer education to Montenegrins and to Slav students from the Ottoman empire. A sharp division appeared between generations.[1] The fathers—the notables who were in high office with little education—had set up a state administration which they expected people to obey and respect. The sons—the junior officials with foreign

---

[1] See Traian Stoianovich, 'The Pattern of Serbian Intellectual Evolution, 1830–1880', *Comparative Studies in Society and History*, IV/3, 1971.

degrees and the teachers in the *Lycée*—were influenced by the ideas of the general European movement of 1848. They did not merely want to take over the state machinery and operate it more efficiently; they turned into a liberal opposition, advocating a Western-style representative system to replace the existing Central European bureaucratic type of government. Meanwhile the Council, which the constitution had originally intended to be made up of representative personalities appointed for life by the prince, turned into a self-perpetuating central committee of the oligarchy.

Like all the young Balkan states, Serbia had conceptualized nationality into a territory, and adopted the idealized form of a 'nation-state'. This was founded on the idea that ethnicity and culture were one. Nationalism was born of opposition to the one-time imperial rulers; everything inherited from the days of 'Turkish oppression' became incompatible with the new national identity. The Ottomans, whose loyalty to the defence of the empire was strong, whatever their ethnic origin and language, could not subscribe to these concepts, and eventually had to leave. They did so as a result of the arrangements stipulated with the Porte; they did so under economic pressure; and they also did so voluntarily. Simultaneously, as populations continued to be extraordinarily mobile in the Balkans even in peace-time, people came to Serbia from Ottoman provinces, as individuals or as whole villages.

The nation-state also increasingly operated as a market. The constitution had established virtual free trade, internal and external. The value of livestock exports to the Habsburg dominions continued to rise, and the value of imports likewise, creating a small trade surplus. The merchant class, who had moved upwards from the peasantry, was turning to a European lifestyle by the 1850s; low Ottoman tariffs, still applicable to Serbia, encouraged the influx of foreign goods. There was little interest in land investment because of measures to protect peasant ownership and the scarcity of hired labour; trade profits went into imports.

The limited concentration of diverse talents and labour in towns, the relative abundance of wood for fuel, and the absence of an organized system of credit at reasonable rates, all postponed the need for industrialization until the end of the century. Serbia still had no domestic money supply. All sorts of coins—mostly Ottoman and Habsburg—were in circulation, with an informal unit of account based on the value of the Austrian gold ducat in terms of Ottoman silver piastres.

The ruling class was open to all through education, and there was a constant filtering up, but the state did not do much more for the peasants, who resented it. They owned the land, but they had no capital and no credit facilities, and there was no one to show them how to get more out of what they had. Trade was free and the peasants traded; they needed money to pay taxes and to acquire things they no longer made. The smallholder was becoming an indebted and a poorer peasant. By promoting a native educated class and a market economy, the Constitutionalist régime indirectly promoted political liberalism. Because these were unsettling times for the peasants, it also laid the basis for the later rise of radicalism.

This was the trend that led to the change of régime in 1858. Caution and power pressure made Serbia's leaders adopt an unpopular neutral stance at the time of the 1848 revolutionary ferment in the Austrian empire, and again during the Crimean war. When the Constitutionalist leaders and the prince—now less malleable—suffered a rift in their relations, the oligarchs wanted to get rid of him. To do so, as in 1842 they had to resort to summoning an assembly, which was hijacked this time by the young Belgrade Liberal intelligentsia.

There was an irresistible popular call for the return of Miloš, whose iniquities had been forgotten or forgiven. What had been intended as a change of prince turned out in 1858 to be the end of the régime. Alexander Karadjordjević went into exile, and Miloš Obrenović was restored—the Porte could do nothing about it. When Prince Miloš returned in 1859, he was eighty years old and had been away for almost two decades. He had forgotten nothing, learnt nothing, and found it convenient to have the whole constitutional system destroyed by popular acclaim, as Liberals argued with Constitutionalists— who now called themselves Conservatives.

Although responsibly cautious, Serbia's Constitutionalist leaders were as nationalist as the Liberals. They had an ultimate aim, which was to strengthen the state they had set up, economically and politically. They aspired to expand its borders, to include fellow Serbs and other Southern Slavs, and to reach the Adriatic in case of a break up of the Ottoman empire, so as to escape being taken over by any other power. An important figure in formulating this thinking was the chief minister Ilija Garašanin (1812–74), who was a link between the older Constitutionalists, the younger Liberals and Croatian nationalists. His formulation of Serbia's long-term foreign policy aims was closely related to the activities of Polish émigrés after the failure of the 1830

Polish insurrection, and the extension of their activities to the Balkans as a potential base for action against Russia and Austria.

From Prince Adam Czartoryski's Paris-based Polish Agency he had received a memorandum of 'advice on action to be followed by Serbia' which became the starting point for his own 'Project', or policy platform, in 1844. In order to prevent Austria and Russia from expanding into the European ruins of the Ottoman empire, the dissolution of which he regarded as inevitable, Serbia should strengthen itself so as to be able to gather kindred populations within a large South Slav state. Unity with Montenegro, and the inclusion of Bosnia, Herzegovina and parts of northern Albania to secure some outlet to the Adriatic sea, were envisaged.

He referred to a restoration of Dušan's empire, as if to supply a psychological reassurance for a project with aspirations that far exceeded Serbia's capabilities. It obviously did not envisage the actual territorial dimensions of Dušan's dominions, and did not look to Greek lands and populations. Serbia was anyway too weak in 1844 for anything more than a long-term vision. Garašanin nevertheless equated the interests of Serbs and other Southern Slavs outside the territory of the principality of Serbia with those of the Serbian state in gestation.

His memorandum was a confidential discussion paper, setting out his thoughts on how to preserve and enhance Serbia's independence to face a disintegration of the Ottoman empire. It was not a public document (it was first published by a historian in 1906), but it expressed a state of mind that prevailed in Serbia's educated class. Its immediate aim was to see how Serbia could avoid becoming over-dependent on its trade with Austria. This could only be achieved in the first instance by acquiring commercial facilities in a port on the Adriatic, and a route to it. In the longer term real independence, both economic and political—not only from Turkey but from Austria and Russia—could only be secured by leaning on the Western powers, and on France in particular.

Garašanin's vision was ambiguous. It moved between subversive action among the subject populations of empires and cautious diplomacy; between an expanded Serbian state and a wider South Slav community; between the nationalist romanticism of Serbia standing alone to show the way and the realistic acceptance of various power interests and of other cultural traditions. It called for full religious freedom, and for cooperation with Catholics and with 'some Muslims'. Special attention was paid to the Franciscans of Bosnia. It suggested inviting one of them to teach Latin at the Belgrade *Lycée*, and to serve a Catholic church there which would not be under Austrian protection.[2] Some of the ideas contained in the memorandum appeared possible a few years later, when Habsburg Croats and Serbs were affected by the subversive wave of 1848 and took up arms against the new revolutionary government of Hungary. The educated youth of Belgrade were in ferment, ecstatic about national liberation, and calling for independence from Turkey, political freedoms at home, and intervention in South Slav lands from Croatia to Bulgaria. Both Russia and the Porte were opposed to any move by Serbia, whose government anyway distrusted such fervour which risked spoiling its own plans. Thus it did nothing beyond turning a blind eye to the money, the weapons and the volunteers pouring over the border, following events through its agents, and keeping in touch behind the scenes with Croatian personalities.

The momentous events of 1848 were to give rise for the first time to something like a popular South Slav movement, or at any rate a Serbo-Croatian one, however inchoate and uncoordinated it might be. Its promoters were recruited from the intellectual élite and youthful idealists. In Zagreb they extolled South Slav cultural unity as a boost to Croatian aspirations. Feeling that Croatia had given in excessively to Hungary against the centralism of Vienna, they felt the need to uncover the substratum of a unified South Slav culture to oppose German and Hungarian claims to preeminence. They adopted the classical name of the 'Illyrians', already used by Napoleon as that of the presumed ancestors of the Southern Slavs. Knowing of Vuk Karadžić's reforms, they likewise adopted the dialect that laid the groundwork for a linguistic rapprochement.

The aim of Croatia's 'Illyrians' was to regroup the Austrian empire into ethnic units, and they needed a broader ethnic base to claim a broader territory—at the least a complete integration with Slavonia, the reintegration of the Military Border territories of Croatia, and Dalmatia. Although they had adherents in Slavonia and Dalmatia, among the Franciscan clergy of Bosnia, and even among educated urban Habsburg Serbs, their movement did not really catch on among Serbs. The memories and myths of medieval Serbia had taken root among the Orthodox of Voivodina and Dalmatia, not to mention those of Ottoman Bosnia.

[2]Since 1991 Garašanin's project has been rediscovered by Croatian nationalists, and read as the manifesto of a 'greater-Serbian' ideology of the post-Yugoslav type.

Serbia becomes a state, 1839–1878

In Belgrade many of the educated young also took up the idea of a common language, but there was little need there for Illyrianism. Karadžić's linguistic vision was that all speakers of his pure and ennobled vernacular were really Serbs, whatever their religious affiliation or self-definition, just as Garašanin's political vision was really that of an open-ended Serbian state. Even the young Serbian Liberals' conception of a common nation was centred on an autonomous Serbia. They were reluctant to give up a name already upheld by their rising statehood. Although in its aspirations the Illyrian movement was truly South Slav, its lack of attraction for other Southern Slavs reduced it to a broadly-based Croatian national movement, which did indeed become the 'National' party of Croatia after 1848.

When the 'Illyrian' Croatian General Josip Jellačić (1801–59) was appointed *ban* or crown representative in Croatia by the Habsburg Emperor Ferdinand in 1848, it was the Orthodox metropolitan of Karlovci, the religious head of the Serbs of Hungary, who swore him in, the Catholic bishop of Zagreb being absent. 'We are all one people; we have left behind both Serbs and Croats', Jellačić told the Croatian diet—the *sabor*. Prince-Bishop Peter II of Montenegro acclaimed him as the saviour of the Southern Slavs.

The Serbian townsfolk of southern Hungary also made language and local demands. The same metropolitan was acclaimed as 'Serbian patriarch', and a Serbian Frontier colonel then serving in Italy was elected to be *voivod* over a territorially defined Serbian Voivodina under the house of Austria, in alliance with a revived 'triune kingdom' of Croatia, Slavonia and Dalmatia. Hopes were expressed for the inclusion of Voivodina into a single kingdom of Illyria. As the Hungarian government became more radical in its demands from Vienna and more intransigent in its attitudes towards non-Magyars, pro-Vienna conservatives gained the upper hand among the latter. Serbs and Croats fought alongside imperial forces to crush the Hungarian rising.

Centralized government from Vienna was restored for all without exception. The Habsburg Serbs got no more than a name. There was one small crown land called the '*Voivody* of Serbia', in order to reduce Hungary, and the emperor took the title of 'grand *voivod* of Serbia'. Beside the autonomous principality of Serbia in the Ottoman empire, there was now also a *voivody* of Serbia in the Austrian empire for a dozen years, but the territory was Serbian in name only. Its 300,000 Serbian inhabitants were outnumbered by Germans and Romanians, and German was the official language. Between and within the various territories and the various movements there were disagreements and misunderstandings, yet representative writers from the Croatian and from the Serbian side did agree on one common literary language, in March 1850 in Vienna.[3]

When Garašanin in 1849 drafted another plan for action, in the 'Slav Ottoman lands', he was disillusioned with what had been achieved in the Habsburg dominions. All he could do was concentrate on Turkey— namely Bosnia, Herzegovina, the sanjak of Novi Pazar separating Serbia from Montenegro, Macedonia and southwest Bulgaria. This was to prepare the ground for liberation and unification with the principality through simultaneous peasant risings.

In practice he wanted to exploit the struggle of Bosnia's Muslim nobility against the Porte, and of the province's Christian peasants against their lords, along with the contacts that he had in Croatia, Dalmatia and Bosnia itself. He was in touch with Peter II of Montenegro and with Catholics (be they the Franciscan clergy of Bosnia or the leaders of north Albanian Catholic tribesmen), on the basis of religious toleration for all. Although he sought to make use of social discontent, he controlled no peasant movement, and contemplated cooperation with the local Slav Muslim lords whose position as well as their religion would be guaranteed.

The Ottoman Porte too had turned to the French model of administration, as its reformist ministers tried to achieve a new type of common political integration to stem the threats of secession and takeover. They had a clear grasp of the problems, but were powerless to change overnight the institutions, symbols and practices that had separated social and religious groups from each other for centuries. They came up against not only the indifference of Christians, but also the resistance of established Muslim groups whose power was challenged by the reforms.

The opposition was particularly manifest in peripheral areas of the remaining European provinces, where new burdens on the peasantry coming on top of the arrival of uprooted Muslims from lost territories caused a deterioration in rural areas from the 1830s, and the emigration of Christian peasants. As Albanian and Bosnian lords

---

[3]These included Vuk Karadžić, the Croatian historian Ivan Kukuljević Sakcinski, the Serbian philologist and translator of the Old Testament Djuro Daničić, who moved between Novi Sad, Zagreb and Belgrade, the Croatian poet and polyglot Ivan Mažuranić, and the Croatian dramatist Dimitrije Demeter.

had rebelled against the sultan's administration to defend their privileges, they had appealed to each other and even to Prince Miloš (both when he was on the throne, and when he was in exile) and to Montenegro, which provided help in order to add fuel to the fire.

To the west, south and east of Serbia there were endemic and sporadic peasant risings, in which the Catholic tribesmen of northern Albania were also implicated. A combination of military intervention, bloody repression and concessions ended the rebellion of the landed nobility in Bosnia in 1850–1,[4] but peasant discontent continued. According to circumstances, Serbia (and also Montenegro) at times supported movements to weaken the Ottoman empire, particularly in areas it coveted, but at other times preferred not to get involved.

During the Crimean war, popular sentiment in Serbia tended to be on the Russian side, but the government was forced to keep it in check, with Turkish and Austrian troops on the borders. The treaty of Paris that ended the war in 1856 placed Serbia's autonomous status (along with that of the Danubian principalities, and all concessions granted to Christians) under the collective guarantee of the European powers, thus ending Russia's unilateral guarantee. In the short term this meant that Austria took over from Russia. Britain and France were distant; they had needed Austria during the war to keep the Russians away from the Balkans but they allowed it, as the power that was the nearest and the most interested, to look after their joint interests. Public opinion in Serbia saw only that the leaders had deserted Russia in the war against Turkey, as they had deserted the Habsburg Slavs in 1848. The further loss of prestige and popularity suffered by both Prince Alexander and the Constitutionalists was a factor that contributed to the change of régime in 1858.

Miloš Obrenović had to wait for more than a year before formal confirmation by the Porte (of his restoration, as he saw it, or of his nomination to a second period of office, as the Turks saw it) allowed him to return to Belgrade. Meanwhile the provisional regency, with the Conservatives of the Council and the Liberals of the Assembly, enacted the formal establishment of a National Assembly, elected by all taxpayers (adult male householders). It would be consulted on institutional changes, on taxation, and otherwise as and when the government wanted.

[4]The Ottoman commander, Marshal Omer Pasha Latas (1806–71), was by birth a Serb from the Austrian Military Border. A specialist in crushing rebellions from Kurdistan and Syria to Albania and Bosnia, he commanded the Turks in the Crimean war.

On his return Miloš was an old man in a hurry, wanting both to consolidate the ruler's authority and to satisfy the peasantry. He sent negotiators to Constantinople to take up the question of heredity and the evacuation of Turkish residents. Both of these he saw as limiting the principality's internal autonomy, since the Porte retained ultimate control over the accession of Serbia's ruler along with direct authority over some of its inhabitants.

He was concerned—demagogically but genuinely—by the plight of the peasants. He feared that their indebtedness to moneylenders might undermine the basis of their landownership. They expected miracles of their peasant prince, but he could only deliver a series of quick-fix measures. After two decades of bureaucratic 'constitutionalism', the restoration of the man who had become a legend to his people had turned into a popular movement against the bureaucrats, but for the older Conservatives and the younger Liberals alike, he was no more than an arbitrary despot grown old.

When Miloš died in 1860, his son Michael, by then aged thirty-seven, returned for the second time to the Serbian throne. During the sixteen years that he had spent in various European countries, he had acquired an extensive education. Refined, dignified and cold in manner, he cut an impressive figure that disguised an honest and shy personality. He had romantic ideals and a programme—to prepare for a rising of the whole Balkan peninsula for a final war of liberation from Turkish rule and the creation of a large South Slav state.

That was the ultimate aim. The preliminary stages were to unite Serbia around its prince, and all Balkan governments and national movements in a Balkan league around Serbia. Appalled by the economic and cultural under-development that he saw on returning home, Michael believed that only enlightened despotism could lead to the rule of law and to material welfare. He wanted a reconciliation of parties under the ruler to make Serbia fit to play the rôle of a Yugoslav Piedmont.

The Porte had no objection to Michael getting a new constitution or amending the existing one, but it wanted this done through the sultan, to stress his ultimate sovereignty and Serbia's dependence. That was precisely what he did not want, and he got round the obstacle by merely enacting a series of organic laws that in fact fundamentally altered the constitution of 1838.

He thus transformed the Council into the apex of the civil service, a body of legal and financial control under the prince. However, it retained its original legislative functions. Law-making was thus effectively transferred to the prince; rule by the Prince-in-Council became rule by Council-under-the-Prince. Michael formalized the Council of Minister under a separate president (or prime minister) and with new ministries. He turned the civil servants from guaranteed and privileged office-holders into trained and tightly-controlled servants of the state.

The evolution of local government was sanctioned by law; local councils were elected by resident taxpayers from among property-holders, and placed under the administrative and budgetary control of French-style district prefects. A new law for the National Assembly kept the same electorate and the same consultative functions as before, but ensured better guidance through a smaller number of members and through appointed officers. The assemblies of Michael's reign were docile affairs, with high abstentionism and short sessions to approve limited government legislation, and otherwise to receive, debate and pass petitions on local affairs.

Michael had wanted to rule with a government of both Conservatives and Liberals, but personal antagonisms forced him to start with technocrats to get through most of his institutional legislation. Then, at the end of 1861, he turned to the Conservatives under Garašanin, because they had the experience of government, and their leader had authority and prestige. They were to remain in office until 1867, and the Liberals went into loyal opposition.

These political groupings were informal and limited to the educated urban class. Michael's policy of reconciling the factions and then ruling with the best statesmen, whatever their party and past dynastic affiliation, was not generally understood. He governed with people who were seen as Karadjordjevićists, who had overthrown Obrenović princes and ruled in their absence, but whom Karadjordjevićists considered renegades since they were now in office under an Obrenović.

Prince Michael Obrenović had set up a personal régime on a legal basis. It was he who carried the weight of the state, yet his aims were greater than his capabilities. He was better at planning than at carrying out his plans, and even his planning was more the product of dreams than of real planning. He was incapable of overcoming serious obstacles or taking quick decisions. He did not really seek outside support.

He was acclaimed as a saviour in 1860, because he came after four years of change and disorder, and the country yearned for order and stability, but as time went by he lost his popularity. For eight years he ruled without restrictions, which was not what the Liberals had hoped for. Their loyal opposition was not allowed any means of expression. By 1864 it had moved abroad to Novi Sad among the Serbs of Voivodina, and even to Geneva, turning against the prince himself on account of his domestic policies. The Conservatives came to dislike the despotism of ministers too long in office; political factions followed with the whole intelligentsia in their wake, and even the peasantry were unhappy because of heavy taxation and military service for the war that never came.

Public opinion, including Liberal opinion, nevertheless continued to support Michael's foreign policy, for he shared the aspirations of all who, spurred by the Italian Risorgimento, dreamed of freeing themselves from foreign rule and of uniting. He succeeded in making his principality the centre of revolutionary and nationalist activity in the Balkans, even though it was still formally part of the Ottoman empire. The Porte, however, in spite of the presence of Turkish garrisons, made little effort to influence its internal affairs.

These internal affairs included the particular attention lavished on the military. Side by side with the small standing army based on intermittent service over four years, a militia was introduced. Rather than take the peasants away from work on the land, it brought basic training to them. Although this auxiliary force was not uniformed, barracked or victualled, it still needed to be armed and officered.

Weapons could not be imported through Turkey, or through Austria. They could only be smuggled through Romania, whose government turned a sympathetic blind eye, with Russian and French diplomatic connivance. The 500 officers trained in Serbia's military academy by the end of the reign were not sufficient. On paper Serbia had some 50,000 militiamen, with another 40,000 in the reserve, and Michael believed that he had thus created an army. In the opinion of foreign experts, 150,000 men could be raised for war out of a population of 1.25 million. Serbia's military effort was then taken most seriously by the Porte and by the powers, which gave Michael great prestige at home and abroad. Opinion caught the fever of wanting to continue the liberation process. People did not realize that it was not enough to give the peasants rifles and a minimum of military instruction. The idea would be tested, and defeated, when Serbia actually went to war against Turkey in 1876.

For some years Michael's foreign policy was supported by all. The Constitutionalists—now Conservatives, who had formulated as their ultimate aim the gathering together of the Southern Slavs—

were still in government—if no longer 'in power'. The 1860s were an important decade for the ideological development of the Southern Slavs. Although the Serbian movement also used religious difference to mobilize the peasantry against Ottoman rule, nationalism had begun largely as an intellectual and secular literary revival. It was in the Habsburg dominions that a Serbian bourgeoisie had developed with a sense of national identity, to which Ottoman Serbs had only become receptive once their social condition began to change.

In Serbia the aims of the emerging national state were formulated by educated people in the secular terms of language, ethnic culture, memories of achievements before the Turkish conquest. The development of a wider Yugoslav movement across the Orthodox-Catholic divide was possible. In Croatia, the 'nationals'—the successors of the Illyrians—gathered around Bishop Strossmayer (1815–1905).[5] Adopting the native name 'Yugoslav', they wanted to forge a common identity on the basis of history, culture and education. They aimed in the first instance at the political union of the Southern Slavs who were under Habsburg rule, and later at union with Serbia and other Southern Slavs. Although the trend on both sides was at an early stage, and historicist in part, the need was never felt to resort to the documentary forgeries or the total immersion in pan-Slavism that accompanied the Czech movement in its desperation to get people to differentiate themselves from Germans.

There were frequent contacts between Zagreb and Belgrade, encouraged by the Serbian government and facilitated by the fact that Strossmayer, bishop of a mixed diocese in neighbouring Slavonia, was at the same time apostolic vicar for Serbia. It was in Belgrade that an agreement was drafted at the end of 1860, and signed in the office of the prime minister, for a tripartite federation of Serbs, Croats and Bulgars which would be called Yugoslavia.

Despite his work behind the scenes with Slav nationalists in Austria, Garašanin was anticipating in the 1860s that a revolt in Bosnia would trigger a general uprising to end Ottoman rule in the Balkans, and

---

[5]Josip Juraj Strossmayer, Roman Catholic bishop of the richly-endowed diocese of Djakovo in Slavonia from 1849 until his death in 1905, was in many ways a personality ahead of his times, although today he is no longer fashionable because of his Yugoslavism. His views have been given a variety of interpretations (and misinterpretations), for he was all at once a spiritual leader, a politician and an educationalist, a nationalist Croat and an idealistic Yugoslav, a Catholic prelate and an ecumenist who worked for unity with the Orthodox. For a long time he imagined that the two sides of the Church could reconcile their differences under Rome.

that is where his attention was concentrated. Prince Michael was certainly not thinking of sending his new army into Bosnia at the first sign of revolt there, in opposition to Austria's wishes, yet the Porte protested against his militia, and applied military pressure on Serbia's frontiers, thereby raising tension. Incidents multiplied on the borders and in garrison towns; one such in Belgrade, in June 1862, led to the death of a child. There were scuffles and more victims, all the Turks were driven into the citadel, and the guns there bombarded the town, luckily causing more panic than harm.

Was this bombardment a deliberate attempt to frighten the Serbs into submission, or the result of disorganization in the overcrowded fortress? Whatever the reason, it was godsend to Michael, who was granted full emergency powers. A call-up was ordered, and a demand made for the immediate evacuation of all Turks. The Porte argued that the Serbian militia posed a threat; the Serbian government that the threat came from the Turkish garrisons.

A conference of ambassadors met in Constantinople. France and Russia backed Serbia, while Austria and Britain backed the Porte. A compromise was found by September. All Turkish civilians were to be evacuated from Serbia, two smaller forts were to be destroyed, but the main ones on the borders (including Belgrade) would remain; there would be mutual compensation for damages. That prevented a war, but it not settle Ottoman-Serbian relations. The Porte went on to protest strongly against the smuggling of weapons through Romania, but solidarity between Romania and Serbia merely ensured that the smuggling thereafter was carried on more discreetly.

The fortresses were the last remaining Ottoman presence in the principality and were therefore resented more than ever in Serbia, and insisted upon more than ever by the Turks, who reinforced them as Serbia armed. The years 1862–7 witnessed a tense armed peace between the Ottoman empire and its vassal. However, the European balance of forces was favourable to Serbia. Napoleon III was in sympathy with the aspirations of emerging nationalities and, after the Crimean war, Russia seconded France in its support for nationalist movements in the Balkans in the hope of regaining influence there. It believed that Britain for one was less likely to defend the Ottoman empire against movements within it than against outside pressure. Austria, weakened by its defeats in Italy and Germany, and by its constitutional experiments, was anxious that Serbia should not 'open the Eastern Question' at that particular moment. Turkey, preoccupied with a formidable revolt in Crete, was on the brink of war with Greece, and worried lest the movement should spread to the mainland, where Serbia was considered influential.

Serbia, as the centre of activities directed at a general disruption of the Ottoman *status quo*, caused concern to the forces committed to its defence. It directed propaganda at Bosnia and Bulgaria; it financed the activities of Bulgarian émigrés; it trained volunteers who would become engaged in the risings. Serbia was the hub of a system of plans and alliances. Prince Michael's inspiration was truly *risorgimentale*, for he believed that the Balkans could 'do it by themselves', through the intrinsic power of a generalized rising and the no less intrinsic decay of Turkish strength. Not only was he a visionary nationalist revolutionary who believed in the right of nationalities to self-determination, but almost everybody on the international scene considered Serbia to be the key to the situation in the Balkans.

In this Michael was cautiously seconded by Garašanin. Plans, agreements and protocols were drawn up in 1866. There were talks about cooperation with existing Balkan governments; Greece in particular keenly sought an alliance with Serbia. A Serbo-Bulgarian state was sketched out with Bulgarian nationalists—a Yugoslavia under Prince Michael that would include Serbia, Bulgaria, Thrace and Macedonia.

Initiatives were also taken again concerning Austrian territory. Strossmayer put a proposal to Garašanin for a Bosnian rising, to be directed from Belgrade and Zagreb, that would lead to a future federal organization of the Southern Slavs of both empires as one nation with three religious faiths. In March 1867 a finalized version for immediate action was returned by Garašanin to Strossmayer.

Since Serbia already had the necessary state structures, it would assume responsibility for the conduct of diplomatic and military activities. The movement would start in Bosnia and Herzegovina that coming summer. It would be directed jointly from Belgrade and Zagreb, and would lead to the setting up of a local administration demanding union with Serbia under Turkey. There would be no direct intervention, in order not to contravene the powers. During these exchanges the Yugoslav area to be envisaged was eventually defined as ranging from Carniola, southern Styria and Carinthia, to northern Albania, Bulgaria and part of Thrace. The plan was accepted by the leadership of Croatia's National Party, a coordinating committee was set up in Zagreb, and in May the Croatian *sabor* passed a solemn declaration that the Serbian nation in Croatia was identical and equal to the Croatian nation.

Austria and Turkey both felt the need to give Prince Michael of Serbia some satisfaction. It was then that he suggested that the sultan might entrust the fortresses to his safekeeping. This was agreed in April 1867, and in return Michael was asked to come and pay homage in Constantinople, a symbol of obeisance which would contribute to calming the Balkan Christians aroused by the Cretan rebellion. He duly went to Constantinople, and the Turkish troops left Serbia. The only tokens of Ottoman sovereignty were henceforth the yearly tribute and the Ottoman flag alongside Serbia's above the citadel in Belgrade. Serbia was a vassal in name only. It set about minting its own small coins, it went on to sign treaties as if it were a sovereign state, and it stepped up its propaganda effort.

In spite of the importance given to Serbia, and of the tense period through which Austria and Turkey were passing, all the plans advocating, envisaging or preparing insurrections leading to union, federation or confederation around Serbia were amateurishly conspiratorial in character. Their goals were basically unrealistic, and they contained no social and economic programme that could appeal to the peasant masses who were expected to bring down Ottoman and Habsburg rule.

The diplomatic situation had also changed after 1866. That year would have offered Prince Michael the best opportunity to launch his pan-Balkan initiative, but it was then that he went for the much smaller but more certain prize of the fortresses. Like everyone else in Europe, he believed that Austria would win the war with Prussia, and France and Russia pressed him to keep quiet during the war. Serbia was not quite ready; Garašanin was as ever cautious. The last date accepted to set the movement in motion was June 1868. By the time all the pieces were in place—the committees and agents preparing the risings, the diplomatic and military conventions with Montenegro, with Greece and with Romania, the military preparations—the opportunity had passed. The great Balkan dénouement turned to anticlimax.

After the Austro-Prussian war France, anticipating a future clash with Prussia, began a rapprochement with Austria. Russia, now isolated, was no longer so keen. The outcome of the war with Prussia had forced the definitive restructuring of the Habsburg monarchy, with the Austro-Hungarian *Ausgleich* (compromise) of 1867 that satisfied Hungary at the expense of the other nationalities and tied it to Vienna.

In Serbia itself a government crisis had ended the Garašanin ministry in November 1867, and Prince Michael was assassinated in June 1868. His régime had been gradually losing popularity at home since 1864. That year a group of some forty Karadjordjevićist plotters were arrested and tried for wanting to use opposition to the newly-introduced income tax for some subversive political action. Only four of them were eventually sentenced to terms of imprisonment, and then freed on appeal by judges who deemed that the evidence pointed to intentions only. Shocked by what it considered a politically inspired verdict, the government enacted a retroactive law on the political responsibility of judges. This was seen as infringing the independence of the judiciary, and turned round public opinion.

Financing the state's army and its diplomatic activity had raised expenditure by over 60 per cent in the ten years between 1858 and 1868, and progressive income tax had been introduced in 1861 to provide more revenue, but it was so widely resisted that it had practically to be given up after a few years. The deficit thus had to be made up from the state reserves, which were running out.

In order to tackle the issue of peasant debt and credit, the Liberals' idea of state credit was adopted, with the setting up in 1862 of a Central Administration of Funds. This lumped together public and various trust funds, and took private deposit accounts guaranteed by the state, from which 6 per cent mortgage loans were made on land. It was a huge step in the right direction, although the fact that the Administration had no branches outside the capital meant that Belgrade traders benefited from it more than poorer peasants. Apart from that, no important economic measure was actually implemented, rather than merely being studied and planned. All available energies and means went to the top priorities—foreign policy and the army.

Garašanin's fall had been occasioned by his opposition to the prince's possible re-marriage after the dissolution of his marriage to a Hungarian aristocrat. The question had become entangled with the Liberals' pressure either to go to war or to give up the dictatorship that had been organized in order to prepare for a war of liberation. Michael had been assassinated just when such decisions were about to be taken—on going to war and on possible political reforms. His murder was, however, hardly the result of a deep-seated political conspiracy; the attack took place while he was out on a walk by three isolated assailants with a grudge.

It was Garašanin, out of office, who got the ministers together, to summon the National Assembly and set up a temporary regency.

Michael had no children, and the only surviving male Obrenović was a fourth-degree orphaned cousin who was at school in Paris. Although the boy, Milan, had not been declared heir, the war minister, Colonel Milivoje Blaznavac (1824–73) immediately had him proclaimed prince at the army barracks, and the Assembly just followed suit. Michael Obrenović had indeed brought political life to a halt, and the army was the only organized force left. His enlightened despotism, his bureaucratic state, and his dreaming-and-scheming nationalist foreign policy had ultimately not satisfied the new generation of Liberal urban youth educated in universities abroad or in Belgrade under foreign-trained teachers.

The 'intelligentsia' at the time simply meant educated citizens. The demands of the first generation that had appeared towards the end of Miloš's first reign had been reduced to the creation of a legal and independent state. They were tinged with strong anti-Turkish feelings and subsequently with pan-Slavism. The second generation, from the 1850s, was made up mostly, though far from exclusively, of sons of bureaucrats, merchants and priests, born in the principality. Over half of them had been educated in the 'West'—Pest, Vienna, Berlin, Munich, Heidelberg, Zurich, Paris. They had codified a literary language, which made communication easier. They shared a taste for Romanticism in literature and were Liberal in politics. They aimed at the creation of an independent and unified Serbia, with political support from Russia. Many of them had wider South Slav aspirations.

Authority within the regency was shared between Blaznavac and Jovan Ristić (1831–99), the Heidelberg- and Sorbonne-educated diplomat who had been the Liberals' failed alternative to Garašanin in 1867. The new constitution which they enacted in agreement with the Liberal-dominated Assembly in 1869 provided Serbia with a veritable constitutional government, if not yet a parliamentary one. It gave the Assembly limited legislative authority over the growing executive, thus turning the elected legislature into a true constitutional factor, alongside the prince and the Council.

Ristić, the constitution's author, looked to the German model of constitutional government. He did not believe that an undeveloped society led by an uneducated parliamentary majority could make any progress. Nevertheless the new legislative functions of the Assembly, the regulation of its sessions, and the electoral process, all specified by the constitutional text, would bring with them the gradual organization of political tendencies. Political life took off when parties had to go to the country.

Idealism and romanticism gave way to realism and positivism. As leaderless Serbia could no longer give a lead, Prince Michael's Balkan league disintegrated, and the regency tried to achieve a diplomatic balance in foreign policy between Austria-Hungary and Russia. At home the new permissive political atmosphere created by the constitution of 1869 was controlled only by the government's prosecution of those—increasingly called 'radicals'—deemed to be subversive of the regency's balanced policy between Conservatives and Liberals. However, the subversiveness of Prince Milan, when he came of age in 1872, could not be entirely controlled. He tried to govern with the Conservatives, who were a party of the past, yet the results of the experiment were interesting. They too now came from a new generation of 'intellectuals'. They had experienced both power-sharing and opposition, were aware of the dissatisfaction of the peasants who were paying the price of an economic progress that seemed mainly to benefit the towns. As the seeds of a radical movement were being introduced on the left fringe of the younger Liberals, a government of Paris-educated Conservatives embarked on a series of reforms. Because they did not control the Assembly, they gave it a real taste of parliamentary government, to carry it along in their concern for European standards.

Serbia may have been perceived as a potential unifier on the model of Piedmont, in the principality and even outside it, but there were other political factors among the various educated communities conscious of their Serbian identity, not to mention other Southern Slavs. For a start, there existed that other, albeit much smaller, Serbian principality, Montenegro, which had consolidated by the 1850s. Until then it had been seen, in the picturesque phrase used by Vesna Goldsworthy, as 'Europe's closest approximation to Tibet'[6]— mountainous, remote and theocratic. With over thirty clans and perhaps 120,000 inhabitants, it was also tribal and extremely small.

Bishop Peter II had cooperated enthusiastically with all the planning and scheming of Serbia's leaders. He had also somehow managed to pay salaries, and thus increased government control over the clans. His successor was his nephew Danilo, who on acceding in 1851 had secularized his position by separating the princely office from the episcopal dignity. He continued the task of modernization, introduced a code of laws, and organized a regular military force.

Recognizing no borders in their blood relationships, or in their pastoral and raiding activities, the Montenegrin clans were a constant threat to Ottoman control over adjacent mountainous territories.

[6]'Diary', *London Review of Books*, 17 February 2000, 41.

Danilo's intervention in the Herzegovinian rising of 1857–8 led to a real war with Turkey, which continued to claim that Montenegro was part of the Ottoman empire. French support and intervention by the powers ended the war, fixed the borders, and thus stabilized Montenegro's position by a *de facto* recognition of its existence.

Danilo was assassinated in 1860. His successor, the Paris-educated Prince Nicholas (1841–1921), would be Montenegro's last ruler to the end. Like his predecessors he considered himself Serbian, was generally supportive of the Serbian cause and willing to cooperate with Serbia, but gave priority to his principality's own territorial objectives. By serving as auxiliary to Michael Obrenović, he also expected to succeed him as ruler of the future joint state, remained diffident, and looked to France for support. Garašanin was no less distrustful of Nicholas, whose separate dynastic claim he considered an obstacle to Montenegro joining Serbia.

The consolidation of Montenegro's statehood contributed to an increase in the sense of its own identity. However, it did not lessen the feeling that it was the bastion of Serbdom, especially as it expanded territorially and came to control other tribesmen who did not think of themselves as belonging to the heartland of old Montenegro. The cult of Montenegro as the surviving part of pre-Ottoman Serbia was important among people, particularly the rural uneducated, who traced their origins to the Dinaric uplands, in the coastal region, Herzegovina, Serbia itself, and Hungary too. There was no contradiction between the duality of history, the uniqueness of ethnic feeling, and inter-clan clashes.

The continued strength of the Habsburg monarchy did not allow Serbia seriously to contemplate, let alone realize, any of its plans there. In these provinces actions developed for the liberation and unification of Serbian lands independent of the foreign policy of Serbia and Montenegro, and often criticized by the two states. That happened even in Croatia, which had the effect of pushing many politically conscious Croats to look to Vienna rather than Belgrade to stand up to Hungary. Ever since the 1840s Serbia's rulers and Croatian nationalists had been in contact; both sides had kept up the mystique of South Slav unity as the ultimate outcome, but used it as an auxiliary to further the realization of their nearer separate aims—that of uniting Serbian (primarily Ottoman) and Croatian (primarily Habsburg) lands respectively, as circumstances permitted.

In 1867 the old family conglomerate ruled over by the house of Habsburg became the Dual Monarchy, or Austria-Hungary. The dynastic lands were turned into two constitutional states with a common monarch and some other joint institutions. The dynasty was under the illusion that it had kept an empire. Hungary's political class believed that it had obtained an independent state within its historic territorial integrity. In fact it provided the model for the nation-state that was really an ethnic state—one ruled by its major ethnic group. Croatia—officially the kingdom of Croatia-Slavonia—was recognized by Hungary as a separate unit linked to the Hungarian crown, with its legislative *sabor* and its executive for local affairs, under a Hungarian-appointed *ban*. Its Military Border territory was finally incorporated in 1881. The political framework of Croatia was then fixed for a long time to come. Dalmatia remained an Austrian crown land. Voivodina was fully integrated again into Hungary, losing any formal trace of a separate identity.

The reorganization of the Austrian empire and the death of Prince Michael brought the scheming and dreaming of both Zagreb and Belgrade to an end. The Habsburg monarchy was stabilized, and the Slavs had to adapt to it. In order to become the governing party in Croatia, the Nationals accepted the limited reforms that gave them some control over affairs, with an electorate that amounted to no more than 2 per cent of the population.

The Serbian community in Hungary went back to its church councils. The military estate was abolished along with the Military Border, and the lay estate was given double representation, but the church councils were politically insignificant since their competence remained limited to ecclesiastical and educational matters. The territorial jurisdiction of the metropolitanate of Karlovci was also reduced, as the Orthodox diocese of Cluj, elevated to the status of a separate metropolitan province, became the centre of the Romanian ethnic community of Hungary.

Relations with official Belgrade had cooled in the 1860s, as a result of new trends in the younger Serbian intelligentsia of Voivodina, and of the presence of Liberal exiles from Serbia in southern Hungary. Svetozar Miletić (1829–1901), mayor of Novi Sad and member of the Hungarian parliament, believed that dualism was there to stay. He founded the new Serbian National Liberal Party to work for equal citizenship within a democratic constitutional Hungary, opposing the conservative Serbian notables who stuck to church privileges and tended to look to Vienna. For a while, until banned in 1871, there was also a dynamic United Serbian Youth in Voivodina, which was meant to work in the field of culture but in fact agitated in favour of democratic republican Serbian nationalism in Ottoman territory, with the ultimate aim of setting up a Balkan federation.

In Dalmatia in the 1860s, Serbs of the urban intelligentsia joined Croats in a National Party to challenge the Italianized autonomists who controlled the provincial diet through the tiny electorate. Whereas the latter wanted an autonomous Dalmatia within the empire, the former aimed at uniting with Croatia. They called themselves 'Yugoslav' rather than 'Croatian' so as to reassure the Serbian minority that it would be treated equally, and not to incense Italian sympathizers.[7] Once the Nationals had obtained a majority in the diet in 1870, Croats and Serbs went their separate ways. By that time union with Croatia no longer seemed feasible.

Plans for Yugoslav coordination had to contend with separate Serbian and Croatian ideas about their respective 'states' (autonomous principality, and separate realm with its own crown) that had evolved since the 1830s in romantic minds, in historicist claims, in cultural investigations and in political practice. They were incompatible not only with each other, but with any wider Yugoslav idea taking in Slovenes at one end, Bulgars at the other, and any other Southern Slavs not attached to such Croatian- and Serbian-based ideas. However, their 'invented traditions' were no different from those used by nationalisms all over Europe at the time.[8]

The political fragmentation of these lands in itself helped to promote the search for a Yugoslav unifying framework over and above the parochial rhetoric, if only to accommodate their mixed and similar populations.[9] It offered national rights based on ethnicity and language in place of both acquired rights and historic rights. Since the dissolution of the Habsburg monarchy could only be dreamed of at the time, Yugoslavism was an ideological framework, one that supported separate efforts in the struggle for emancipation because of existing common aims, and one that was questioned, challenged, revived and altered. However fluid, the Yugoslav idea was at the root of Austria-Hungary's distrust of Serbia thereafter, and of its relief at developments in the principality after Prince Michael's death.

Most of the land in the Ottoman Balkans was still in Muslim hands, and although a general rising of Christian peasants did not take

---

[7] Austria's Serbo-Croatian Military Border regiments had participated prominently in the North Italian campaigns and were not popular with Italian nationalist opinion.

[8] See E.J.Hobsbawn, *Nations and Nationalism since 1780*, Cambridge University Press, 1990.

[9] John R.Lampe, *Yugoslavia as History: Twice there was a Country*, Cambridge University Press, 1996, 40.

place, the atmosphere was favourable to regional movements that occurred for local reasons, influenced by propaganda from across the borders. Wedged between Austrian Dalmatia, Hungarian Croatia and autonomous but nominally Ottoman Serbia, Bosnia remained one of the most backward areas of the Balkans. Economic decline after the end of the transit trade of the Napoleonic era had increased exploitation of the peasantry by landlords, giving rise to jacqueries, reprisals and emigration.

Population figures should be treated cautiously. Of a total population of some 1.3 million in the late 1860s, perhaps 400,000 were Muslims, of whom 7–10,000 formed the landowning élite, where a strong autochthonous Slav element had assimilated the later Turkish and other Muslim settlers. Their relations with Christians varied from paternalistic or friendly to jealous or fanatical. The distribution of their settlement tended to coincide with their control of towns, plains and valleys.

There were some 500,000 Orthodox, the overwhelming majority being peasant sharecroppers on the estates of Muslim lords. A small but developing Orthodox urban commercial class was the first segment of the population to modernize, alongside a prosperous Jewish urban community. The 250,000 Catholics, largely concentrated in Herzegovina, did not have a similar commercial élite. Ottoman reforms there since the 1850s had in many ways improved the administration and the state of the population in towns, but they had done little for the peasants. Indeed, administrative efficiency had increased both expectations and tax collection. Christian churches provided their local communities with schools; this was especially the case in towns, where many schools were endowed by the Serbian merchant community, which spoke up for its co-religionists and looked to Serbia. Although most of the Bosnian Muslims were no better off, the presence of Catholic and Orthodox clergy added a confessional justification to the grievances of the Christian peasantry, most of whom had been affected by the ideas propagated by Belgrade and Zagreb in the 1860s.

Herzegovina was in the south-eastern corner of what had become a vast single province of Bosnia in 1864. It had remained a hot spot, mountainous and tribal, involved in the warfare of Montenegrins and pashas. The peasant rebellion there in 1875 was spontaneous; the area had suffered a disastrous harvest the year before, and resisted the violent measures resorted to by tax collectors. Peasants took to the mountains to withhold payments. The revolt extended quickly without a central organization, moving from a social to a political and national level. It turned into the great Eastern Crisis, as it spread to the whole of Bosnia, and to Macedonia, Bulgaria and Albania.

The South Slav lands of the Habsburg monarchy were affected, as well as Serbia and Montenegro. Serbian involvement was far from monolithic. Quite apart from Montenegro's objectives, there were 'non-governmental organizations' operating in the region. All strands played down the religious differences. Catholics took part in the rebellion in Herzegovina; in Bosnia it was mostly limited to the Orthodox; the Muslim areas of central and north-eastern Bosnia remained loyal.

Pressed by domestic opinion, Serbia and Montenegro sent their troops into Bosnia and Herzegovina in June 1876, effectively going to war against the Ottoman empire of which they were still formally part. Official propaganda stressed the Yugoslav aspect of the war, which was neither religious nor social, and tried to reassure the Muslims. In Croatia the *sabor* had to be threatened into giving up its support for the rebels. The Serbian militia was no match for the reformed Ottoman army, and Russia intervened in October to save Serbia from total defeat.

When Russia itself went to war the following year, Montenegro and Serbia returned to the fray. Tennyson was inspired to write his poem 'Montenegro'. In the House of Commons Gladstone praised the Montenegrins as 'heroes such as the world has rarely seen', taking up and expanding the myth that they were the descendants of those Serbs who had rejected Ottoman rule after 1389. The rising in Herzegovina and Bosnia had turned into one of the greatest guerrilla wars of modern European history, with violence on all sides. By the time it ended, an estimated 150,000 lives had been lost and 200,000 non-combatants had sought refuge in Austrian territory.

The Eastern Crisis ended with the wholesale revision of the Balkan territorial *status quo*, by the powers assembled at the Congress of Berlin. The treaty signed there in July 1879 brought formal independence to both Serbia and Montenegro. They obtained more Ottoman territory, but not all that they had managed to capture, and had to accept the transfer of Bosnia and Herzegovina to administration and occupation by Austria-Hungary. That put an end to the illusion that all Serbs could be unified in an independent Serbia, or that Bosnia could become a bridge between Serbia and Croatia for a future Yugoslavia, for as long as the Habsburgs continue to rule. Serbia had to turn its attention southwards and eastwards to the remaining Ottoman provinces, entering a struggle with other Balkan states that would poison inter-Balkan relations and foment bloodshed in unpartitioned Macedonia.

4

INDEPENDENT SERBIA – RIVAL DYNASTIES AND POLITICAL PARTIES 1878–1914

Independent Serbia in 1878 had a territory of 48,600 sq. km with a population of 1.7 million. It had been extended by 11,000 sq. km and 350,000 people, yet it was landlocked, and its Serbs were but a minority of those who thought of themselves as such. Over 87 per cent of the population were rural. Only Belgrade, the capital, and Niš, newly-acquired, had more than 10,000 inhabitants. During the capital's chaotic development in the 1880s its population almost doubled, reaching 54,200 in 1890. This mostly first-generation urban population provided the carriers of development. They were a thin layer of merchants, craftsmen, civil servants, officers, priests and teachers.

The contrast between the educated minority and the illiterate mass (over 80 per cent, including 87 per cent of urban females) was characteristic of developing societies. Primary education was made compulsory in 1883, but there were not enough schools or teachers, and parents were not keen. Secondary education was available in towns. There were 5,621 registered secondary-school pupils in 1885/6. What was called the intelligentsia was recruited from the graduates of Belgrade university (fully-fledged since 1880) and of foreign universities. In 1879 the government spent 119,000 dinars on study grants abroad—more than on parliament. Right at the top, cultural life was intense, with a remarkably high number of books, periodicals and dailies being published, in comparison to the market.

Peace, security, control of epidemics and the availability of land all contributed (in Serbia as in neighbouring Balkan states) to a population density never equalled before. The population had increased from 678,000 in 1834 to 1,353,000 in 1874, through immigration more than through natural increase. Relatively high and predictably collected money taxes had pushed peasants into producing marketable crops, which were quicker and cheaper to generate than livestock. They returned to the under-populated and more fertile lowlands. Land under grain cultivation doubled from the 1860s to the '90s. However primitive the methods, the yields initially surpassed those of the Habsburg lands. The systematic development of a cereal economy and a change in eating habits then increased the birthrate, which continued long after the initial fertility of the land had reached its natural limit.

Serbia was a land of smallholders, with 73 per cent of agricultural land in units of less than 5 hectares. By 1897 only 12.5 per cent of the grain harvest was available for export. The cereal share of Serbia's export value was never more than 30 per cent before 1905, so that the country still depended on its livestock exports to Hungary. It was as a result of the 1881 commercial convention with Austria-Hungary, which afforded advantages to Serbia's farm exports, that its trade balance became favourable after 1887.

The changes needed to turn growth into sustained development had hardly begun. Apart from mining and railways, foreign capital did little to promote the growth of Serbian industry. Although the 1880s saw the beginnings of manufacture, the largest enterprise remained the Kragujevac ordnance factory, with over 2,000 employees by 1900. The rest was made up of breweries, flour mills and sawmills. Serbia (with Montenegro) was the only rail-less country in Europe. The government had undertaken at the Congress of Berlin to complete Serbia's section of the Orient Express. European loans enabled the completion of the Belgrade-Niš section by 1884, and by 1888 of the remainder to the eastern borders. In that year Serbian railways already transported 270,000 passengers, but the service of the debt on foreign loans had reached one-third of the budget, and there was no industrial take-off.

The new states of the Balkans were the last in Europe to industrialize, but they could not compete. When they tried to adopt protective tariffs, the industrialized countries raised impediments in order to retain the region as a reservoir of raw materials. Serbia would have needed a rate of growth at least as great as that of the advanced countries for its own economy to take off. Even though it passed through a period of economic expansion during the remainder of the century, Serbia fell behind while moving ahead.

The Eastern Crisis and its outcome had dealt a blow to its dream of becoming the Piedmont of the Southern Slavs. Defeat in war when Serbia alone faced Turkey had revealed the gap between the dream and the capacity to realize it. Russia had shattered the assumption that it necessarily supported Serbia's leadership rôle among the Balkan Slavs; it had made it clear that Vienna would now be Serbia's patron. The new frontier with Bulgaria became one between rivals for the remains of the Ottoman empire in Macedonia—a rivalry that knew or cared little about the ethnic composition of the area.

Bosnia, regarded as something of a natural heritage, and the sanjak of Novi Pazar, separating Montenegro from Serbia, were now out of bounds. Vienna imposed on Prince Milan agreements by which the newly-independent state became a satellite of the Habsburg monarchy. Austria-Hungary wanted favourable terms for its manufactured goods, and Serbia needed markets for its crops. Access to them had previously been at the price of heavy dependence on Austrian coinage and credit; the price now consisted of locking Serbia into Austria-Hungary's economy.

A greater danger was that of political strings. The secret political convention made Serbia's position all too clear, and caused a ministerial crisis. In exchange for Vienna's readiness to support its elevation to the status of a kingdom, and its interest in Macedonia, Serbia undertook to look away from the Dual Monarchy and the Habsburgs' sphere of influence. Milan had gone so far as to give an undertaking that he would not enter into any treaty without Austro-Hungarian approval. After that the principality was duly proclaimed a kingdom in March 1882.[1]

Serbia faced the problem of integrating new territory with a population that included 29 per cent Muslims who had no emotional attachment to the new nation-state. The additional triangle of territory had suffered from the war, and was generally below Serbian standards. There were Muslim property-owners, some with Christian tenants. As part of the Ottoman resettlement policy in sensitive areas, a continuous Muslim belt had surrounded pre-1875 Serbia—Albanians to the southwest, inserted Circassians to the northeast, and the 'Turks' who had left Serbia after 1862.

During the wars, the forces operating against Serbia had been

---

[1]Church autocephaly followed from state independence. Distinctions between 'church', 'state' and 'nation' were blurred; autocephaly was no longer perceived as interdependence between territorial churches, but as jurisdictional independence from Constantinople. At least, the Belgrade government was the only one in the Balkans to have the courtesy not to place the ecumenical patriarchate before a *fait accompli*. Autocephaly was negotiated, and granted in 1879.

made up to a large extent of Albanians—mostly from Kosovo and Macedonia. After the fall of Niš, Serbian units had gone on to penetrate Kosovo, and had stepped up their offensive due to the resistance of local Albanian conscripts until their advance was stopped by the armistice. Local Serbs had shown greater hostility towards Albanians than the soldiers from Serbia.

Although emigration from Serbia's new territories was less significant than that from Bulgaria and Bosnia, Muslims were, in one way or another, encouraged to leave. Their number has recently been estimated at 71,000, including at least 49,000 Albanians.[2] Most of them had gone before the end of hostilities. On the eve of its transfer to Serbian rule, Serbs made up no more than half the population of Niš; Turks were one-third, with Jews, Greeks, Gypsies, Armenians, Albanians and Bulgars accounting for the rest. By 1884, the Serbian share had risen to 80 per cent.

The Serbian government was bound to respect the Muslims' property rights, but tenants were pressed to buy, landlords sold on a depressed market, and speculators bought urban property at cheap prices. Many public buildings, including mosques, were subsequently neglected and destroyed as reminders of Turkish times. Most of the remaining Muslims were poor urban Turks. Albanian refugees settled in northern Kosovo, along the new border, replacing Serbian villagers who had fled to Serbia during the 1876 war, and taken over abandoned Albanian homes. The arrival of Albanian villagers worsened the lot of local Serbs, whose emigration continued after the treaty of Berlin.

Forced to come to terms with Austria-Hungary, Serbia concentrated on domestic issues. In spite of some financial scandals linked to rail contracts, and its king's tumultuous married life, the country made real progress, not least with mass politics and modern parties. The nationalist and popular Liberals had come to the end of their rôle. The intelligentsia turned away since they had nothing new to offer, and so did the peasantry who had to pay for the wars.

The influence of the educated élite had grown along with the bureaucratic structures of government. Most of them had by now obtained their higher education at home. Those who had been abroad had studied in Germany and Austria-Hungary as well as in France, but also in Russia and in Switzerland. Military officers, medical prac-

---

[2]Miloš Jagodić thinks that the figure of 30,000, suggested by Jovan Cvijić in 1911, is too low ('The Emigration of Muslims from the New Serbian Regions 1877/ 1878', *Balkanologie*, II/2, Paris, 1998, 109, 120).

titioners and engineers tended to study in central Europe. French influence remained strong, as students went to Paris to complement their education, and to acquire literary and political skills, which often went hand-in-hand.

With independence, the younger wing of the one-time Conservatives joined their Liberal counterparts. Their proclaimed war against backwardness, ignorance and lassitude was no less heroic than that to liberate kindred populations. For them the positivist virtues of progress, order and modernity were the essence of European culture. They believed that the modernization of the state should be initiated by the educated élite, in co-operation with the crown.

In 1881 they set up the Progressive Party; Radicals and Liberals also formally organized themselves as political parties. The Progressives were the pioneers of constitutionality and modern legislation. They saw respect for law as the only way to overcome absolutism, and the condition for social progress. They advocated shock therapy to drag Serbia out of its backwardness; the country had joined the modern family of European nations through independence,[3] and if it wanted to survive in that world, it had to be modernized—Europeanized.

This was a challenge, for such values were not widely appreciated. The peasant was attached to the collective, preferably local, and his craving for material goods was limited. He was broadly patriotic rather than nationalistic. One peasant member of the Assembly is recorded as having said in 1876: 'If we get Bosnia, that won't make my plot any bigger!' He distrusted the state and the towns which were the main beneficiaries of the much-vaunted progress. Most of all, he disliked increased taxation.

Although they moved away from their original Slavism and their utopian rural socialism, the Radicals feared that the country was so backward that it could only survive by holding on to its identity. They organized themselves as the first mass party, and obtained popular support with their call to cut down the state bureaucracy 'radically' and to extend 'self-government' at the local level. They were more and more influenced by the French republican left, by Swiss Radicalism, and even indirectly by British parliamentary practice, as they called for universal suffrage, government by the majority party in parliament, less bureaucracy, and less power for the crown.

---

[3]In 1881 Cunard launched a 'grand Ocean liner' called *Servia*. The first one, in 1840, had been the *Britannia*. A model *Servia* was exhibited at the Victoria and Albert Museum's 'Victorian Vision', London, spring 2001.

The emotional debate in parliament on the railway contracts symbolized the issue of modernization. Rail was the price of independence, and a requirement of modernization, but the peasants feared they would end up by paying for railways that would be advantageous to towns and to foreigners. Radicals argued that they would lead to economic bondage to foreign interests, and that the distinctive social and economic equality of Serbia would be destroyed.

The contracts were adopted. The Progressives, in office for most of the 1880s, carried out major reforms. They joined the Latin Monetary Union, setting Serbia's currency unit, the dinar, on a parity with the French franc. They founded a National Bank. They reformed education and taxation. They abolished the militia and improved the regular army. They strengthened the independence of the judiciary, and the freedoms of expression and association. They were more reformist that the Constitutionalists, and more enlightened than the Liberals, but they did not have popular support.

The reforms notwithstanding, the first decade of independent Serbia was marked by intense shocks, which could not be offset by the proclamation of the kingdom in 1882. There were scandals as the first railway contractors collapsed, and opposition to Milan's subservience to Austria-Hungary increased. The 1883 elections—the first to involve electioneering by organized parties—returned a 2:1 Radical majority.

King Milan nevertheless called the Progressives back to office. They adjourned the newly-elected Assembly, and ordered the collection of all privately-held weapons. Peasant resistance turned to real rebellion in the Timok area of eastern Serbia, which had suffered from the war, and where Radical agitation was rife. The rebellion was crushed by the army, and its leaders were executed or imprisoned, or fled abroad. The Radical party was temporarily neutralized.

Bulgaria had become a haven for Serbian émigrés. They came and went over a disputed border, and caused incidents. Milan was obsessed by Bulgaria's future moves. When in 1885 Eastern Roumelia was unified with Bulgaria, he saw it as a breach of the balance established in the Balkans by the treaty of Berlin, and launched a preventive war—to yield compensation, bring about a European intervention, and divert attention. Bismarck mocked the talk of 'balance of power' between Balkan statelets, but Serbian opinion too did not see the issue in such terms. Radicals and Liberals viewed the conflict as one between allies in a common cause. The Conservatives believed that an understanding could have been reached over spheres of influence in

Macedonia. Serbia's reluctant conscripts performed badly, and the unpopular war turned to humiliating defeat, from which Milan was rescued by Austrian intervention. His position had become untenable. He began to prepare his own exit with a flourish. He accepted a freely-elected Radical parliament. A new constitution was drawn up by an all-party commission, which sent personalities to study on the spot the electoral systems of France, Belgium, Denmark and Greece. Passed by parliament, the constitution of 1888 introduced parliamentary government tempered by the influence of the crown.

The Liberals were by then clearly the party of the past. The Progressives had had to attach themselves to the palace, and to use force. They were pushed aside by the Radicals, who voiced the aspirations of the masses. Their remaining rebels were amnestied, and they were asked to form a government. At the age of thirty-five, King Milan abdicated in favour of his thirteen-year old son Alexander (1876–1903).

The new constitution was a compromise between the parties, and between the crown and the parties. It spelt out civil liberties, strengthened local government and enhanced the Assembly by enabling it to share legislative initiative with the executive. Elections were direct and secret, the tax threshold for the franchise was further reduced, and there had to be at least two graduate representatives from each district. The Radicals, who were closer to the peasants' collectivist and egalitarian mentality, were going to build a party organization to obtain power through elections. They gained the peasant voters' numerical advantage, and in return their People's Radical Party (its full name), along with the other parties, enabled the peasants to take an active part in politics.

Their leader Nikola Pašić (1845–1926) still distrusted the way in which the older parties and King Milan had aspired to turn Serbia into a pale imitation of a small Western state, whereas the Serbian people had many good institutions of their own which only needed to be supplemented with technological and scientific knowledge. He advocated a foreign policy that relied on Russia, linked to an internal policy that sought to preserve what was good, rather than satellite status to Austria-Hungary and slavish imitation of Western institutions.[4]

[4]The Dalmatian legal scholar Valtazar Bogišić (1834–1908), who worked in Vienna, Paris and Russia, and was for a time minister of Justice in Montenegro, studied the institutions of the Southern Slavs. His enhancement of the *zadruga*— the extended family—helped it to serve as a sign of an allegedly distinct Slav, South Slav, Serbian and/or Croatian identity.

Considering itself to be the only true representative and defender of the Serbian people's interests, the Radical Party used the constitution to accede to power. Once in power, it would work not so much for allegedly Slav institutions as for parliamentary government, a limitation of the rôle of the crown, and guarantees against an intensification of Austro-German influences. In government the Radicals went on with much of what had been begun by their predecessors. They used parliament, but they also used the crown when convenient, and although they started off as the peasants' party, their representatives in government were no longer so rural.

They had their own way of interpreting the popular epic tradition, to show that medieval Serbia had been free, self-governing and egalitarian until the quarrelsome greed of its potentates had delivered it up to the Turks. As in other parts of Europe, the motivation was not to return to the past but to use the past as a way of moving into the future.[5] As the fifth centenary of the battle of Kosovo approached, the church calendar started to mark Saint Guy's (Vidovdan) as a holy day, the romantic theme was picked up by painters and playwrights, and Radicals agreed with Progressives to use the celebration in order to strengthen the kingdom's prestige. When 1889 came, however, an under-age King Alexander was on the throne, and Serbia was under Austrian influence. The main celebration was held in Kruševac, Prince Lazar's city, as a memorial to the fallen heroes of the battle of 1389, but care was taken not to turn it into a manifestation against Turkish rule over Kosovo.

The centenary also marked the beginning of a more scholarly approach, pioneered by the writings of Archimandrite Ilarion Ruvarac (1832–1905), whose controversial monograph on Lazar was published on the eve of that anniversary.[6] Most of his career was spent struggling against traditionalists and romantics, but there was no turning back after him, since he inspired other historians to investigate the past critically.

It was as though culture, politics, the economy and society moved at different speeds, without synchronization, and incapable of mutual

---

[5] It is interesting to note that, at the other end of the continent, Icelandic scholars and politicians were constructing a narrative based on the sagas—of a country once free, egalitarian and democratically self-governing, until the greed of its élite delivered it up to the king of Norway in the 1260s. In Finland the national epic, the *Kalevala*, laid the groundwork for the illusion of national continuity of Finnish culture.

[6] Ilarion Ruvarac, *O knezu Lazaru* (Prince Lazar), Novi Sad, 1888.

support.[7] Very soon after his accession King Alexander Obrenović displayed the same authoritarianism as his father. By a series of coups, starting in 1893 when he was not yet seventeen, he dismissed his regents and then proceeded to turn constitutional government into a farce. He became an adept at playing party factions against each other, at managing a palace group within each party, at manipulating elections through administrative pressure, and at obtaining parliamentary sanction of sorts. In 1900 he married his mistress, a widow older than himself, with a past. Even the Radicals came to accept a compromise as a way back to a more parliamentary régime—a new constitution granted by the king in 1901. This introduced an upper house for the first time, a senate of which three-fifths of its members were crown appointees, and a possible succession other than through male heirs since the royal couple were childless and there were no other male descendants of Miloš Obrenović. Public opinion turned against King Alexander. In 1903 a group of army officers murdered the twenty-six-year-old monarch and his queen who had made their kingdom into an object of international ridicule. Serbia offered a mixed picture at the end of the nineteenth century. In spite of undeniable progress, it was not an altogether attractive proposition even for Serbs outside the kingdom, let alone for other Southern Slavs.

Relations with Montenegro had become cool, as the sister state continued to affirm itself under Prince Nicholas, who remained an autocratic monarch. It too had been internationally recognized as independent in 1878, when it was doubled in size—to 9,433 sq. km, with 116,000 more inhabitants to a total of some 286,000 (of whom about 25,000 were Catholics and as many Muslims).

The new acquisitions included a small coastline, but its waters were closed to warships of all nations, and Austria-Hungary was entrusted with policing its shores. Surrounded on three sides by Habsburg possessions or occupied territory, and with some sort of a naval protectorate, it continued to receive Russian subsidies. The government was able to fund enough primary schools to decrease urban male illiteracy to just under 50 per cent by 1900 (when the 31,400 town-

[7]Cf an interesting point made by the historian Dimitrije Djordjević, *Ogledi iz novije balkanske istorije* (Essays on Modern Balkan History), Belgrade: Srpska književna zadruga, 1989, 198.

dwellers made up less than 11 per cent of the population). Students went on to university in Zagreb and, especially, Belgrade. However, Montenegro could not make up for the decline in prestige of the larger Serbian state. It found difficulty integrating old Montenegro, the new territories and the coast. Its inhabitants continued to emigrate to Serbia, where they settled the border regions abandoned by Muslims.

In Croatia-Slavonia, whose separate identity attached to Hungary had been acknowledged after the *Ausgleich*, Serbs formed a quarter of the 1.9 million population; as refugees from the Ottoman dominions, they had once been placed under the direct authority of the court in Vienna, but had lost that status with the abolition of the Military Border. Whenever they felt worried by Croatian claims, they would turn to Budapest, to Vienna or to Belgrade. Since Croatia's public opinion had generally placed much hope in Serbia as the nucleus of a future Yugoslav community, part of its political class came to fear an alliance between Serbia and those Serbs whom the wars had displaced westwards.

Such a link, even more than the one with Vienna, was felt as a potential threat to the very historicity of Croatia. The mentality of Hungary's ruling gentry, which sought to establish a unitary nation-state over 'historic' lands that included other ethnic communities, affected political thinking among neighbouring nationalities. At the same time the Hungarian authorities would use such feelings to control rising discontent against their Magyarization policies.

At the time of the Compromise, a smaller part of Croatia's politicians had wanted a separate Croatia. These defenders of their country's 'state' rights formed the Rights Party, headed by Ante Starčević (1823–96). Born of a mixed Border family, and in his youth an ardent Illyrian, disillusioned with Serbia's lack of response and with Slavism of any kind, he sought a clear identity for Croatia, based on his arbitrary reading of history. Spreading his Croatia across Slovenia, Croatia-Slavonia, Dalmatia and Bosnia-Herzegovina, Starčević argued that all its Slavs, however they spoke or worshipped, were really Croats who did not realize it and could be Croatized (or re-Croatized). His party, which had been in the ascendant in the 1870s, went into decline in the 1880s and split at the end of the century. While its main stream settled into moderation, its Pure Rights splinter became more antagonistic to Serbs.

The 1868 constitutional arrangements meant at first that the Budapest government's Magyarization measures were not implemented in Croatia-Slavonia to the same degree as elsewhere. However, after

Independent Serbia, 1878–1914   75

Károly Khuen-Héderváry took over as *ban* in 1893, remaining in the post for the following twenty years, Magyarization intensified. The *sabor* was controlled through the small electorate, party divisions, the presence of hereditary and official members, and the exploitation of Serbian-Croatian differences after the full incorporation of the Border. This brought more Serbs into political life. Indeed, with Serbia virtually a dependency of Austria-Hungary, more Serbs were encouraged to enter the administration.

The voice of political Serbs in Croatia was the Serbian Independent Party—until the 1890s, when it was challenged by the Serbian People's Radical Party of Hungary, which extended its activities to Croatia. The Radicals in Hungary looked to eventual union with Serbia; their attraction was their call for universal suffrage, along with cultural and religious autonomy at local level.

The Austrian province of Dalmatia had a population of under half a million, of whom 16 per cent were Serbs. Their exponents had gone along with the National Party until that party, on gaining control of the diet in 1889, turned to being more Croatian and styled itself the Croatian National Party. The Serbs then shifted to the Autonomists, but since these were led by urban Italian-speakers who increasingly defined themselves as ethnically Italian, Serbs went their own way with the Serbian National Party.

Such were the political shifts among the élite of the Habsburg Serbs. The last decades of the century saw growing dissatisfaction among the non-Magyar nationalities, as cultural Magyarization, added to political control, went with accelerated change in rural areas. After an agrarian crisis due to the competition of foreign grain, protectionism and more modern techniques produced an agricultural revolution in Hungary, which worked to the benefit of the great landowners and the detriment of the smallholders. The effects were particularly hard in Hungary's borderlands, where owners of estates were largely non-native. Indebted over the compensations they were paying for having acquired their plots, smallholders became landless labourers or emigrated. The Hungarian part of the Monarchy saw a wave of emigration, in which minorities were over-represented. The drift of Croatian and Serbian peasants to towns and overseas was the result of the paucity of land, a growing population and rising food prices. The one-time Military Border was one of the areas particularly affected. In Voivodina at the turn of the century, Serbs formed the majority of the rural landless 40 per cent.

At the same time, added to the established social élite of Hungary's

Serbian community and the small number of educated and partly Catholic urban Serbs in Dalmatia, there was a growing and prosperous Serbian urban commercial and professional class in Croatia. Its Serbian Bank founded in Zagreb in 1882 grew to attract a capital surpassing that of any Belgrade bank, with extensive commercial operations and direct investments in Serbia.

Bosnia-Herzegovina was a special addition to Austria-Hungary, which acquired there 1.2 million more Southern Slavs. The takeover on a mandate from the treaty of Berlin was practically a conquest, in which one-third of the Monarchy's fully-mobilized combat capability was committed in three years of intermittent warfare. The resistance was offered by paramilitaries assembled from the Bosnian Muslims around the local conscripts who formed most of the Ottoman forces on the spot, and who remained with their kit after the Turkish army had officially been evacuated. Serbian leaders and agitators worked alongside Muslim activists. Further rebellions and guerrilla action were led by Serbs from Herzegovina, with Muslim support. Serbia kept out, unwilling to confront Austria-Hungary.

The region did not finally settle down until the autumn of 1882. Muslims had immediately started to leave in large numbers for other parts of the Ottoman Empire. No exact figures exist, but perhaps as many as 100,000–180,000 of them, mainly peasants, had emigrated by 1914. Another 100,000 Serbs and Croats may also have gone— temporarily for the most part—to Serbia, Hungary, Romania and, even more, to America. By the time of the 1910 census, with 180,000– 200,000 immigrants coming in from the rest of the Monarchy, Muslims were down from 39 to 33 per cent, Catholics were up from 18 to 23, and the Orthodox remained at 43 per cent.

Taken over as one unit, Bosnia-Herzegovina was immediately treated as if it were a permanent possession, administered colonially under the crown by the joint Austro-Hungarian Ministry of Finances. Habsburg rule moved efficiently but carefully, so as not to upset further the balance between the religious communities. During his long tenure of the ministry, Benjámin Kállay took special care of the new territory, for he was Austria-Hungary's Balkan expert. A diplomat who had been consul general in Belgrade until 1875, he was a Serbo-Croat-speaker and had written a 'History of Serbia' (1877). A much improved administration was put in place, infrastructures were enhanced, the exploitation of natural resources was encouraged, and returning refugees and newcomers were successfully accommodated.

Because agriculture was left largely untouched, the Muslim landowners were reconciled, in spite of measures to assist dependent peasants to buy their plots. Three-quarters of the sharecropper families who worked on 6–7,000 Muslim-owned estates were Serbs. By 1910 that glaring ethnic-religious difference between owners and sharecroppers obscured the fact that free smallholders had become twice as numerous as dependent peasants, but the free peasants spent all their money on paying out compensation to the landlords, making the Orthodox a generally frustrated minority looking to Serbia.

With increasing emphasis on ethnic definitions, the great question in Bosnian politics for both Serbs and Croats was to claim the Muslims in order to become a majority. To insulate the province from nationalist tendencies, the administration promoted the idea of a Bosnian identity. While it generally failed in all three communities, it did appeal to some Muslims, most of whom wanted to be neither Serb not Croat.

The administration's exploitation of Catholic-Orthodox rivalries, and its inability to advance state education, contributed to growing Serbo-Croatian tension. Both Christian communities got their own church hierarchies; nevertheless, a favoured Catholic hierarchy, imported clerics from Croatia, an expanded network of Catholic schools, and the staffing of state schools by immigrant Croatian teachers, who were considered more reliable than local Serbs, all contributed to Serbian apprehension. Since no form of political expression was yet tolerated, a movement for autonomous education developed among the very small number of urban Serbs (parallel to that of the Muslims).

The Ottoman empire had come out of the Eastern Crisis seriously weakened. Having suspended the constitution of 1876, Sultan Abdülhamid II returned to authoritarian rule. This was a personal despotism which both continued reforms and used Islam as a state ideology. The Westernized teaching establishments produced a new élite which harked back to the constitutional order so as to modernize the empire. The Ottoman cadres in the European territories provided a base for a more nationalist identification in the Muslim majority. The emphasis on Islam further contributed to the alienation of non-Muslims.

Albanians acquired weight as the predominant Muslim group in what remained of the Ottoman Balkans. The League of Prizren was a turning-point. As the powers gathered in Berlin in 1878, Albanian leaders met in Prizren to prevent the assignment to Christian states of territories inhabited by Albanians. Born of such resentment, the Albanian movement thereafter received encouragement from various sources, including at times Montenegro and Serbia, as a way of sapping Ottoman power. There was growing anarchy in the peripheral regions of the empire inhabited by Albanians, as rebellion against the central government mixed with action against the non-Albanian population— with or without official help. Albanians continued to expand into the better lands of Kosovo and Macedonia, as Slavs continued to emigrate.

Macedonia—defined as the three provinces of Salonika, Monastir (Bitola) and Üsküb (Skopje)—occupied an important strategic location in the centre of the peninsula. Several ethnic groups overlapped and blended into one another. The majority spoke South Slav variations that ranged from established Serbian to established Bulgarian, and felt no strong identity. In the 1880s and '90s the territory became the focus of competing nationalists, who sought to carve out their stakes among the crumbling Ottoman possessions. The rural world was one of largely absent Muslim landlords and Christian sharecroppers. Although more land was passing to the peasants, it could not support the population. Ottomans could only seek to divide and rule in a region where social and economic unrest was added to religious and ethnic rivalries.

Austria-Hungary had diverted Serbia's view to the south. Although in their time Prince Michael's plans had been a source of inspiration there, they had concentrated on Bosnia. Partly as a consequence of reforms of the Serbian literary language, speech traffic with Macedonia had declined. Bulgarian influence had been the first to challenge the position of Hellenism among the educated, and came out on top in the competition since the establishment in 1870 of a separate Bulgarian church organization—the Bulgarian exarchate. The mass of the Slav peasantry were subjected to varying external influences, which an incipient autochthonous Macedonian movement wanted to exclude.

The fears in Serbia that it was being left behind in the competition led it after 1885, with Austro-Hungarian support, to step up its efforts. The foreign ministry set up a special department for schools and churches outside Serbia, consulates were opened, talks were initiated with the patriarchate and the Porte for the appointment of some ethnic Serbian bishops. By the end of the century the sees of Prizren and Skopje had been filled by Serbian prelates, and a network of Serbian schools established. Official Serbia saw this expansion of influence southwards into Ottoman territory as a way of defending itself against increased Austro-Hungarian control.

Initially played by consuls, priests and teachers, the competition had been taken over at the turn of the century by armed bands supported by governments and nationalist lobbies, while landlords employed private militias of Albanians to intimidate their peasants. Influenced by Bulgarian and Serbian socialists, the young urban Macedonian autonomists hoped to lead abused peasants into social rebellion. However, the response of Christian peasants was increasingly to emigrate to neighbouring Balkan states or to America.

The pattern of great power alliances and antagonisms had little direct effect on the ground. No power wanted to be distracted by events in the Balkans; Serbia had politicians and diplomats who took advantage of opportunities, and were ready to compromise.

The way in which the last Obrenović king had been killed by the military plotters shocked European opinion but upset few people at home. A provisional government was immediately formed of representatives of the political parties. It summoned the last regularly-elected parliament, which restored an amended version of the 1888 constitution, and elected as king, in succession to the extinct Obrenović line, the only obvious candidate: Peter Karadjordjević (1844–1921), son of the last reigning prince of that family, and widowed son-in law of Nicholas of Montenegro. Educated in France, he had fought in the French army, participated in the Bosnian rising, and lately been living in Geneva with his children. Having spent his life in exile, he was not closely acquainted with internal conditions.

In order to show that a new era had begun, a coronation was held for the first time, but not until 1904, to coincide with the centenary of Karageorge's rising, and to give Europe time to come to terms with the new monarch. The following decade has often been described as the golden age of parliamentary democracy in Serbia—which it was, relatively and retrospectively. The tax threshold for the right to vote had been reduced yet further. This was not quite full male suffrage, but in terms of the percentage of the population entitled to vote, Serbia was third in Europe after France and Switzerland.

At the elections that followed, the Radicals obtained 90 per cent of the seats. Their hegemony was mitigated by their division, for although they had obtained absolute majorities since 1883, a fraction had been formed in 1901 that disapproved of the concessions made to the crown: these 'independent' Radicals would secede in 1905, even though the original reason for the division no longer existed.

The Progressive Party had dissolved in 1898. The Liberals were still there, but did not play any significant part. The Social-Democratic

Party, formed in 1903, was based on a tiny industrial working class. The political scene was thus practically the preserve of two parties originating in the same movement, and indeed sharing the same programme. They were equally nationalist in foreign policy, were hostile to Austria-Hungary, considered Russia to be Serbia's natural protector, but looked also to France and Britain. With a more urban and educated electorate, more 'left' and Yugoslav-minded, less prone to compromise and demagogy, the new Independent Radical Party grew to virtual parity with the mainstream Radicals, joining them, or alternating with them, in government.

Two shadows were cast over the 'golden age'. One was the Radicals' tendency to use their parliamentary majority to place themselves above parliament. The other was the section of the officer corps that had made it all possible. There was a tacit division of power between parliamentary government, dominated by one party, and the military which looked after its own, with constant meddling by the conspirators of 1903, generally known as the Black Hand. The problem was that, as elsewhere in the Balkans, modernization went with fear of the unknown, and that a state-dependent bourgeoisie did not provide strong support for development. There was no really wealthy class, the state apparatus absorbed most of the educated, and the social mentality remained fundamentally egalitarian, even collectivist.

Nevertheless, the last decade before the First World War was alive with modern party politics—in five organized parties—and press debates—around a dozen dailies. The expanding state education system, by drawing increasingly on Western European secular ideas, assimilated the small non-Serbian urban minority of Jews and various Christians (Vlachs, Czechs and others), and stamped itself particularly on the upper reaches of the civil service, of political parties and of the free professions.

By 1910 half the country's 12,000 secondary and vocational school pupils were in Belgrade, along with the university's 1,600 students. The capital city became the centre of a culture led by a new generation of intellectuals who advocated 'French' ideas of political 'liberty' in opposition to the Central European notion of historic 'privileges'. They provided a Serbian expression of the Yugoslav idea that was also being aired by some Croatian writers in reaction to the historicist tradition of 'state rights'. The French-educated founders of the influential journal *Srpksi književni glasnik* (Serbian Literary Herald) even invented the 'Belgrade style'—a simple, direct, lighter, elegant way of writing Serbo-Croat.

The centenary of the First Rising combined with the coronation were also celebrations of South Slav solidarity, as Croatian, Slovene and Bulgarian delegations attended them. That profile of Belgrade made Serbia more attractive to Serbs and other South Slav neighbours still under Ottoman or Habsburg rule, even though there was no generally agreed vision of what Yugoslavism entailed. In Belgrade the momentum for, and the focus on, modernization could easily be confused with an attraction to join Serbia.

Belgrade had a population in 1910 of 90,000—3.1 per cent of a total population that had increased to 2.9 million. Industry employed 7 per cent. Serbia remained predominantly agrarian. The Hungarian agricultural revolution had turned the Dual Monarchy into a net exporter of livestock by the end of the century, and Hungarian agricultural interests, concerned for their imperial internal market, demanded protection. The decennial renewal of the Austro-Hungarian customs union in 1906 led Vienna to press Belgrade to make concessions on tariff increases.

Controversy had already arisen over railway loans and military purchases, when the Serbo-Bulgarian rapprochement caused alarm in Vienna. Austria-Hungary applied pressure to force Serbia away from its 1905 treaty with Bulgaria, and interrupted negotiations over its own trade relations with Belgrade, finally countering Serbia's reluctance to comply with a veterinary embargo. This was the start of the 'Pig War', which turned on Budapest's protectionism as much as on Vienna's more general anxiety over Serbia's increasing independence.

The potential for continued expansion of its cattle export was by that time limited, and Serbia was forced to find new outlets and to process its exports for more distant markets. French loans ensured its survival during the tariff war, and the switch of military purchases to France. Germany, Austria-Hungary's closest ally, took the bulk of Serbia's wheat and processed meat exports; corn still went to Hungary's cattle breeders. Austria-Hungary's failure to retain sufficient economic leverage enabled Serbia to emerge strengthened from the tariff war in 1911, but with the fear that the Monarchy's one-time dominance might be revived.

In the meantime the 'Pig War' had merged with the crisis over the annexation of Bosnia-Herzegovina in 1908. Vienna decided on this in order to strengthen its position in the Balkans and on the Adriatic, and also to alter the course of the South Slav movement that it saw as being increasingly attracted to Belgrade. It was hastened by the revolution of the 'Young Turks' which that year reactivated the Ottoman constitution of 1876 formally over the whole empire, including Bosnia and Herzegovina. However, by the will of the Dual Monarchy, the sanjak of Novi Pazar remained Ottoman in order to keep Serbia and Montenegro separated.

The annexation was felt in Serbia as a heavy blow, a manifestation of Austria-Hungary's intention to end once and for all the aspirations of its own Serbian population to unite one day with Serbia. In Serbia itself an inflamed opinion, expecting a rising in Bosnia, seemed ready for war. The powers meanwhile called on the Belgrade government to recognize the annexation, and a three-party coalition government accepted that there was not much Serbia could do in the circumstances. The emergency and the indignation caused by the annexation somewhat sidetracked the developing multiparty system which had promoted democratic reforms since 1903. An official consensus was reached on a restrained foreign policy, with unofficial support for nationalist agitation outside the kingdom.

It was only after the crisis that the Black Hand officers began to meddle more directly in politics. Having decided that the political parties could not be relied on to carry out the task, they undertook themselves to organize nationalist propaganda and the action of armed bands (*chetas*) in 'unredeemed' territories. In 1911 they set themselves up as a secret society under the name of 'Unification or Death', whose statute listed as 'Serbian provinces' to be united to Serbia: Bosnia, Herzegovina, Montenegro, 'Old Serbia', Macedonia, Croatia, Slavonia, Srem, Voivodina and Dalmatia.

Serbia concentrated its sights once again on Macedonia and the sea; Balkan cooperation returned to the fore. Macedonia was particularly vulnerable. In the anarchy that prevailed, the small left-leaning Internal Macedonian Revolutionary Organization (IMRO) staged the abortive rising of August 1903, leading a minority of peasants against landlords and warlords. The brutality of the repression drove the powers to initiate a policy of reforms, to be enforced by international monitors and an international gendarmerie, through ethnically-based districts. These moves triggered off, and were stopped by, the Young Turks' coup, which promised effective equalization and Ottomanization. The population of the European provinces at first welcomed it, and all groups in Macedonia took advantage of the period of freedom and uncertainty that followed, until ruthless authoritarianism prevailed in the new régime.

Talks were resumed between Belgrade and Sofia. The war that Italy started against Turkey in 1911 over Tripoli, and the great Albanian

Independent Serbia, 1878–1914

revolt that followed on disappointment with the Young Turks, hastened the resolve to agree. By March 1912 Serbia and Bulgaria had conceded Greek claims to southern Macedonia, and attempted a division of the north—agreeing to disagree on a contested zone, the fate of which was left to Russian mediation.

Fearing that Austria-Hungary would obtain a mandate over Macedonia as it had over Bosnia, and threatened by the new régime's Ottomanization, and by the possible setting up of a great Albanian autonomous unit if the Porte gave in to the rebels, the Balkan states combined. Now that the annexation of Bosnia-Herzegovina had put an end to Austro-Russian cooperation, Russia was willing to support policies that led to a re-opening of the Eastern Question.

Bulgaria, Greece, Montenegro and Serbia went to war to vindicate the cause of their oppressed co-nationals still under Turkish rule, but they were also attracted by territorial expansion into Macedonia and Albania. They justified their adoption of European-style imperialism by historical memories more than by the defence of Christian peasants against Muslim landlords, or by the contradictory claims of ethnicity. The Porte had hurried to settle with Italy, and had come close to settling with the Albanian insurgents. The powers, divided among themselves, did not intervene.

Within a month the Balkan armies had won spectacular victories on all fronts. The well-reformed Serbian army had fought a successful campaign, even though its war plans since 1908 had been defensive. Serbia and Montenegro had played Albanian clans against each another. The Serbs had eventually entered Skopje and joined the Montenegrins in Novi Pazar. The realization that Kosovo could finally be liberated and avenged fired the conscripts' imagination. 'Kosovo' had by then become a complex whole interweaving several elements— the battle which symbolized the end of medieval Serbia and the beginning of Turkish domination, the religious values of martyrdom and hope, and the territory of what had come to be called 'Old Serbia'.

Austria-Hungary threatened Serbia and Montenegro with war if their troops did not withdraw immediately from the Adriatic. The decision taken by the powers to set up an Albanian state between the mountains and the sea blocked Serbia's extension to the Adriatic, prompting its refusal to compromise on its gains in Macedonia. Bulgaria tried to reverse these by launching the Second Balkan War against Serbia in 1913. Turkey joined in to defeat Bulgaria. At the treaty of Bucharest which brought about a final settlement in August 1913, Serbia gained 40,000 sq. km.—including Kosovo and a common frontier with Montenegro. The prestige of the Serbian army, and with it the influence of the military, had been enhanced.

The cost had been high—60,000 dead and wounded, and military expenditure estimated at four times the state revenues of 1911. Serbia was exhausted. All participants in the wars had behaved in such a way as to show that their aim was not only to acquire territory, but to get rid of rival or antagonistic ethnic groups, at least by cultural or statistical means. Racked by a decade and more of disorders and ethnic rivalry, the new territories of Macedonia and Kosovo needed to be integrated politically, economically and culturally. Their neglected and disparate population included many Orthodox Slavs with no clear national consciousness, some of whom looked to Bulgaria, as well as an important proportion of Muslim Turks and Albanians.

The Muslim Albanians in particular felt hostility towards Serbia. The avenging violence of Serbian and Montenegrin troops when they moved into Albanian-inhabited territory had further embittered feelings, leading to a rebellion in September 1913. This of course was damaging to Serbia's freedom-loving image, and was denounced by Dimitrije Tucović (1881–1914) the leader of Serbia's Social Democrats who had himself taken part in the war.[8] Serbian opinion hardly realized that only few Serbs were left in 'Old Serbia'.[9]

The army continued to have the upper hand in the new territories pending the full extension of constitutional rule, which had not yet been achieved by 1914; this caused tension both with the civil authorities in Macedonia and with the opposition in Belgrade. Driven by officers more loyal to the Black Hand than to the government, the military stifled the government's efforts to give the largely Slav population of Macedonia at least the immediate right to local government. They sanctioned the dismissal of local officials, teachers and priests who were not willing to declare themselves Serbs, and in the circumstances few ventured into what was a provisional legal vacuum to rebuild war-torn infrastructures.

---

[8] Dimitrije Tucović, *Srbija i Arbanija. Jedan prilog kritici zavojevačke politike srpske buržoazije* (Serbia and Albania. A Contribution to the Critique of the Serbian Bourgeoisie's Policy of Conquest), Belgrade, 1914.

[9] Serbs amounted to some 21 per cent of the 439,000 population of the area at the time of the first Yugoslav census in 1921. The census recorded only language (26 per cent Serbo-Croat-speakers) and religion (21 per cent Eastern Orthodox) (Bogoljub Kočović, *Etnički i demokratski razvoj u Jugoslaviji od 1921. do 1991. godine* (The Ethnic and Demographic Evolution of Yugoslavia from 1921 to 1991), Paris: Bibiothèque Dialogue, 1998, 346).

Whereas Orthodox Macedonian Slavs were deemed to be Serbs, no attempt was made to Serbianize the Albanians, but they were generally accused of having forced some 150,000 Serbs out of the area since the mid-1870s, and of terrorizing those who remained. They were considered rebellious against all authority, and as having been pushed to nationalism by Austrian and Italian intrigues. Some emigrated to the new Albanian state, or to other havens in the shrinking Ottoman empire. Those who stayed resisted Serbia's authority whenever and however they could.

Nevertheless, Serbia's victories inspired most Serbs in the Habsburg lands, and once again more Croats and Slovenes, to think of a new Yugoslav state as an alternative in the nearer rather than the remoter future. The Croatian sculptor Ivan Meštrović (1883–1962), who had grown up as a shepherd in Dalmatia under the influence of the Kosovo epics, became obsessed in the years between 1907 and the outbreak of war in 1914 with his project of a temple to the Kosovo heroes, as symbols of the long struggle of the Southern Slavs against foreign oppression. Public opinion in Serbia may even have been convinced that the kingdom was indeed destined to lead a future united Yugoslavia. The permanent break with Bulgaria over Macedonia also meant that Serbia was isolated against Austria-Hungary. Pašić and the Radical leaders began to talk of a possible future union, and to explore cooperation with the coalition of parties that controlled the diet in Croatia-Slavonia.

Montenegro's enlargement was even more of a strain. Many Muslims emigrated from the sanjak of Novi Pazar after their villages had been scorched in the war in retaliation for what had been done to Christian villagers at the time of the Eastern Crisis. The rising opposition to Prince Nicholas's autocratic rule from the younger and mainly Belgrade-formed generation of a small intelligentsia was partly neutralized by his foreign policy, which followed that of Serbia. In 1905 he granted a constitution—which was little more than a change of form to improve his image and attract foreign money, since it left power in his hands. An assembly, partly elected through open voting, provided a forum for an organized opposition, but was dissolved in 1907. The opposition went underground, and caused strained relations with Belgrade, as Nicholas believed that support for his opponents came from Serbia.

Montenegro had more than quadrupled its territory since Nicholas's accession. By 1913 he ruled over highland clans who had not been stamped by Montenegro's identity, and who felt a closer bond to

Belgrade than to Cetinje. His state had an outlet to the Adriatic, and it had acquired Metohija, with the historic patriarchal monastery of Peć. He too remembered the glories of the Nemanjić period, and dreamed of uniting the Serbs, at least in his poems. On the fiftieth anniversary of his accession in 1910 he promoted himself to be king of Montenegro, and gathered representatives of the ruling houses of Europe in Cetinje to celebrate the event. By that time he was nicknamed the father-in-law of Europe; his sons-in-law were King Victor Emmanuel III of Italy, King Peter of Serbia, two Russian grand dukes, and Prince Franz Joseph of Battenberg (brother of Alexander, the first prince of Bulgaria, and of Louis, the British naval officer).

In spite of all its acquisitions, Montenegro's basic problem remained: namely, that it could not support its population. It is estimated that by 1914 over a third of men of working age were away on seasonal jobs or had emigrated, usually to the United States. The number of expatriates may even have been as high as half the population. Montenegro subsisted on their remittances, as well as on foreign loans and subsidies.

Expatriates and the educated youth viewed Serbia as a rising state that was superior to Montenegro in every aspect, and branded Nicholas as conducting a policy that was narrowly Montenegrin as well as reactionary. Montenegro's reputation declined. When a 200–km-long common border was established with Serbia, many Montenegrins demanded immediate unification. King Nicholas met the challenge by allowing free elections, which brought the opposition People's Party to power in March 1914. Negotiations were opened with Belgrade for a military, diplomatic and financial union. However, the complete loss of identity implicit in unity with Serbia was as difficult to envisage as the survival of a second, smaller and economically non-viable Serbian kingdom. The dilemma made the third option of a larger Yugoslavia attractive to sections of Montenegrin opinion. All three options had their supporters.

Austria-Hungary went through a constitutional crisis in 1905 when the Hungarian opposition Independence Party won the elections. The sovereign's threat to introduce universal suffrage, as was intended in the Austrian part of the Monarchy, brought Hungary back to order. The *Ausgleich* remained unchanged, and Hungary retained a franchise limited to just over 6 per cent of the total population. Coming as it did soon after the changes in Serbia, the tension between Budapest and Vienna once again brought Serbo-Croatian solidarity to the fore. Intellectuals and even politicians in Zagreb and Belgrade had intermittently been in touch with each other through visits, congresses, exhibitions and other events, and regarded the mystique of South Slav unity as an ultimate aim. In Croatia a new political generation resented the way in which Hungarian policy had successfully broken up Croatian parties, or used concessions to promote Hungarian rather than Serbian interests. The young in both communities were joining to demand reforms. In 1905 Croatian opposition deputies met in Fiume (Rijeka) to try and exploit the crisis, by offering their support to the Hungarian Independentists in exchange for improving the status of Croatia-Slavonia, and for working towards the incorporation of Dalmatia into a reconstituted Triune Realm.

What was intended primarily as a statement of political strategy obtained no response in Budapest, but it was made on behalf of one Serbo-Croatian people, and was warmly endorsed by the representatives of the Monarchy's Serbian parties meeting in the Dalmatian city of Zadar.[10] Both groups and the Social Democrats then merged into the Croat-Serb Coalition, which won an absolute majority of seats in the Croatian diet in 1906.

The two Serbian parties were 'ethnic' parties, in the sense that they spoke for the Serbian 25 per cent of the population of Croatia-Slavonia, although most Serbs there did not even have a vote. The Serbian Independent Party, which had been expanding since 1903 under the militant leadership of Svetozar Pribićević (1875–1936), had taken the lead from the Serbian People's Radical Party, by getting rid of the 'Military' Serbs' image as supporters of officialdom, and by returning to the earlier idea of Croats and Serbs as one people.

Pribićević offered the willingness of the Serbs to respect Croatia's rights, and to struggle for the unification of Croatia, Slavonia and Dalmatia, in exchange for a full acknowledgement of their equal partnership. For many leading Croats at the time, the future common state was indeed seen as an extended autonomous Triune Realm of equal Croats and Serbs. Although it remained the majority political force in Croatia until 1918, the coalition—never more than an umbrella organization—followed a highly opportunistic course of action.

The annexation of Bosnia-Herzegovina complicated matters.

---

[10] The ethnic minority parties of Hungary proper had teamed up for the elections of 1905, and one Serbian representative from Voivodina had been elected to the Budapest parliament along with Slovaks and Romanians.

There was some sympathy for Serbia's indignation, and tough measures were taken. The *sabor* was adjourned. Ill-conceived treason trials, and the writings of a Vienna historian aimed at showing that coalition leaders had conspired with the Serbian government, misfired. The coalition was given a new lease of life, and the Hungarian government had to come to terms with it; it agreed to work again within the system, and the number of voters was increased from less than 50,000 to 190,000, out of a total population of 2.6 million. New elections again gave the coalition an absolute majority of seats.

The Balkan wars increased the prestige of Serbia. On the one hand, its victories frightened many Croats, who came to see Belgrade as an obstacle to the establishment of a South Slav unit within the Habsburg monarchy, and on the other, many of the young turned against legal action. The moderation of the coalition was criticized; the situation deteriorated. There were pro-Serbian demonstrations, strikes and acts of terrorism. The diet was again dissolved, but new elections in December 1913 returned the same majority, reinforced.

On the eve of the war in 1914, there was a strong feeling of South Slav solidarity. Serbia once more focused hopes, as a growing and restless student population turned to terrorism. Openly anti-Habsburg aspirations were nevertheless still limited to a fringe. The strongest political grouping worked within the constitution. The coalition had brought to an end the manipulation of Serbo-Croatian differences; it stood strongly for cooperation of all the Southern Slavs within the Monarchy.

However, Croatia's limited economic upsurge in the years leading to the First World War had exaggerated the already sharp differences between its one-time civil and military areas. Light industry had progressed. The proportion of the total population in agriculture had decreased from 84 per cent in 1900 to 70 in 1910. Yet the grain output was not much greater than in Ottoman Macedonia. The estates did not respond to export opportunities or even to the advantages of the imperial market. The old Border's low-yield cultivation, a literacy rate of barely 20 per cent and virtually non-existent industry further prompted the emigration of almost a quarter of a million pauperized peasants (more Serbs than Croats) to North America in the final pre-war years. The situation in Austrian Dalmatia was even worse; it enjoyed universal male suffrage, but could not support its population.

South Slav solidarity, agricultural ferment, and the impatience of high-school pupils and students were particularly strong in Bosnia-Herzegovina. The Sarajevo conspiracy was not born in isolation. It was linked to the students's and workers' strikes, the demonstrations and repressive measures, and the previous attempts—numbering about a dozen—on the lives of state dignitaries throughout the Yugoslav territories of Austria-Hungary. In Bosnia contacts with various organizations in neighbouring Serbia were easier.

The reforms enacted between 1903 and 1912 had, if anything, aggravated ethnic antagonism in spite of their attempt to promote modernization. The formation of ethnic political organizations was allowed. In 1907 a Serbian National Organization was set up, and the number of Serbian Orthodox church schools increased sharply. A Croatian organization had been founded the previous year, and the Muslims had theirs the following year. All three placed similar emphasis on separate school networks; the clergy played an important rôle in defining their respective communities. With respectively more and less legality, Croats looked to Croatia and Serbs to Serbia.

In 1910 Emperor Francis Joseph granted Bosnia-Herzegovina its own constitution. The administration was flanked by an advisory diet, elected with a limited franchise and colleges divided according to social position and religious affiliation. The elected deputies reflected exactly the size of their respective confessions. The parties even cooperated tactically within limits, usually the Muslims with a majority of Croats, leaving the Serbs in a minority.

In spite of measures to help the voluntary buying-out of sharecropping tenants, there were few transfers. In 1911, 91 per cent of landowners with dependent peasants were Muslims, and so were 56 per cent of free peasants, whereas 74 per cent of dependent peasants were Serbs. A scattered uprising of Serbian peasants that year helped to accelerate the implementation, but in 1914 there were still nearly 90,000 sharecroppers working for landowners who had declined the redemption. A special bank had been set up to provide loans, but the interest was high, and landlords were not keen to give up. Serbian representatives in the diet had pressed for obligatory redemption, but they had been opposed by the Muslims supported by some of the Croats. Eventually most Serbian members abandoned efforts to work within the legal framework, and stood by as radical students justified terrorist action as tyrannicide.

The reaction to Serbia's victories had been a mixed one in Slovenia and Croatia. The appeal of a Yugoslav state linked to victorious Serbia was strong among students. Some had even tried to enlist in the Serbian army. The Croat-Serb coalition had organized a mass demonstration in Zagreb to celebrate, and to call for the creation of a South Slav state. However, Pašić had been quick to restrain the coalition leaders. At the same time the Pure Rights Party also seemed to have gained more support for a third, Croatian-led unit in the Monarchy which might absorb a defeated Serbia. In Dalmatia, demonstrations across the province flaunted Serbia's victories in the face of the authorities. Donations were made for war relief, and volunteers actually enlisted in the Serbian army. The provincial diet adopted a resolution praising the Balkan alliance, and condemning Austria-Hungary's policy towards its South Slav subjects.

The impact had been strongest in Bosnia. Serbian celebrations in Sarajevo and other towns following the Turkish defeats had created anxiety among the Muslim élite, whose leaders moved closer to the Habsburg administration. The feeling had been heightened by the arrival of Muslims leaving the territories newly acquired by Serbia and Montenegro. Some even came from families that had originally left Bosnia-Herzegovina in the wake of the Austro-Hungarian occupation. The total number was probably less than 10,000, but it led to rumours that many more had come, or would do so, and that they would be settled in Serbian majority areas. Croatian opinion was divided, Serb-Muslim relations were affected, and the constitution was suspended.

From Bosnia came the strongest advocates of romantic, revolutionary and ill-defined Yugoslavism. Serbs had taken the lead in forming the Serbo-Croatian Progressive Organization in 1911, with a membership composed largely of students and schoolboys. It opposed the official organizations, and also included Muslims. The small and secret groups loosely defined as Young Bosnia (whom the authorities called *Jugoslawen*) drew their inspiration from German romanticism, anarchism, Russian revolutionary socialism, Nietzsche and Kosovo. Young men of peasant stock, they believed in personal sacrifice and tyrannicide, sought radical solutions to everything, and were under permanent police surveillance. Mistrusting elected political leaders and lacking confidence in the zeal of peasants, they moved to overt revolutionary propaganda and action in 1913, attracting Croats and even some Muslims.

Contrary to enduring assumptions, it was they who sought connections in Belgrade, and the cover of agents of the nationalist organizations through which the Black Hand officers also operated. Like their Greek, Bulgarian and Ottoman counterparts, these soldiers felt that politicians were holding back. Not only did they oppose government policy in the new territories, but they encouraged militant action for the unification of all Serbs. As for the Bosnian youths, they wanted radical Yugoslavism vaguely defined as the only possible solution to the problems of their provinces. Openly anti-Habsburg aspirations, some expressed through violence, were limited to a fringe. The organized parties kept well clear. They came from a small segment of the population, and claimed to speak for their national groups, but historians still find difficulty in determining what the 'people' thought. A showdown was expected, on the death of the aged monarch, between his heir Archduke Francis Ferdinand and the Hungarian ruling class. Both sides were preparing for it by trying to win over the other nationalities. Francis Ferdinand let it be said that he was ready to set up a Slav unit, equal in status with Hungary. The Hungarian government restored constitutional government in Croatia. The party leaders could once again entertain the hope of legal reforms. However, the Austro-Hungarian general staff, seeing all the trouble as being masterminded from Belgrade, were convinced of the need for a preventive war against Serbia.

Far from plotting the downfall of Austria-Hungary, the Serbian government was recovering from two years of warfare, considering some form of union with Montenegro, and bracing itself to grasp the nettle of its own military. In the spring of 1914, the Radical prime minister Pašić was trying to counter the Black Handers' influence, while they were trying to get rid of him. By conniving with the Bosnian youngsters Colonel Dragutin Dimitrijević (1876–1917), nicknamed Apis, leader of the Black Hand officers and head of Serbia's military intelligence, probably wanted to do no more than cause tension with Austria-Hungary in order to weaken Pašić.

The officers practically blackmailed the weak and prematurely aged sovereign, whom they had brought to the throne, into promising that he would get Pašić to resign. Crown Prince Alexander (1888–1934) and the Russian minister intervened, and Pašić remained. The Assembly was dissolved, and new elections called. On 11 June King Peter retired because of ill-health, and entrusted the exercise of the royal prerogative to Prince Alexander.

Without understanding the difference, public opinion seemed to move between the concept of an extended Serbia and that of Serbia acting as the unifier of all Yugoslavs. Only among the higher intelligentsia were there people beginning to entertain a genuine Yugoslav idea. There were certainly no plans, and there was no broad popular support in Serbia in 1914, for the creation of a Yugoslav state in any near future.

Archduke Francis Ferdinand's ill-planned visit to Sarajevo on 28 June had not taken into account the symbolism of the date: the anniversary of the battle of Kosovo (15 June, according to the Julian calendar to which the Serbian church adhered, and still adheres). Security was careless as a result of rivalry between civil and military authorities. The evidence suggests that the initiative for an assassination attempt came from a small group of very young men, who used Black Hand weapons and channels, to carry out the bungled yet successful assassination of the heir to the Habsburg empire.[11] The First World War was about to be launched.

---

[11] Its manifest deficiencies notwithstanding, the essential work on the conspirators' motives, milieu and links is Vladimir Dedijer, *The Road to Sarajevo*, London: MacGibbon & Key, 1967.

5

SERBIA AT WAR – BETWEEN DESTRUCTION AND YUGOSLAVIA 1914–1918

It was not obvious that a 'great war' was about to break out as a result of the fact that there were Serbs in both Austria-Hungary and Serbia. However, on both sides there were influential people and sections of opinion who were led by obsession with international status, fatherland or nation to contemplate war as a possible way of overcoming the limitations of the balance of power. The war party in Vienna gambled on a death-or-glory solution to Austria-Hungary's difficulties.[1] Serbia was not prepared for war, but it was ready to face, if necessary, heroic death to defend its independence.

Crown Prince Alexander had just taken over as regent, elections were due, a concordat with the Holy See had settled the status of the Roman Catholic church in Serbia to everyone's satisfaction, the prime minister was out campaigning, and the chief of the general staff was convalescing in Austria. Vienna's ultimatum of 23 July 1914 was designed to be rejected. Extreme caution was taken in dealing with it. Belgrade's moderate reply expressed readiness to accept even Austro-Hungarian participation in the investigations to be carried out in Serbia, in so far as it did not contravene international law or Serbia's judicial procedures. This was not considered satisfactory, war was declared on 28 July, and Belgrade was immediately subjected to an artillery bombardment. The clarion call was 'Serbia must be destroyed'.

Austria-Hungary carried out its mobilization smoothly, including

---

[1] Alan Sharp, *The Versailles Settlement: Peacemaking in Paris, 1919*, London: Macmillan, 1991, 8.

that of its ethnic Serbs, but the authorities' behaviour was fuelled by an irrational fear of pro-Serbian feelings. Serbs in the empire were viewed collectively as sympathizers with the enemy, although most of them actually performed loyally throughout the war in Austria-Hungary's armed forces. They were harassed, interned and deported from the border regions. Everywhere anti-Serbian feelings were encouraged.

In the autumn constitutional rights were curtailed in Croatia-Slavonia. If military rule there was impeded by rivalry between the Hungarian government and the military, it was imposed in Bosnia-Herzegovina. Catholic and Muslim volunteers were recruited for 'defensive anti-bandit' units which carried out executions and deportations of civilians accused of supporting Serbian rebels. By the repressive measures that they took and the violence that they encouraged, the 'hawks' in Vienna gradually pushed the Serbs of Bosnia into Serbia's arms.

Serbia was in mortal danger. A small state of 4.5 million inhabitants, exhausted by the Balkan wars, it faced the Habsburg monarchy's 52 million population. Apart from tiny Montenegro, its allies were far away and concerned with defending themselves against Germany. It was Germany that had been the transmission belt between what Austria-Hungary had envisaged as an operation of domestic policy and what became the First World War—fought between the Entente Powers (Britain, France and Russia) and the Central Powers (Germany, Austria-Hungary and Turkey).

The elections were immediately cancelled, and the dissolved National Assembly was recalled and evacuated to Niš, where Pašić at the end of the year expanded his government by bringing in Independents and Progressives. Half-a-million men were mobilized by September. Serbia managed to survive by a thread, in a desperate struggle to repel the invasion. The battle of Cer in August was the first victory against the Central Powers in the Great War. Belgrade was then lost and regained. After another resounding victory at the river Kolubara in December, Serbia just managed to hold its own, helped by the Russian advance in Galicia and by supplies from the Entente sent through Greece and up the Danube. Yet the future was bleak. High losses, in combat and from typhoid fever, could not be made good.

The war had suddenly thrown forward the question of Yugoslav unification. The very existence of the Serbian state was at stake. The Pašić government immediately understood that the outcome of this war would, for better or worse, bring great changes to the country's position. If defeated, it risked being turned into a protectorate of

Austria-Hungary, or even integrated into the Dual Monarchy. Defensive considerations dominated. To pose publicly the Yugoslav question—the creation of a state of all Serbs, Croats and Slovenes—was at least a way of weakening the enemy, perhaps even of guaranteeing the future.

There had been ambivalence between a more narrowly Serbian identity, expressed in striving for a greater Serbia—on a par with a greater Greece, a greater Bulgaria or a greater Romania—and a hazier Yugoslav identity, with Serbia as the Piedmont of South Slav unification. As a military Piedmont, Serbia had shown its worth at the expense of the Ottoman empire in the Balkan wars, but its plans had been no more than defensive as far as Austria-Hungary was concerned. The dissolution of the Habsburg empire in the foreseeable future was not seriously envisaged by a government preparing to impose its control over an army whose influential Black Hand officers thought in the simpler terms of the Serbian question.

Pašić quickly went out to supersede the possible resolution through war of the 'Serbian question', by posing the 'Yugoslav question', even though it was to be resolved on Serbia's initiative. The war aim of setting up a Yugoslav state to take in the Slovene region, Croatia-Slavonia, Bosnia-Herzegovina, Dalmatia and even possibly Bulgaria was immediately discussed by the cabinet. In September Pašić spoke of the postwar borders of the South Slav state reaching halfway across the Istrian peninsula.

In December, from Niš, the government proclaimed through the National Assembly that the war was being fought for the liberation and unification of all Serbs, Croats and Slovenes. The Niš Declaration replaced the notion of a Serb nation-state with the new but less clear concept of a state for the Yugoslav nation of the three ethnic groups of Serbs, Croats and Slovenes.[2] The Serbian government thereby also indicated its intention to lead the way, operating as it was within the familiar parameters of liberating kith-and-kin from foreign rule.

Its declaration was far from being a precise proposal for a postwar settlement. It was in the first instance meant to attract support from the Southern Slavs of Austria-Hungary, and to create interest among

---

[2] The new territories acquired after the Balkan wars were in the end fully integrated into the constitutional order by a royal proclamation. This was a confirmation that they belonged to Serbia, a statement that the Macedonians were regarded as Serbs, an acknowledgement of their loyal participation in the war effort, and a symbol of the government's control of the military.

Serbia's Entente allies. The latter would decide it all in the peace treaties, but for the time being they were totally oblivious of the 'Yugoslav question'. In order to internationalize it, the Serbian government invested huge energy in propaganda, calling on the country's best scholars to argue the case for the geographic, geological, ethnic, linguistic and literary unity of the area, and for Serbia's rôle in the unification process. This had begun as early as August 1914, on the assumption that the war would be a short one, and that postwar demands had to be quickly formulated.

The government was also helped in this task by a number of South Slav personalities from Austria-Hungary, generally belonging to the Croat-Serb coalition, who had gone abroad to Serbia and neutral Italy when the war started to advocate the union of the Habsburg Yugoslavs with Serbia and Montenegro. From Niš in October the government suggested that they should form a Yugoslav committee to propagate the aim of a Yugoslav state.

Once again it was led partly by fears that the Entente might be more interested, in the short term, in winning over neutral Italy and Bulgaria with territorial promises on the eastern side of the Adriatic and in Macedonia; or, in the long term, in a federal reorganization of the Dual Monarchy. The exiled Yugoslavs learnt in St Petersburg that the Entente was about to conclude a treaty with Italy that would satisfy its aspirations to acquire the former Venetian and mostly Yugoslav-inhabited lands of Austria. This coincided with pressure on Serbia to consider giving up some of its recent Macedonian gains in order to attract Bulgaria.

Early in 1915 offers were being made and pressures applied to all neutrals in the region to join one or the other side, until secret treaties secured Italy for the Entente in April, and Bulgaria for the Central Powers in August. Italy was promised Austrian and Albanian, and Bulgaria Serbian and Greek, territory, in return for immediate involvement. In October, Serbia was struck down by the full weight of a German-led combined German-Austrian-Bulgarian offensive. French and British troops had just landed in Salonika, on the territory of neutral Greece, invited by the prime minister Venizelos. His split with King Constantine was thus started, but it was too late to prevent Serbia's lifeline to the Aegean being cut off.

Facing the alternatives of capitulating or risking a mid-winter retreat through the hostile mountains of Albania to the Adriatic coast and Allied shipping, the Serbian government chose the latter. Albania was in chaos, set up as an independent principality in 1912 under a

German prince, with contested borders still to be fixed. The new ruler had arrived in March 1914, and left in September. One of the rivals for the succession was the self-proclaimed president, Esat Pasha Toptani, who had Italian and Serbian support. In June 1915 Serbian and Montenegrin troops moved in to thwart Italy, and succeeded in their fourth attempt since 1912 to get to the sea through northern Albania.

The retreat in December across Albania has found a permanent place both in Serbian popular memory and in representations of the First World War. The aged and ailing monarch, officialdom, parliamentarians, army and countless refugees trekked over the uplands to the sea, dying of hunger, cold and disease, pursued by the Austro-Hungarians, with the hostile Albanian highland clans wreaking their revenge on the dejected Serbs. Kosovo Day had only just become a state public holiday. The retreat gave the legend new strength, with the accent again on sacrifice in battle—'better die as free men than live as slaves'. More than 240,000 died or were captured on the way.

When the decimated Serbs arrived in the ports of Scutari (Shköder) and Durazzo (Durrës), the French navy was sent to rescue them. By the end of February 1916, 135,000 soldiers had been taken to the Greek island of Corfu; 50–60,000 civilians had also been evacuated. Serbia was no more. The exiled remnants of the state maintained a symbolic continuity in the most precarious situation on Corfu, by courtesy of the Allied powers. This was Greek territory, which had been occupied by Entente troops to provide safe haven for the Serbs.

Montenegro was even worse off. Negotiations on union with Serbia had been pointing to a German type of arrangement, with a Petrović-ruled kingdom retaining its separate identity, when Austria-Hungary declared war on Serbia. King Nicholas expressed solidarity in defence of 'our Serbian nation', a Serbian general was appointed chief of the general staff, and Serbian officers were seconded to other important positions in the Montenegrin army. However, there were confrontations over military moves, when Nicholas pushed for separate forays to back his kingdom's territorial claims.

As the Austrians moved in, Nicholas made his way to Scutari, and thence to Italy, leaving behind a rump government which capitulated to Austria-Hungary. While his sons dispersed, he set up a government in exile in France, out on a limb, increasingly sidelined both by the opposition among the few hundred émigrés from Montenegro and by the Serbian government.

The French had rescued the Serbian army and brought it back to life. They also took upon themselves the burden of looking after most of the civilian refugees. King Constantine's government in Athens would not, however, allow Serbian troops to go overland to Salonika to join the Allies' Macedonian front. Only when Venizelos formed his counter-government there with Allied support, were 115,000 men of the restored Serbian army, with the regent and commander-in-chief Prince Alexander, placed at the centre of that Allied force. Before the end of 1916, after the battle of Mount Kajmakčalan, they had even managed to take back a portion of their country, with the town of Bitolj (Bitola).

The government preferred to remain in Corfu rather than go to France or Italy, where it would have been under greater pressure from its hosts, but it still depended on loans provided by the Allies, and faced old challenges that had reappeared in the dangerous climate of defeat and exile. To explain away the defeat, it had changed the entire supreme command, thus embittering the military. To the Black Hand group was added a rival coterie of officers, nicknamed the 'White Hand', who gathered around Alexander. There were various combinations among the exiles, aimed at removing Pašić. His government faced criticism when parliament (108 out of the original 166 members) was reconvened in Corfu in September 1916, only to be recessed after six weeks for the rest of the war.

A wave of Serbophilia swept through public opinion in Allied countries,[3] and Pašić survived with Entente support. He remained loyal to the political course followed by the Allies, despite the vacillations of their territorial offers, and continued to invest much effort in acquainting them with the Yugoslav question. He was helped by, no less than he helped, the gathering of Yugoslav exiles from Austria-

---

[3]Directives were sent by the French Ministry of Public Instruction in 1915 for talks to be given in all schools, so that Serbia be better known and *aimée*. Schoolchildren were to be told about the history of its long struggle against its Austrian and Turkish oppressors. Those learning to write were made to copy out: '*Braves Serbes, la France est avec vous! Vive la Serbie, vive la France!*' For several weeks in the summer of 1916 Paris was covered with posters to mark 'La Journée Serbe' (28 June), and London had its posters urging people to `pray for Serbia'. British schoolchildren were encouraged to write essays about the importance of Kosovo to Serbia. (Jean-Jacques Becker, 'L'ombre séculaire du nationalisme serbe', *Vingtième siècle*, 69, 2001, 7; 'Le conflit vu de France', Laurent Gervereau and Yves Tomic (ed.), *De l'unification à l'éclatement. L'espace yougoslave, un siècle d'histoire*, Paris: Musée d'histoire contemporaine-BDIC, 1998, 68–9; Tim Judah, *War and Revenge*, New Haven and London: Yale University Press, 2000, xvi).

Hungary who had formed the Yugoslav Committee in Rome in November 1914. After Italy entered the fray, and they came to know of the terms of the secret treaty of London, they moved to Paris, and eventually to London. Under its Croatian chairman Ante Trumbić (1864–1938), the committee formalized its existence with a memorandum claiming borders for a future Yugoslavia that took in much of what had been promised to Italy.

The Yugoslav Committee had no legal status and no mandate to represent the Yugoslavs of Austria-Hungary, where the elected Croat-Serb coalition in Zagreb continued to profess loyalty to the Habsburgs. Although its only support came from the Serbian government, which saw it as a Yugoslav public relations auxiliary, the committee was no instrument of the exiled government. While it interpreted Serbia's determination to fight as an expression of the Kosovo spirit, and an inspiration for all Southern Slavs in their struggle to unite, it boldly set out to proclaim the right of nationalities to self-determination rather than to liberation. Refusing the constraints of Serbian support and Entente policies, its propaganda was directed against Italy as much as against Austria-Hungary, and in the course of time its differences with the Serbian government became more serious.

The Serbian government was constrained by international and military realities. Apart from the fact that Pašić did not realize how different a future Yugoslavia would have to be from the Serbia he knew, he had to act cautiously in order to safeguard what had been attained, and to obtain from the Allies what he felt was feasible. For that reason he was intent on keeping control of the unification process. Differences with the Yugoslav Committee were not the only ones. Black Hand officers were more anxious to fight for the restoration and extension of Serbia than for the unification of all Serbs, Croats and Slovenes. At the same time neutral Geneva was the centre of Serbian intellectuals critical of the government; gathered around the government-run Serbian press office, they believed that the simple restoration of a smaller or greater Serbia, not united to a larger whole, would be retrogressive for all.

Meanwhile Serbia was under harsh enemy military occupation. The southern areas of Niš and Skopje were under Bulgarian rule, which imposed instant Bulgarianization through churches, schools and conscription, even in areas that had been Serbian since 1878, and where people definitely did not feel Bulgarian. Cutting across the Bulgarian occupation zone, the valleys of the Morava and Vardar formed a German logistical area.

The greater part of Serbia was under an Austro-Hungarian military government which wanted to neutralize all politically active individuals. Peasants reacted by refusing to handle the currency issued by the occupation authorities, and by joining armed bands operating in the woods and hills. 40,000 people were deported to Austria-Hungary and another 10,000 confined to concentration camps in Serbia, not to mention 60,000 prisoners of war in Austria-Hungary, Bulgaria, Germany and Turkey. Belgrade's population of 90,000 in 1914 had fallen by early 1916 to 15,000. A typhus epidemic in the autumn of 1915 had taken 150,000 lives, and still more died of hunger, disease and maltreatment during the rest of the occupation.

The following year, 1917, was one of confusion. The United States joined in the war, Russia dropped out, and both its new leaders and President Wilson talked of the self-determination of nationalities. The death of Emperor Francis Joseph at the end of 1916 raised hopes of a reorganization of the Habsburg monarchy and of a separate peace. Many of the emergency war measures were rescinded, except in Bosnia-Herzegovina.

Elected South Slav parliamentarians in Zagreb and Vienna bargained for their loyalty. Those of the Vienna parliament, formally united in a Yugoslav group, expressed their loyalty to the new Emperor Charles. They demanded the unification into one unit of all the territories of the monarchy where Slovenes, Croats and Serbs lived—based on the principle of nationality and on the rights of the Croatian state. The Entente Allies were in a shaky position, and examined the possibility of detaching Austria-Hungary.

Military operations had slowed down; the Macedonian front was stuck. In total uncertainty about the future, the Serbian government concentrated on union with Montenegro to counteract Austro-Hungarian and Italian plans for the little kingdom. As one after another of the Montenegrin personalities in exile abandoned King Nicholas, a former prime minister formed a Montenegrin Committee for National Unification in Paris with political support and financial backing from the Serbian government.

In the dark about what was going to happen, the Serbian Radical leadership in exile was gripped by apprehension of the festering problem of civil-military relations. It managed to pass its fear of the Black Hand to Crown Prince Alexander, leading to the trial in Salonika, before a Serbian court-martial, of a number of officers on ill-supported charges of an attempt on the life of the regent and of conspiring to overthrow the government and dynasty. The execution there in June 1917 of Colonel Dimitrijević and two of his associates eliminated what potential threat there was from the Black Hand, but left a bad impression of foul play. Pašić's coalition broke up as Independent and Progressive ministers resigned. The Serbian government's image suffered as a result.

The reorganized and French-backed Serbian army in Macedonia, which had reached a strength of 150,000, was its major asset. In spite of the Salonika crisis, the troops performed loyally and dutifully. Eager to fight for the liberation of their homeland, Serbian soldiers were used to the full by the French, whose own manpower was stretched and depleted. French support went with a strong dose of paternalism, and the relationship was not without stress.[4]

Nevertheless Serbian combatants viewed France as a saviour, and French comrades in arms as friends. To this should be added the substantial number of civilian refugees in France, notably children of school age and students, taken in by French schools and universities. By the beginning of 1918 there were some 3,300 of them, many with French scholarships, and numbers increased in the course of that year.[5] Those young people who had been welcomed and educated in France during the war years would later exert a decisive influence on the educational, cultural, economic and political life of their country. French politicians were well aware of it, and soldiers and students figured in various plans to extend French influence in the region. They would form the basis of both the reality and the myth of French influence, and of feelings towards France, in all ranks of Serbian society after the First World War.

Neither the Serbian government nor the leaders of the Habsburg Southern Slavs knew what was going to be the outcome of the war, and what would happen to Austria-Hungary. In the circumstances the lines between envisaging a greater Croatia or a greater Serbia on the one hand, and a true Yugoslavia on the other, were hazier than

---

[4]French officers tended to treat the Serbs as they would their own colonial troops, and it was at times said in Salonika that the Armée d'Orient was fighting to its last Serb, Russian and Albanian (there were Russian troops on the Macedonian front, as well as Albanian units that had come with Esat Pasha, who had also set himself up in Salonika).

[5]Ljubinka Trgovčević, 'Školovanje srpske omladine u emigraciji 1916–1918' (The Education of Serbian Youth in Exile 1916–18), *Istorijski časopis*, XLII-XLIII, Belgrade, 1996, 161.

ever. Both sides aimed at ensuring what could be obtained, while keeping contact with the Yugoslav Committee.

The Serbian government and the Yugoslav Committee both saw developments in the Habsburg monarchy as a danger. Not only had neither so far been able to sell the Yugoslav project to the Allies, but friction between the two had contributed to the impression that it was a questionable proposition. Both had been shaken by recent events, and were eager to use such disaffection as there was among Habsburg Croats, Serbs and Slovenes, who accounted for 17 per cent of the armed forces.

Desertions among them increased, by Serbs in particular, and on the eastern front. There were already overseas emigrants and defectors from Austria-Hungary serving as volunteers in the Serbian army. The Yugoslav Committee was keen to form a specifically Yugoslav legion, to show the reality of the Yugoslav idea and to boost its own prestige. There were fraught negotiations between government and committee on the status and name of such troops.

In 1916 the government, with Russian support, had proceeded to organize two volunteer divisions in Odessa. However, non-Serbs were not on the whole eager to return to the front. Officers of the Serbian army, sent out from Corfu, imposed draconian discipline, anxious to weed out revolutionaries. The use of these units by the Russians in Dobrudja was not a success, and the tension exploded after the February 1917 revolution. Having dwindled by May from the original 30,000 to 20,000, they were transferred to Salonika and attached to the Serbian army as the Yugoslav Division.

It was essential to repair the strained connexion between the Serbian government and the Yugoslav Committee. Both realized that to present to the world and to the Southern Slavs of Austria-Hungary a unified and concrete programme was the best way to internationalize the Yugoslav question at a time when the Allies were seriously exploring the possibility of a separate peace.

A delegation of the Yugoslav Committee representing its several tendencies, and one of the Serbian government, including the opposition parties, met in Corfu in June to discuss the future Serb-Croat-Slovene state. The Corfu declaration that they jointly issued in July was a compromise. It set out the principles on which the new state would be founded, but glossed over its different conceptions.

Over all the lands on which the three-named Yugoslav nation of the Serbs, Croats and Slovenes lived in a compact and continuous mass there would be a single independent state known as the kingdom of the Serbs, Croats and Slovenes, with one citizenship, one territory and one crown—a constitutional, democratic and parliamentary monarchy under the Karadjordjević dynasty. It would guarantee the equality of its three national names (Serbs, Croats and Slovenes), its three main religious denominations (Orthodox, Catholic and Muslim), and its two scripts (Cyrillic and Latin). Its constitution would otherwise be drawn up by a constituent assembly elected, after peace had been restored, by universal, direct and secret suffrage, and adopted by a 'numerically qualified majority' not otherwise specified.

One should not overstate the longer-term importance of the Corfu Declaration for its signatories at the time. The committee realized that unification depended more than ever on Serbia's success; its only alternative would have been to give in to Italy's claims under the treaty of London. Its shorter-term aim may have been no more than to project again the Yugoslav question which had been somewhat overlooked since the Serbian government's unilateral Niš Declaration, and to commit that government again to a Yugoslav solution.

Serbia was only a very small part of the Entente's war effort. The Allies were ready to use slices of South Slav territory, Austro-Hungarian and even Serbian, as bargaining chips. In the circumstances Pašić's shorter-term aim may have been no more than to improve his government's standing, to counter the threat of a Habsburg Yugoslavia, to secure a larger Allied force in Macedonia to break through the front, and help in the liberation of Serbia.

The Corfu Declaration had immediate effects. Its text was published by newspapers in Zagreb, and even in Sarajevo. Negotiations between the Serbian government and the Yugoslav Committee continued. Contacts were made in Switzerland with Habsburg South Slav politicians. The claims of Italy and the occupation régimes were countered. Bulgaria's occupation of southern Serbia and Serbian Macedonia had done more damage to pro-Bulgarian feelings there than all Serbia's heavy-handed efforts since 1912. An uprising in February 1917 had been brutally put down. More and more young men were joining the armed bands hiding in the hills, to avoid the conscription that would have sent them to fight against their fathers who were in the Serbian army.

At the beginning of 1918 the Allies were still in two minds about Austria-Hungary. Even Wilson's Fourteen Points spoke only of restoration and access to the sea for Serbia, and of autonomous development for the peoples of the Dual Monarchy. Austria-Hungary's refusal to make concessions precipitated events. The naval mutiny at the Kotor (Cattaro) base indicated a distinct change of heart in the South Slav military personnel. Prisoners of war returning from Russia did not want to go on fighting.

Rather than return even to the Italian front, they regrouped in woods in bands known as the 'green cadre' in Croatia, or swelled Serbian guerrilla bands in Bosnia. By the summer anti-Habsburg manifestations and military mutinies were spreading. The military authorities estimated that by then the whole of Dalmatia, 60 per cent of the population of Croatia-Slavonia, and half of Bosnia-Herzegovina were 'infected with the Yugoslav idea'.

The collapse of the Central Powers began in the summer, on the Western and North Italian fronts. In September an Allied offensive with the Serbian army broke through the Macedonian front, put Bulgaria out of action, and started liberating Serbia. The authority of the Vienna and Budapest governments then crumbled rapidly.

The Serbian government (as indeed its great allies) had not anticipated the total and immediate collapse of the Habsburg monarchy. The appearance of local autonomous forces compromised Serbia's rôle as liberator and unifier; as the Serbian army hurried to Belgrade, the Yugoslavs of Austria-Hungary were liberating themselves by default and presenting unexpected interlocutors to the Serbian government. All over the empire *ad hoc* regional councils appeared, set up on ethnic lines, and began to take over. The initiative to create one such council for the Southern Slavs was taken as early as March by the opposition parties of the various provincial diets. Disagreements over the extent of unification, and the reluctance of the Zagreb *sabor* majority coalition to break with the continuity of historic institutions, delayed action, until pressure from Slovenia and Dalmatia, provinces more vulnerable to Italian claims, got everyone together.

By 8 October the representatives of the various South Slav parties from Croatia-Slavonia, Bosnia-Herzegovina, Dalmatia and other Austrian and Hungarian provinces had set up the National Council of the Slovenes, Croats and Serbs. Unification then simply occurred, unplanned, with no liberation by anyone, as Austria-Hungary disintegrated. Emperor Charles's manifesto of 16 October to his 'faithful peoples of Austria', announcing the federal reorganization of the empire, came too late. Yugoslav unification within the Habsburg monarchy was anyway made impossible by Hungary's refusal to tamper with the integrity of its territory.

Pressure from below and from the periphery for the Croatian *sabor* to break with the Hungarian crown, was added to the fears of military commanders of a breakdown of law and order. Having gone to Vienna to consult the emperor on the possibility of the National Council taking over authority, and having been told to do what he wanted, the *ban* summoned the *sabor*. In a euphoric session on 29 October, at which the Croatian anthem, Serbia's anthem and '*La Marseillaise*' were sung, the diet broke off all links with Hungary and Austria. It proclaimed the integration of Dalmatia, Croatia and Slavonia into a common national sovereign state of Slovenes, Croats and Serbs over 'the whole ethnographic territory of that nation, whatever its local and state borders'. Authority was handed over to the National Council, which formed a government for the state of Slovenes, Croats and Serbs.

The 'SCS state' was in a critical situation. It had no borders and no army, and it was unrecognized, except in a roundabout way, by the moribund monarchy. When the Austro-Hungarian command had asked an armistice a few days later, it handed over the fleet to the Zagreb council, but when the armistice was signed it gave the Allies the right to penetrate up to a line that coincided with what had been promised to Italy. As chaos developed everywhere, Italian troops began to occupy what was technically enemy territory. The breakdown of law and order was particularly serious in Bosnia-Herzegovina, where social revolt combined with revenge for wartime events as Serbian peasants had their own back on Muslim landlords and members of special units. For many it seemed that the Serbian army was the only force that could restore order in the countryside and turn back the Italian army.

The pace of the unification process with Serbia and Montenegro, started in Geneva, quickened. On the initiative of the Serbian opposition leaders, who were negotiating with him for a new coalition government, Pašić himself came to Geneva for a meeting with them, with the Yugoslav Committee and with a delegation of the National Council. On his own he faced the opposition politicians and the 'Yugoslavs'. Hard pressed, he renounced the position that the Serbian government, as the only participant that was an Allied power, should represent all Southern Slavs until peace was established. He recognized the National Council government in Zagreb as the legitimate government of the Southern Slavs who lived on the territory of the former Habsburg monarchy, and agreed to support their cause with the Allies.

The Geneva Agreement of 9 November, signed by all parties, set up transitional dualistic arrangements, the SCS government and the Serbian government retaining authority over their respective territories until the adoption of a constitution for the new united state. Trumbić was also successful in obtaining a joint ministry to look after common affairs and to prepare the constituent assembly. Pašić was less interested in the details than in an affirmation of Yugoslav unity for the Allies; Serbian opposition leaders were more interested in forcing Pašić to retreat.

The agreement was repudiated in both Corfu and Zagreb. The Serbian government under its acting premier Stojan Protić (1857–1923), supported by the regent, resigned. They considered the agreement an expression of mistrust in Serbia, were opposed to any form of dualism, however transitional, and believed that the government in Zagreb no longer represented the real forces that had emerged in the SCS state. The National Council under its acting president, the Serb Pribićević, also claimed that it had given its representatives no such mandate. Some feared that Serbia's strength would unbalance the transitional arrangement. For others immediate unification with Serbia was a question of survival.

The situation was indeed changing by the day as chaos spread and Italian troops continued to advance. Pressure from Slovenia, Dalmatia and Bosnia increased. Zagreb was accused of dragging its feet, of being too preoccupied with the threat of Serbian power at the expense of other threats, closer at hand. Pribićević and the Serbian government, and in particular the military, made use of the situation.

Pašić was asked to form a new coalition government, which he did from Paris, where he had gone to be available as the Supreme Allied Council met to discuss the situation in the Balkans. Prince Alexander and the government returned to a liberated but war-ravaged Serbia. From Belgrade they now wanted to come to an agreement with those elements who pushed for immediate unification. Representatives from various local councils turned up for direct negotiations from southern Hungary, Bosnia-Herzegovina and Dalmatia, asking for troops.

Under the terms of the armistice arrangements, Serbian troops had gone to areas of Hungarian territory, as Italians had done in Austrian territory. Token detachments of Serbian troops also eventually turned up in parts of Bosnia-Herzegovina and Dalmatia. They raced to Kotor and Dubrovnik to get there ahead of the Italians. They were greeted with various degrees of enthusiasm, by ethnic Serbs but also by non-Serbs. Serb districts proceeded to unilateral declarations of unification with Serbia. Voivodina proclaimed itself part of Serbia in this way. Even the diet of Bosnia-Herzegovina voted by 42 out of 54 to join Serbia. The National Council had tried, and totally failed, to organize a military force of its own, and had to resort to returning Serbian prisoners of war. It eventually asked for a detachment of Serbian soldiers to be sent to Zagreb.

Meanwhile Montenegro had been liberated by troops of the Yugoslav Division of the Serbian army working with local guerrillas. The population, embittered against Austria-Hungary after three years of harsh occupation, was worked on by returned émigrés of various opinions, by Serbian and Italian agents, and by partisans of King Nicholas who had remained in France. The Serbian government did not want him back and regarded the Committee for National Unification as the virtual government. Amid public demonstrations of local partisans of unilateral unification with Serbia, the committee organized elections for an *ad hoc* Grand National Assembly to decide on the future status of Montenegro.

The proponents of unilateral unification were known as 'whites', because their propaganda was printed on white paper, and the opponents as 'greens', again after the colour of their leaflets and proclamations. The voting was public and indirect. The assembly met not in the old capital Cetinje, the centre of pro-Nicholas sympathizers, but in Podgorica where the mood was in favour of immediate unification.

On 26 November 160 of the 168 elected representatives met. They proclaimed the deposition of the Petrović dynasty and the immediate unification of Montenegro with Serbia in a wider joint fatherland of the Serbs, Croats and Slovenes. The white majority—generally urban, better educated and in the younger age-group—included most of the merchants and of the administrative and military élite. It left the greens to nurse their wounded pride at the way in which Montenegro's rôle had been brushed aside. With Italian support a rebellion was stirred up at Christmas in the Cetinje area, but it quickly collapsed as whites set upon greens.

The day before, the National Council in Zagreb had taken the decision to unite the Yugoslav territories of the former Austro-Hungarian monarchy with Serbia and Montenegro in a single state, and to send a delegation to Belgrade to agree on its organization. There were differences between the delegates over the modalities. Pašić was still abroad, and it fell to the regent to play the key rôle in the talks. The Zagreb deputation eventually agreed on an address, which invited Prince Alexander to proclaim the union and assume the regency of the new state. It expressed an unconditional will for unification, left the form of the united state to be decided by the future constituent assembly, and made no reference to a specific majority.

On 1 December 1918, in the presence of a delegation from the National Council and of members of the Serbian government, Alexander, having received the address, proclaimed in the name of King Peter the unification of Serbia with the lands of the state of the Slovenes, Croats and Serbs in a united kingdom of the Serbs, Croats and Slovenes. In the same interval of a few weeks in November 1918 a united Romania had similarly come into being, as a variety of *ad hoc* councils and assemblies had sprung up under the pressure of events, and precipitated the unification of Austrian Bukovina, Hungarian Transylvania and Russian Bessarabia with Romania. In the Romanian case too the process had ended on 1 December with the unification of Transylvania.

Unification had been no more than an intellectual concept and a distant ideal at the beginning of 1914. At the end of 1918 it had become a political priority. Serbia's suffering at the hands of the Central Powers and its military contribution to the Allied cause, the cautious realism of the leaders of the Habsburg Slovenes, Croats and Serbs within Austria-Hungary, and the determined idealism of those who had gone abroad to propagate the cause of unity and independence— all these had contributed to the outcome, but it would not have been precipitated in the last few months of 1918 had it not been for the sudden collapse of Austria-Hungary. Serbia's prestige in the international community had never been higher. Nevertheless, and in spite of pushes here and there, it did not control the process of unification.

Unification just happened, in a way that nobody had anticipated, and there was probably no alternative to the way in which it was achieved. The National Council in Zagreb faced the option of a Yugoslav union at any price, or partition of the formerly Habsburg Southern Slavs between Italy, Serbia, Austria and Hungary, with a residual Croatia not unlike Albania.

Counter-factual claims have been expressed by various Serbs since the disintegration of Yugoslavia that Serbia should have tried to extend its borders rather than lose its identity in a joint state of the Serbs, Croats and Slovenes. But any solution except a Yugoslav one would have left ethnic Serbs outside Serbia, however much extended, and any addition to its territory would have taken in more non-Serbs. On the eve of the First World War, Serbia already faced the problem of integrating new territories and new citizens in a state that was no longer homogeneous. With further enlargement in Voivodina and in Bosnia-Herzegovina it would have acquired Muslim Slavs, Croats, Magyars and Germans, and for them Serbia was more difficult to accept than Yugoslavia.

It is almost impossible to gauge how much the population at large supported the idea of unification during the war. Pressured, drafted into embattled armies, living under an occupation régime, a state of emergency or constrained loyalty, harassed, interned, deported or captive, isolated from the political actors abroad, they waited for the outcome of the world conflict.

By the end of 1918 a majority of the population were probably in favour of some sort of unification, but the Yugoslav idea had not penetrated in depth, except perhaps in Dalmatia. It cannot be questioned that some 'common ethnicity' had established a solid foundation for the development of the ideology of Yugoslavism, and to precipitate Yugoslav unification. The scholars who had studied it knew it, and they also wanted to promote it, but we still do not know how conscious the average educated citizen, let alone the average peasant, was of this common ethnicity.

The precipitation of events meant that these questions were not asked. The leaders of various sections had not had the time to work out beforehand clear ideas about how the union would be implemented in practice. Pašić certainly wanted to ensure that Serbia retained the political advantages of its status in bringing about unification once the war had started, and yet he was not out to achieve a Yugoslavia over which Serbia would rule.

The problem was that Pašić, and many with him in Serbia, did not really understand the difference between Serbia and Yugoslavia. Influenced in part by those Yugoslavs of Austria-Hungary who, for tactical reasons, exaggerated both their suffering and their interest for Serbia, Serbian politicians believed that they were facing populations eager to be freed from Habsburg enslavement. Croatia-Slavonia at least was, within restricted limits, a self-governing territory, on the basis of the historic continuity of its 'rights', linked to the house of Habsburg through the crown of Hungary. Elsewhere Serbs, Croats and Slovenes enjoyed limited political rights, cultural rights and, for some, access to economic advantages. There was an almost total lack of understanding in Serbia for the historicist constitutionalism that dominated Croatian political thinking. In its insistence on *ancien régime* rights, it seemed archaic at a time when national sovereignty and the self-determination of nationalities were deemed to be universally accepted.

In fact Serbia had not gone to war in July 1914 in order to liberate and unify the Serbs, Croats and Slovenes. That came in December. In July its sole purpose had been to defend itself. Instead of destroying Serbia in a quick military operation, the centuries-old Habsburg empire had broken up at the end of a four-year world war. Serbia had almost been destroyed in the process. It may have lost as many as 1,000,000 of its people, but it had survived, and it was now part of the new kingdom of the Serbs, Croats and Slovenes. It no longer existed as a state.

6

SERBIA INTO YUGOSLAVIA – BETWEEN THE TWO WORLD WARS 1918–1941

The First World War had ended as unexpectedly as it had begun. The winners claimed that the outcome had been bound to happen, but they were not prepared for it. This was the case with Serbia as it was with the major Allied powers. The Paris peace conference of 1919 was conducted in a haphazard manner. The settlement was meant to be based on the principle of national self-determination, but there were caveats, contradictions and compromises. Some nations were more successful in their self-determination than others.

The kingdom of the Serbs, Croats and Slovenes, known as Yugoslavia (South Slavia) for short, was no invention of the Allied powers, nor was it a creation of the treaty of Versailles. It had been in existence for over a month, unrecognized, and in direct confrontation with one of the 'Big Four'—Italy—when the peace conference opened in January 1919. Neutral Norway was the first to recognize it, on 26 January. The United States followed in February.

Its delegates insisted that they represented the kingdom of the Serbs, Croats and Slovenes, but the conference knew only of the kingdom of Serbia, which no longer existed.[1] If Britain and France came round to recognizing the new state in June, it was because the peace treaty with Germany—the treaty of Versailles—was ready. Serbia had been at war with Germany, and the signature of its successor-state

---

[1] The delegation was headed by the Serb Pašić, seconded by the Croat Trumbić, wartime chairman of the Yugoslav Committee and now Yugoslavia's first foreign minister, by the Slovene Ivan Žolger (1867–1925), until recently a minister in the Vienna government, and by Serbia's well-connected minister in Paris, Milenko Vesnić (1863–1921).

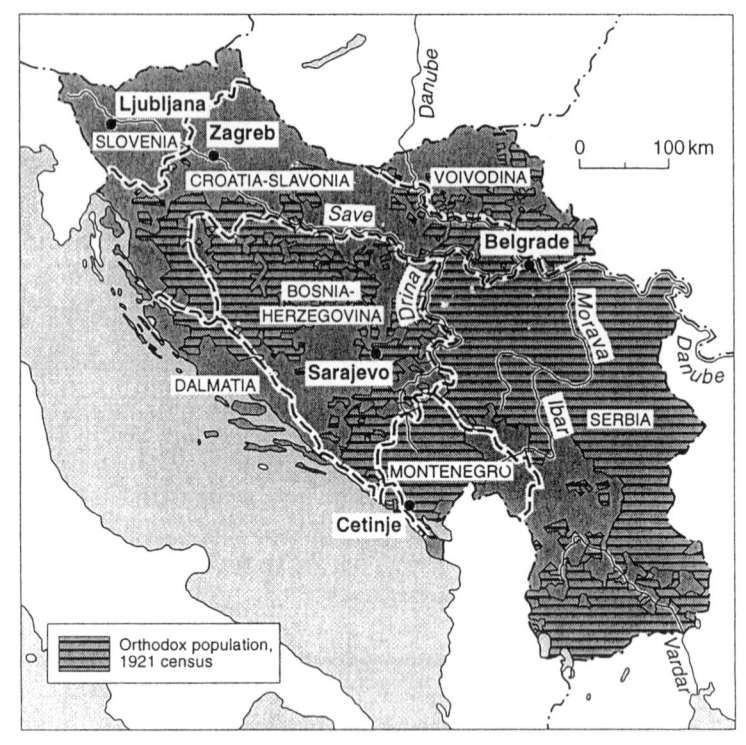

Serbia and the other Yugoslav lands on the eve of unification, 1918.

was necessary. Only by being included as a signatory was Yugoslavia a creation of the Versailles treaty.[2]

It had no frontiers and no constitution. Its territorial claims clashed with those of all its neighbours except Greece. The conference approached the task in a piecemeal fashion, as the various treaties were being drawn up. After the border with Italy had been agreed in November 1920, only Albania was left, but that problem went back to the setting up of the Albanian state in 1912 and was not part of the peace settlement.

Once in place, Yugoslavia extended over 247,500 sq. km and had 12 million inhabitants. It was made up of very different components. There were two Serb-feeling independent states—Serbia and Montenegro—

---

[2]The treaty of Versailles was signed on 28 June 1919, the anniversary of the Sarajevo assassination. Did anyone at the Quai d'Orsay or in Whitehall realize that it was also Vidovdan?

which included territories that had been Ottoman until 1912, and there were one-time Habsburg lands. Some had been part of Austria, and some part of Hungary. There was also a realm under the Hungarian crown with its own home rule—Croatia-Slavonia—attached to but not part of Hungary; and an Austro-Hungarian condominium that had been formally Ottoman until 1908—Bosnia-Herzegovina. Montenegro and predominantly Serb-inhabited parts of various Habsburg lands had unilaterally declared their unification with Serbia.

The chaotic situation of Yugoslavia was the result of warfare, which for Serbia and Montenegro had been almost continuous since 1912. Nevertheless it was one of the great beneficiaries of the principle of national self-determination. As the union of the Southern Slavs it had been set up without the Bulgars who had their separate state, but the overwhelming majority of the Serbs, Croats and Slovenes were now united in one state.

According to the first census, taken in 1921, which carried data on mother-tongue and religion, ethnic 'Yugoslavs' (Serbo-Croat-speakers, including Macedonians deemed to be Serbian speakers, and Slovenes) made up over 80 per cent of the total population, with a proportion of 'minorities' below that of Romania (24.6 per cent), Poland (31) and Czechoslovakia (35.6).

Pre-war Serbia represented 35 per cent of the territory and Serbs 39–40 per cent of the population.[3] They called themselves Serbs and were conscious of common roots. The overwhelming majority had come to look on Serbia as a unifying force, and professed the Eastern Orthodox faith.[4] Otherwise, they differed among themselves as much as the other Southern Slavs did from each other. The descendants of

---

[3]Even by taking in Macedonians, not recognized as such and officially Serbs, they were less than 44 per cent. According to Bogoljub Kočović's calculations, Serbs represented 40.02 per cent, Croats 23.34, Slovenes 8.51, Bosnian Muslims 6.17 and Macedonians 3.88, making up a total of 81.92 per cent ethnic Yugoslavs (*op.cit.*, 252). According to Ivo Banac, Serbs were 38.83 per cent, Croats 23.77, Slovenes 8.53, Bosnian Muslims 6.05, and Macedonians (to whom he adds Bulgars) 4.87, adding up to 82.05 per cent (*The National Question in Yugoslavia*, Ithaca, NY: Cornell University Press, 1984, 58). In 1921 there were 4,813,460 Serbs in Yugoslavia's population, according to Kočović, and 4,665,851 according to Banac.

[4]There were 9–10,000 Catholic, mainly urban, Serbs on the coast; perhaps 10,000 Jews of the old kingdom were assimilated (author's estimates, after Kočović, xxix, xxxiii); and there were Muslim Slavs who, for cultural, political or genealogical reasons, considered themselves to be Serbs. The Orthodox church, unified canonically under one restored *Serbian* patriarchate in 1920, grouped all the Eastern Orthodox faithful of Yugoslavia.

the soldier settlers of Austria's Military Border differed from the middle-class Serbs of Zagreb, the landowning and professional Serbs of Voivodina and the educated Serbs of Dalmatian towns; the Serbian bourgeoisie of Bosnia from the tied peasants of the Muslim-owned estates; the Montenegrins from the Ottoman Serbs of Macedonia and the long-suffering Serbian minority of Kosovo; and all of these from the Serbs of the kingdom of Serbia who provided about half the total number.

That nucleus had a mixed periphery. To the north the formerly Hungarian Voivodina contained, apart from 526,000 Serbs and 133,000 other ethnic Yugoslavs, 365,000 Magyars, 331,000 Germans, 68,000 Romanians and others, who amounted to 57 per cent of the population. The new territories of Macedonia were inhabited by 543,000 ethnic Yugoslavs (461,000 of whom were unrecognized Macedonians and 35,000 Muslim Slavs), as well as by 119,000 Turks and 111,000 Albanians. As for Kosovo, 288,910 or 65.8 per cent had Albanian as their mother-tongue (and 11,000 Turkish), compared to 109,090 Serbo-Croat.[5]

The government was confident that it could control these minorities. Macedonians were to be assimilated, but there was no question of turning other South Slavs into Serbs. All that Serbian politicians wanted, from Belgrade to Zagreb, was to ensure that all Serbs were gathered together in one state. They had come to realize that this could only be a united Yugoslav state of the Serbs, Croats and Slovenes, and they hardly distinguished between Serbs and Yugoslavs.

Serbia had come out of the war with huge losses. Its military losses were proportionately 2.5 times higher than those suffered by France.[6] For many of the survivors, that alone seemed to justify that its state structures should be the heart of the Yugoslav body. It had a king, a government, an administration, an army and parliamentary parties based on near-universal male suffrage. The army had not only contributed to the defeat of Austria-Hungary, but had been

[5] 1921 figures (calculated for the territory of present-day republics and provinces) according to Kočović (322–5, 328–9). Comparing demographic data from 1910 and 1921, it is estimated that some 70 per cent of the Muslim population of the new territories may have left (Gordana Krivokapić-Jović, 'Tipologija balkanske elite i radikalska baza 1918–1929' (A Typology of the Balkan Elite and the Radical Rank-and-File), *Tokovi istorije*, 3–4, Belgrade, 1997, 77).

[6] The combined loss of population suffered by all the regions forming Yugoslavia, as a result of the wars from 1912 to 1918, is estimated at slightly under 2 million (Ivo Lederer, *Yugoslavia at the Paris Peace Conference: A Study in Frontiermaking*, New Haven and London: Yale University Press, 1963, 221–5).

called to stake out frontiers and prevent disorders. In a tense period the new authorities in Zagreb, Ljubljana, Split and Sarajevo had exaggerated the revolutionary situation; the presence of a few thousand Serbian soldiers had been sufficient to maintain order at the very end of 1918.

The government in Belgrade was all too conscious of the fact that such use of its troops could feed anti-Yugoslav propaganda, and it gave priority to the borders. It did not want to intervene in Russia or in Hungary, and it was keen both to set up a peacetime gendarmerie for the whole territory by recruiting former Austro-Hungarian personnel, and to extend army recruitment. Thus in 1919–20 over 3,000 officers from the former Austro-Hungarian and Montenegrin armies were taken into the army of the kingdom of the Serbs, Croats and Slovenes. A little over half of its total active officer corps and of the command structure generally were for from the Serbian army.

The hurried creation of the united state and its unsettled territory created a confused constitutional situation which lasted until 1921. Crown Prince Alexander as regent was head of state. Discussions for the composition of a cabinet to represent all major political groups and provinces had resulted in its appointment on 20 December 1918. At Alexander's behest, the prime minister was not Pašić, who had remained in Paris to head the delegation at the peace conference, but Protić, with the Slovene Korošec, head of the Zagreb SCS government, as deputy prime minister, and the Croat Trumbić, chairman of the wartime Yugoslav Committee, as foreign minister. Compared to Serbia's pre-war cabinet of eight, the first Yugoslav government was a big one, with twenty-one members (eight from Serbia), because of the need to represent a much wider spectrum, and to tackle a large number of economic and social problems.

The various local executives continued to function outside Serbia for a while, at least until the setting up in March 1919 of an interim parliament. Under the name of Provisional Representation, it was intended to give backing to the government, provide a legislative counterpart, and prepare the elections for a constituent assembly. It was made up of 296 delegates of the Serbian parliament, the Zagreb National Council and the other regional councils, selected by the parties in proportion to their strength in these bodies and to the population of the regions. A number of elected members were included for Serbia's new territories of Macedonia and Kosovo, chosen by open and well-controlled ballot. The Croatian Peasant Party (CPP), which at the time was also republican, was offered two seats, but refused them as its protest against the way in which the union had been carried out.

As the territorial crisis postponed the holding of general elections, and a state of uncertainty continued, it was difficult for a majority to emerge which would agree on what sort of Yugoslavia it wanted. Only when the new state and its borders had been internationally accepted was the Constituent Assembly elected. Universal male franchise and a proportional system had been adopted; 419 representatives were returned in November 1920.

Of Serbia's pre-war parties the Radicals not only retained their hold over the peasantry in the old kingdom, but attracted many of the other Serbs as well. With sixty-nine members in the pre-parliament, it had already looked beyond Serbia, and sought alliances with the Slovene People's Party—the Catholic party that had ascendancy over the Slovenian countryside—and with the Muslims, whose parties were dominated by the landed interest. At the general elections, the Radicals had ninety-one seats with 17 per cent of the votes. Through their exercise of power in the decade before the war they had acquired, over and above their richer peasants, local merchants, priests and teachers, a new generation of better-educated activists, and the image of a modern party promoting European democratic values. The war had killed many of its voters as well as most of its younger and better-qualified cadres; the newcomers changed its character.

The new recruits from Serbia were those who felt they had lost out in the war, and wanted to restore their pre-war standing through the most influential party. Outside Serbia they were joined by people who considered that they had won the war—the adherents of Serbian ethnic movements, who had dreamed of uniting with Serbia. It was they who gave the Radical Party a 'Greater Serbian' flavour. It wanted to be a pan-Yugoslav party, it did not attract non-Serb votes, it failed to link Serbs and Croats locally, and it could only paper over the heterogeneity of its Serbian militants. It gradually became more conservative, and lived on through its party machinery and the prestige of its leader Pašić.

The Independent Radicals too immediately went out to extend their base. In Sarajevo in February 1919 they had set up the new Democratic Party, with Pribićević's Serbian Independents of Croatia, who had been encouraged by Prince Alexander to reinforce the Radicals' rivals. The remains of Serbia's Progressives and Liberals, various groups of the Croat-Serb coalition, and the Slovenian Liberals had also joined. Although predominantly Serbian, the Democrats were the first party to represent all parts of the state. They rejected sectional interests as a basis for political action or territorial division. Already the largest group in the pre-parliament with 115 delegates, they were confirmed as such by the general elections with 92 seats (one more than the Radicals) in the Constituent Assembly, and almost 20 per cent of the vote.

The common, if differing, centralism of Radicals and Democrats had got the better of their rivalry; they had come together in the pre-parliament to enact the electoral law and hold the elections. They then joined in a government, which Pašić headed again in January 1921. Two major newcomers to the parliamentary stage expressed opposition to the shape that the new state was taking. Founded in 1904, the Croatian Peasant Party obtained over 14 per cent of the total vote; it voiced the aspirations of the newly-enfranchised Croatian peasantry, tired of fighting for and being ruled by a government in a distant capital. Its leader Stjepan Radić (1871–1928), though a believer in South Slav brotherhood, had become so suspicious of Serbia's state machinery that he decided to boycott the work of the Constituent.

The Communist Party of Yugoslavia had been formed in April 1919 on the initiative of the very radical Social Democrats of Serbia. It had quickly established its network, joined the Communist International (Comintern), and obtained impressive results at local elections in many towns, including Belgrade. At the constituent elections its 12.4 per cent share was made up of disparate protest votes from every region—urban centres, frontier areas, and especially under-developed Montenegro and Macedonia.

Even before the assembly was opened on 18 December, the Radical-Democrat government had decided that the constitution would be passed by an absolute majority of the total number of deputies (whereas the Corfu Declaration had stipulated a 'qualified' majority). This had led to the CPP decision to stay away. Having called for revolution and a Soviet republic, the Communists threatened a general strike to exploit what they perceived to be a revolutionary situation. The government took a series of temporary measures of dubious legality, aimed at curbing their subversive potential, but Communist deputies stayed on.

The government's draft kept the essentials of Serbia's 1903 constitution: the monarchy, a single-chamber legislature, a centralized state territorially divided into French-style districts. Its supporters argued that to institutionalize existing differences was wrong, and that the play of parliamentary and local government would prevent the ascendancy of any one community.

At the other end of the spectrum the CPP published a draft constitution for a loose union, in which Croatia figured as a 'peasant republic'. Its boycott weakened the case against centralism, and was interpreted as being tantamount to separatism. The old-kingdom politicians mistrusted as much as they misunderstood the very notion of federalism, but they were not all adverse to regional autonomy. The former Radical prime minister Protić even boldly stressed the need for decentralization. It was Pribićević's Austro-Hungarian Serbs who wanted rigid centralism. They believed that there had to be one unitary state for one nation, and spread the fear of federalism.

Pašić in Paris had seen how difficult it had been to get Yugoslavia accepted. Two years had passed since unification, and the state still had no more than makeshift structures. He feared the disruptive potential of the Communists and of Radić's group. He wanted a proper working constitution to set the seal on Yugoslavia, and he could not do it without Pribićević and the Democrats. Like many others, he failed to see that most Croats, and certainly most of those elected in 1920, did not go for the 'one-nation-state' concept.

In the government draft victorious Serbia kept its concept of the state, and could accept the loss of its name. Croats would lose the continuity of their age-old political forms just as they emerged from imperial rule. However, there were others besides Croatian Serbs, including Croatian politicians mainly from Dalmatia, who were on hand to argue that special historic rights were no longer needed now that freedom was guaranteed to all. Few understood that a compromise was necessary.

Pašić in fact played a larger part in getting the constitution through than in shaping it. The government draft, as tabled, updated the Serbian constitution by stipulating equality between the main religious communities, and by incorporating a social charter inspired by Germany's Weimar constitution. It kept the name of Kingdom of the Serbs, Croats and Slovenes, although the Democrats would have preferred Yugoslavia.

As the date of the vote approached, more opposition deputies withdrew—the old Croatian parties, the Slovenian Populists, the Communists .... Bargains were made with the Muslim deputies to make sure of their vote.[7] Of the full total of 419 deputies, 258 were

[7] The administrative units would not cut across the territory of Bosnia-Herzegovina,

present on the symbolically set date of 28 June. The required majority was 210, and 223 voted in favour of what would henceforth be called the Vidovdan constitution.[8] Serbia's state tradition had won the day.

The union government had tackled right from the start the task of making the land of the Serbs, Croats and Slovenes theirs both to live in and to own. In pre-1912 Serbia and Montenegro, smallholding was already the rule, but in the former Habsburg lands there were large estates, many owned by German-Austrian and Magyar nobles, while in the former Ottoman territories ownership with dependent tenants survived.

Promises of land redistribution had been made by the Serbian government and by the Zagreb National Council, and these were confirmed in the regent's first pronouncement. The Yugoslav government immediately set up a special Ministry for the Agrarian Reform and issued an interim decree setting out the general lines. Large estates would be redistributed, their owners being compensated in state bonds; recipients would contribute through payments to the state over thirty years, except for veterans who had fought for the liberation of the Serbs, Croats and Slovenes. Sharecropper land would be handed over to tenants. Because conditions varied, legislation had to be passed for each area. In spite of often long delays, an area of 2.5 million hectares, or a quarter of the arable land, was eventually parcelled out in the territories outside pre-1912 Serbia and Montenegro to 518,000 families, or a quarter of the total number of peasant households.

The question of Ottoman estates should have been simple, with ownership transferred to the peasants who already held their plots by releasing them from their obligations to largely absentee landlords, whose rights were deemed to be 'feudal' and thus not subject to compensation. Legislative delays complicated matters. Returning soldiers did not wait for implementation, but went for the land, and settled scores against Muslims—Bosnians, Turks and Albanians alike,

---

Muslim religious courts and schools would be safeguarded, and compensation would be extended to Ottoman-type sharecropper tenures.

[8]The majority was made up of 87 Radicals, 89 Democrats, 34 Muslims (23 from Bosnia, 11 from Kosovo and Macedonia), and 14 others. The Radicals were Serbs. The Democrats included 11 Croats, 3 Slovenes and a few Macedonians. The Bosnian Muslims were Serbo-Croat-speakers of the Yugoslav Muslim Organization; the other Muslims were Turks and Albanians of the Society for the Defence of the Rights of Muslims of Kosovo and Macedonia. The 'others' included ten Slovenes.

landowners or otherwise. This happened especially in Bosnia-Herzegovina, where predominantly Muslim auxiliaries had been used by the Austro-Hungarian administration to fight against guerrillas, but also to intimidate the Serbian population. In Kosovo too the Austro-Hungarian occupation had raised Albanian detachments to make the best of existing anti-Serbian feelings.

Muslim landlords had the time to organize, bargain for their parliamentary support, and obtain compensation. The Bosnian Muslims found a comfortable place in the Yugoslav political arena, and yet their one-time landowning élite were irremediably impoverished by the reform, for they could not adapt to the modern world. Ownership of their land went to 113,000, mainly Serb, tenant families.

Legislation provided for colonization where there was surplus land. That included uncultivated, state, communal, abandoned and reclaimed land. Only in the south was there a surplus. Owing to the insecurity that had prevailed in Macedonia even before the long period of warfare, peasants had emigrated to towns, for temporary work to neighbouring territories, or overseas. There had been massive Muslim emigration ever since the withdrawal of Ottoman sovereignty, and there was continued emigration to Turkey after 1918. Because of the incursion of armed bands from Bulgaria across a porous frontier the prevailing sense of insecurity remained. In spite of its efforts to develop the area, the government was resented for its imposition of Serbianized surnames, its attempts to Serbianize the language and its encouragement of settlers—4,200 families coming by 1940.

The aims of the reform were to appease the revolutionary potential of the peasants, eliminate the foreign landowning class linked to the empires, and reward war veterans. For obvious reasons the veterans were overwhelmingly Serbs—43,500 families, land-hungry peasants from the barren mountain regions of Montenegro, Herzegovina and Lika in 'Border' Croatia. In Kosovo the reform was carried out against the Muslim landlord class, Turkish or Albanian, but there was also general discrimination against the local Albanian population. As a result of measures against terrorist action, land belonging to outlaws was confiscated, but it was often difficult even for law-abiding Albanian peasants to prove their claims in the absence of regular title-deeds.

Thus was initiated a timid reversal of the Ottoman policy of encouraging the settlement of supposedly loyal Muslim Albanians in the plains of Kosovo and Metohija, and in the Morava-Vardar corridor. The Yugoslav government tried to secure the border with Albania, restore the ethnic balance, and improve economic conditions. Its efforts were not generally successful. If the Serbs were generally and relatively more prosperous in Kosovo, the newcomers—in all some 60–70,000 people by 1940—often struggled to survive in a difficult environment, and many left before the Second World War. The Albanians, illiterate and unfavourably treated in the land reform, were dissatisfied; many had to go to other parts of Yugoslavia as unqualified seasonal labourers, or emigrate. Serbian historians have worked out that, in the period 1878–1912, 150,000 Serbs left the area while according to Albanian counter-claims an equal number of Albanians left after 1912.

Ethnic minorities were not all treated equally.[9] Yugoslavia had signed agreements on minority rights that came with the peace treaties and the League of Nations, but Kosovo and Macedonia had been part of pre-war Serbia. In practice the rights of minorities depended essentially on bilateral relations, and Yugoslavia's ethnic Albanians were its least protected minority.

Kosovo was the most backward region and a disturbed border area. Albania's frontiers had been recognized in 1921 when the country was assigned to Italy's protection under League of Nations provisions, but Yugoslavia was unhappy. Prominent émigrés from Kosovo nudged Tirana's post-war government towards an irredentist policy, and they organized resistance, raids and the smuggling of weapons. This was entangled with robbery, kidnapping, blood feuds, and the Yugoslav authorities' attempt to disarm the population. Settlers and state officials were the target of retaliation.

[9]The 'White' Russian refugees were almost a minority in their own right. They peaked at 42,000 in 1924, most of them in Serbia and Voivodina. More than half were from General Wrangel's southern Russian armies. They were well received by the authorities; help was also provided by international organizations and Western governments (eager then as now to keep refugees as near as possible to their country of origin).

At first they were almost a state within the state, with Wrangel's command and the exiled synod of the Russian Orthodox church established at Sremski Karlovci. The Russian legation in Belgrade became the Delegation for the Protection of Russian Refugees. Wrangel did not manage to have Cossack settlements in parts of Macedonia and Kosovo, but 4–5,000 of his men were enlisted in the Frontier Guard on the Albanian border, and forty-seven subalterns were accepted into the Yugoslav army. However, Serbia was hardly the West the refugees had dreamed of. Even its perfunctorily practised Orthodoxy was different. The better-off soon moved on, and by 1940 numbers were down to 25,000. In 1930 there were still more than 8,000 in Belgrade, where their educated élite were a boon to academia, the arts, science, medicine and even religion (they fostered female monasticism).

Nevertheless, most of the victims of the ongoing war across the border between the Yugoslav army and Albanian armed bands were local Albanians. The landowners who had stayed behind negotiated with Belgrade to safeguard their interests, and local government was generally staffed by the same people who had held on to their jobs from Ottoman times through the Austrian occupation to Yugoslav rule. Yugoslavia intervened between factions in Albania, and having given refuge to Ahmet Zogu, it supported his return to power in Tirana in 1924. Because he placed internal consolidation before irredentism, the raids stopped and a border settlement was achieved in 1925, but Italian interference subsequently brought about renewed tensions.[10]

Though it had been voted for by a clear majority, the constitution of 1921 was unacceptable to, or disapproved of by many others. The Communists had sprung from the pro-Yugoslav tradition of the Socialists. Having at first exploited all manner of discontent, they had followed the Comintern into believing that there was a revolutionary situation, and came to accept that Yugoslavia was no more than the expression of Serbian hegemony over non-Serbs, supported by the victorious imperialist powers.

Frustrated militants missed the regent as he was returning from taking the oath to the constitution, but assassinated the Democrat politician Milorad Drašković (1873–1921), who had been responsible for the anti-Communist regulations. Ironically, his assassination closed off the parliamentary debate on whether these regulations should be sustained, and secured the easy passage in August 1921 of the stricter Law for the Protection of Public Security and Order. A change in the public mood enabled a nervous government to outlaw the Communist Party. No longer able to channel discontent, the Communists were driven underground and abroad.

The smaller Croatian parties gathered around the CPP to strengthen the demand for a federal union. In fact this was a desire for dualism. It expressed the Croats' distrust of the psychological strength of Serbia which, if it had not 'liberated' them in the Serbian sense, had certainly provided exclusive protection against Italian expansionism. They were bitter that the Radical-Democrat-Muslim government

---

[10]In 1938 talks were started between Belgrade and Ankara for an orderly emigration of 'Turks' (obviously including Albanians) from Macedonia and Kosovo to Anatolia. The Yugoslav government was anxious to avert the growing danger of instability on the south-western border, and its Turkish counterpart eager to attract more Balkan Turks and other Muslims for resettlement. The plan did not materialize because financial terms could not be settled.

insisted on implementing its constitution to the full under their onetime coalition partner in the Zagreb *sabor*, for it was Pribićević who had taken over from Drašković at the interior ministry. Pašić's intransigent government faced the boycott of the Radić-led Croatian parties. The government acted as if Yugoslavia was just an extended Serbia that took in other Southern Slavs as well; the Croatian opposition acted as if it was an improved South Slav version of Austria-Hungary where Croatia would be Serbia's Hungary. Radical in terms of self-determined unification and land-ownership, the élites were conservative in their political conceptions, and their failure to understand the novelty of what had been achieved fuelled mutual resentment. It hampered the work of reconstruction and integration. Governments concentrated their efforts on surviving through unstable coalitions. The royal prerogative was thus pushed well beyond the spirit of the constitution, particularly since it was exercised by the authoritarian-minded Alexander, regent and then formally monarch on the death of King Peter I in August 1921.

Whereas the Radicals survived on the strength of their old prestige and leadership, holding on to government but also to their far from homogeneous post-war cadres and voters, the more sensitive and modern Democrats were soon cracking under the strain of government intransigence. As more and more began to see the need for a third way, they parted from the Radicals at the end of 1922.

The electoral law was changed in an effort to reduce the number of parties, and the elections of March 1923 were fought on the issue of a revision of the constitution. The results merely hardened the differences. Serbs broadly speaking voted to keep things as they were, and Croats for a change. Radicals and the CPP came out on top, the former with 25.8 per cent of the vote and the latter with 21.8. The Democrats lost out, because they were in the middle and because their more scattered votes had been favoured by the previous system of proportional representation.

Pašić tried negotiating with Radić, but the Croats stayed away and Pašić formed a minority Radical cabinet. Radić reacted with a series of provocative speeches challenging the legitimacy of the constitutional framework, and then went abroad to rouse foreign support. The Democrats split. Because the mainstream had come to favour a compromise with the Croats, Pribićević and his anti-revisionists seceded to form the Independent Democratic Party; they went over to the government, thus saving the Radicals. Meanwhile, however, CPP deputies took up their seats, attracted by the opposition coalition gathering around Ljubomir Davidović (1863–1940). He had brought Serbia's Independent Radicals into the Democratic Party, whose leader he now was.

Pašić resigned. Davidović's alternative team was ready and calling for CPP support, but it was only reluctantly accepted by King Alexander and by Radić, who had just returned. His tour of European capitals had led him to Moscow, where he had been well received, the Comintern having come out in favour of a break-up of Yugoslavia. The visit to Moscow had been intended to put pressure on Belgrade. Back home, he applied more pressure with renewed attacks against the monarchy, causing tension in Davidović's newly-formed cabinet, and prompting Alexander to argue that he had wanted, and still wanted, a broader coalition. Davidović gave way after one hundred days in office. Pašić was recalled, and granted a dissolution.

The Radical leader was reduced to bargaining for the continued existence of a government based on shifting coalitions, which caused extraordinary somersaults. In tandem with Pribićević again, the government decided to apply the Law for the Protection of Public Security and Order to the CPP as being linked to the Comintern. The Democrats and others protested. CPP candidates were allowed to stand, but judicial proceedings were initiated against their leaders. The government platform was that the constitution was the only alternative to disintegration.

The peasantry in Serbia, no longer actively enrolled in parties as they had once been, were now more sensitive to slogans and personalities. The Croatian peasantry, by contrast, had been well organized by the CPP. The Radicals had become the party of all those who wanted to be associated with the government, but were divided into several trends. The Democrats, their principal rivals in Serbia, in urban and in more prosperous areas, had had high hopes of becoming a Yugoslav-wide party, but had failed to hold their ground.

Crucial in their decline was the split with Pribićević, who. removed the Croatian Serb constituency that he had brought with him. He had also aroused among Croatian Serbs fears of Croatian domination, and among Croats fears of Serbian centralism. The government parties resorted to their control of the state machinery to try and improve their chances, but a 77 per cent participation allowed only marginal pressure.

The February 1925 elections gave the government parties an absolute majority of seats with 43 per cent of the vote. Branding it as made up of crypto-Communists had not weakened the CPP, but

Radić's game with Moscow had weakened his potential Serbian allies and practically destroyed the chances of a wider opposition coalition under Davidović. While CPP deputies in parliament acknowledged the constitution and rejected all links with Moscow, Radić was negotiating with Pašić in order to extricate himself. In the summer came the surprise announcement that the largest Croatian party would join the largest Serbian party in government. Proceedings against the CPP leaders were dropped, and Radić was received by the king and entered the government. CPP ministers replaced the Independent Democrats.

The new government was welcomed with relief by the country at large and abroad, and tension abated. King Alexander went to Zagreb for the millennium celebrations of the Croatian realm, and was received with enthusiasm. However, there was no real worked-out compromise, and teamwork between the two parties was difficult.

If Radić's tactics were difficult to understand, Pašić's were all too simple: he clung to power. Although Radicals held the key posts, they had little by way of a comprehensive programme of legislation. Their base was in Serbia and among the Bosnian Serbs, but they had lost support in towns. They had been forced to seek uneasy alliances in order to obtain working majorities. People went on voting for them out of habit, because they defended the unity of the state, and because they were the government party.

Pašić at eighty no longer controlled it, and was fast approaching his end. He had been a Balkan revolutionary in his youth, and in his prime a great party leader, able diplomat and skilled parliamentarian, but he had not been either a Yugoslav prophet or a constructive statesman. Yet he remained a legendary figure, in whom much of the Serbian peasantry saw the main architect of unification. In March 1926 a corruption scandal broke out in which his son was implicated, and the old prime minister resigned. Away from government, he died before the year was out.

The Radicals limped on, increasingly divided, distraught by the loss of Pašić, and losing support. The other parties were also divided, as the king interfered among factions. Second-rate prime ministers headed what were becoming 'palace' governments of ill-fitting coalitions, until new elections were called in September 1927 in an attempt to try and clarify the situation.

There were interesting attempts at extending constituencies, by the CPP to attract Macedonian votes, and by the Democrats to link up with the Bosnian Muslims. However, participation fell to below 70 per cent for the first time. The Radicals were down to 32 per cent, and the Democrats up again to 16.42, more than the CPP's 15.81. Surprisingly, while in Belgrade Radić had developed good relations with King Alexander, who defied the fading Radical establishment by asking him to form a government. Radić came up with the most unlikely combination of the decade. He teamed up with the archcentralist turned federalist, Pribićević, in a Peasant-Democratic Coalition, but that was not enough for him to become prime minister.

Parliament met in a heavy atmosphere, with strong complaints of electoral irregularities and of corruption. As a Radical tried to patch up a government, parliament turned into an arena for insults, threats and obstructionism. Extremist Croats openly talked of the need to break away. Radić in his turn invited the king to intervene as arbiter, and appoint an extra-parliamentary government under a general.

In June 1928 a debate turned to pandemonium. It had been triggered by government efforts to secure the ratification of agreements with Italy, countered by Radić's call for recognition of the Soviet Union. A Radical deputy from Kosovo answered insults with revolver shots, killing two Croatian colleagues, and wounding three others including Radić. Opinion was numbed. The king hurried to Radić's bedside, to be told: 'Now only the king and the people are left'.

The eighty-three deputies of the Peasant-Democratic Coalition left for Zagreb, demanding a dissolution, new elections and a revision of the constitution. Radić himself died soon after. The government resigned. Radicals and Democrats feared that another dissolution would merely aggravate the situation. There were half-hearted attempts at wider coalitions, triggered by the fear that the king might otherwise dispense with parliament.

Alexander did try a general with an all-party government, before turning reluctantly to the Slovene Populist leader, the Catholic priest Anton Korošec (1872–1940), who had been president of the National Council in Zagreb at the time of the unification. Korošec rallied Radicals, Democrats and Muslims as well as his own Slovenes, but the boycotters in Zagreb would not join. He was the one and only non-Serb to head a government in inter-war Yugoslavia. For five months he soldiered on with a truncated parliament that was breaking down. Although the tenth anniversary of unification, on 1 December 1928, was played down, student protests in Zagreb turned into riots that caused a dozen deaths. The Democrats then decided to leave the government in order to break the deadlock with the opposition in Zagreb. Korošec resigned at the very end of the year.

Vladko Maček (1879–1964), Radić's successor, told King Alexander that the Croats wanted a new federal constitution, and that the process should be initiated by an extra-parliamentary government appointed by him. The plan that he sketched out was deemed by Radical and Democrat leaders to be tantamount to Austro-Hungarian dualism, but they were willing to talk about it. The monarch was not.

On 6 January 1929 Alexander issued a proclamation: it was his sacred duty to preserve the unity of the nation and the state, and since this could no longer be done through parliament, he was taking it upon himself to organize institutions that would best correspond to the country's needs. The Assembly was dissolved, the constitution invalidated, and a new government appointed. The king had been meddling behind the scenes. Essentially a soldier, not schooled in civil government, he had been thinking for several years of an extra-parliamentary solution. He would tolerate no rival, and had developed an aversion to Pašić, even though the Radical leader had helped him against the Black Hand. He had had, right from the start, excellent if ill-informed intentions towards the creation of a united state to which non-Serbs could feel as loyal as Serbs, and was still carried along by a sincere if nebulous Yugoslavism.[11]

Yugoslavia finally had an extra-parliamentary government headed by a soldier, but Alexander's General Petar Živković (1879–1947) was merely his agent at the head of his cabinet. Reflecting the king's desire for widely-based advice, the ministers were known parliamentarians with experience of office, coming from all major groups, including the CPP. Nevertheless, apart from the outgoing prime minister Korošec, who could claim to have his party's backing, the others were all individuals occupying their positions as mere royal appointees, some against their party's wishes if not as outright dissidents. All powers were transferred to the crown; the law-and-order legislation of 1921 was strengthened and extended.

Alexander could count on much Serbian support. He enjoyed popularity among the peasantry of Serbia as military commander, and those Serbs who rallied to him did so because they wanted to uphold at any cost the unity of the state. However, the dictatorship was not an exclusively Serbian affair and it was easily set up. Most Croats welcomed the repeal of the constitution. The dictatorship

[11] There is as yet no scholarly biography of King Alexander.

had been announced as temporary—to allow passions to subside, create a sense of national unity, and accelerate integration. No time was lost. The country was officially renamed Yugoslavia, legal codes and school curricula were unified, Serbia's old regimental flags were replaced with new Yugoslav ones, and the territory was reorganized into nine large geographical provinces called 'banovinas', that broke up the historical pattern.

A weary public opinion had been at least willing to give King Alexander a chance, but different sections expected different things. Croatian opinion had not expected a crash programme of Yugoslav patriotism imposed from above. Even though there were many more— unrepresentative—Croats in government than during the parliamentary régime, King Alexander's Yugoslavicizing dictatorship was perceived by most Croats as a more efficient way of implementing the Serbian style of centralism, even Serbian hegemony, over the common state.

From abroad, a former Pure Rights member of parliament from Croatia, Ante Pavelić (1889–1959), launched his Ustasha (insurgent) movement to fight by all means possible for the independence of Croatia. As a fringe group operated from abroad, increasingly Fascist-inspired and sheltered by Italy and Hungary which used them as a weapon to threaten Yugoslavia, the Ustashas had few supporters among Croats at home, but the dissatisfaction on which their movement fed was widespread.

In 1931, as the economic crisis hit Yugoslavia, King Alexander reflected that his aims had not yet been accomplished, but that he could not carry on as a temporary dictator. In September he granted a new constitution. There was to be a bicameral legislature, but government was responsible to the king alone—'guardian of the unity of the nation and of the integrity of the state'. Elections took place in November: only countrywide lists were allowed, voting was public, and the list heading the poll received two-thirds of the seats. The government's was the only list, and one-third of registered voters did not bother to vote. In order to give the king's government popular backing and organize its supporters, a Yugoslav National Party was set up, made up of dissidents from across the whole political spectrum around a nucleus of onetime (and mostly right-wing) Radicals.

Realizing that there was no chance of deeper moves, Maček from Zagreb issued a call in November 1932 for a return to the beginning—to 1918. This important political reaction attracted expressions of sympathy from different quarters. At the same time the Ustashas stepped up their propaganda, accompanied by acts of terrorism. An allegedly seditious interview given by Maček landed him in prison in April 1933.

King Alexander had concentrated his energies on foreign policy. He considered that his efforts to strengthen Yugoslavia's external security had been quite successful, but he remained pessimistic about his achievements at home. There is evidence that he was thinking of new initiatives in 1934, in particular of negotiating with Maček to find an issue to the Croatian problem. Because of these indications, because of the relative success of his diplomacy, and because he had become the only authority, the Ustashas decided to strike at the king. On 9 October 1934 he was shot dead soon after landing at Marseilles at the start of a state visit to France. He was aged forty-six.

The immediate effect was not to split Yugoslavia apart, as the Ustashas hoped, but to bring it together. King Alexander was respected by most Serbs, and most Croats at least approved of his foreign policy. The general grief showed that he had been removed because he had become the symbol of the country's unity and independence. Paradoxically, however, he had dealt a death-blow to unitary Yugoslavism in wanting to forge a new nation from above, but his tailor-made constitution survived him. His will entrusted the regency for his eleven-year-old son Peter II (1923–70) to his cousin Prince Paul (1893–1976), accompanied by two little-known worthies (a Croat and a Serb from outside Serbia). A new government was sworn in under Bogoljub Jevtić (1886–1960), who had been Alexander's foreign minister. Maček and other political detainees were released, and elections were held in May 1935.

The government ran these as a plebiscite for the dead monarch. In order to fulfil the now rather more manageable conditions for nationwide lists, Davidović revived the Belgrade-based opposition coalition, and with the support of Muslims came to an agreement with Maček for a single Combined Opposition list to be headed by the CPP leader. The platform was to win the elections, and reorganize the state according to a subsequent all-party agreement. As parties they were technically illegal, and many of their cadres had gone over to the government, but despite open voting and manipulations their combined presence attracted a participation at the polls of over 73 per cent. Encouraged by the 37 per cent of the votes that it secured, the opposition went on to protest against the conditions under which the ballot had been held, and to call for fresh elections under a new electoral law and a neutral government.

The prince regent had another plan. He asked the ex-Radical, British-connected and successful finance minister Milan Stojadinović (1888–1961) to form the next government. Stojadinović had built up his own following within the government party. He had approached leading Radicals, Slovenes and Muslims, with a view to launching a new party that would draw together more effectively pro-government supporters. From a Serb-Slovene-Muslim base, he would seek the cooperation of the CPP on a reform programme. Prince Paul wanted a solution within the 1931 constitution. Formally it could not be revised during the monarch's minority, and Paul did not want to jettison the safeguard of its prerogative.

Most political detainees were amnestied, parties were tolerated, the ideology of one-nation Yugoslavism was no longer stressed, and Stojadinović organized his new Yugoslav Radical Union. A majority of deputies elected for Jevtić's party went over to it, and it obtained genuine support in Slovenia and from Bosnia's Muslims, but failed to build up more than a time-serving following in Serbia. Yet Stojadinović was able to remain in the saddle until the crisis over the Concordat, without any real concessions to the CPP or to the Serbian opposition.

The issue of a concordat with the Holy See to settle a unified status for the Catholic church in Yugoslavia had lingered on since 1920, when negotiations had first got under way. It was initialled under Jevtić and signed under Stojadinović, and its ratification was put to the National Assembly in July 1937. The Serbian Orthodox church raised an unexpected storm, objecting to most of its terms, which it alleged would have granted the Catholics a more favourable position. With its organization and influence, the Catholic church did stand to gain from a unified regime of relations with the state, but Orthodox churchmen felt insecure in a state where they were no longer the established church of the overwhelming majority of the population (48.7 per cent Orthodox in the 1931 census, to 37.8 Catholics).

However, the storm was more than a clerical reaction. The Concordat was seen as a first step in the direction of a foreign realignment in favour of Italy. It passed the lower house by only 169 votes to 129. When Patriarch Varnava, who had led the opposition, died that very night, there was talk of foul play and the Concordat was shelved. The episode had exposed the lack of homogeneity of Stojadinović's party. He had tried, and failed, to lure the CPP into government before making any concessions to it. The CPP and Maček were uninterested in the Concordat issue. Meanwhile Stojadinović had turned to building the Radical Union into his own ruling party, with mock-Fascist trappings. The country was tired of veiled authoritarianism and pseudo-representation. Opposition was appearing, and there was a revival of the Communists' fortunes as the Soviet Union turned from an anti-Yugoslav to a pro-Yugoslav and popular front line. Nevertheless, the opposition to the Concordat produced neither a popular front nor a Serbian anti-Croat upsurge, but a more closely united opposition. In October 1937 the Serbian-based parties, the CPP and its partners jointly issued a call for a national government to work out with the regency a transition to a new constitutional structure, to satisfy a majority within each of the three acknowledged national communities.

The appeal was greeted with a wave of enthusiasm. By then most Serbs wished to come to an arrangement with the Croats, if only to remove the threat of secession and the arguments against a return to parliamentary government. Huge crowds greeted Maček when he came to Belgrade in August 1938. In December Stojadinović called an election. He expected that the international situation would favour his argument that this was not the time to count on Franco-British support or to tamper radically with the constitution, but he fared worse than Jevtić had done in 1935. His authoritarianism had caused adverse reactions even in government, and frightened Prince Paul.

With a ballot that was still public, the opposition obtained 1.3 million votes to the government's 1.6 million. Stojadinović went in the same way as he had come. The regent had started confidential negotiations with Maček, and found an alternative within the government party, determined to settle quickly with the Croats and formally within the constitution. If Stojadinović had remained longer in office at one stretch than any other Yugoslav prime minister before or since, it was essentially because he had an economic policy with which to confront the Depression. Yet the expansion of the state-financed industrial sector, which favoured the newer plants of Bosnia and Serbia, had not gone unnoticed in the older enterprises of Croatia. His gamble on the economic advantages of trading with Germany, and his general readiness to move towards Germany and Italy, had caused fears in Francophile Serbia.

In February 1939 Dragiša Cvetković (1893–1969), minister under Stojadinović and also of Radical origin, became prime minister, and took up the talks with Maček. The CPP leader had worked on several fronts, with Serbian opposition leaders, with the government, and even with the Italians. Eventually he decided in favour of a bargain with the crown. He had suggested that his Serbian friends should trust him and the regency to come to a quick arrangement, because of the threatening international situation. They, however, would not be stampeded into half-measures that dropped the key demand for a democratic constitution, that satisfied only Croats and the crown, and separated them from Serbs. In order to break the opposition alliance, Prince Paul had not opposed the development of the CPP as an all-embracing pan-Croat movement, while he had marginalized the Serbian opposition. Furthermore, he did not have the prestige of his cousin Alexander, and was not popular with Serbian opinion.

The Cvetković-Maček *sporazum* (agreement)—in fact an *Ausgleich* between the crown and the CPP leadership—was formalized in August 1939 by royal ordinances. A self-governing *banovina* of Croatia was set up over 26.6 per cent of the national territory (Croatia, Slavonia and Dalmatia, with some districts from Bosnia-Herzegovina), and 28.6 per cent of its population.[12] It had its elected *sabor* and an executive under the *ban* who represented the crown. The central government retained control of foreign affairs and trade, defence, transport and communications.

A new government was formed under Cvetković, with Maček as deputy prime minister, and ministers from the Radical Union, its Slovenian and Muslim components, the CPP, its Independent Democratic partners and the smaller (Serbian) Agrarian Party. Parliament was dissolved. The government was given full powers to modify legislation on elections, parties and the press. In an about-turn for which the regency gave no explanation, a process of constitutional revision had been started, implicitly and ambiguously. Explicit revision could not take place until September 1941, when King Peter II came of age, but the ordinances were taken under the crown's reserved emergency powers (in case of war or any other threat to the security of the state)—to be subsequently submitted to parliament.

The *sporazum* put an end to the United Opposition. It gave short-term satisfaction to the CPP leadership and to a minority of the Serbian opposition, but for most Croats it was a first step towards a general solution of the Croatian question, or too little too late. Serbian opinion felt frustrated and humiliated. Relations between Serbian and Croatian politicians, which had improved considerably, came under

[12] 4 million, including 768,000 Orthodox Serbs and 144,000 Muslims (1931 census).

strain. Many in the opposition were bitter against Maček; they had adopted him as leader, and saw him now as having abandoned the common goal of changing the Yugoslav political system, in order to come to power in Croatia by agreement with the crown.

Serbs generally considered that the 'Serbian question'—the question of their community's integration—had been solved by the mere fact that they were all gathered in Yugoslavia (with the exception of a few in Romania and in Hungary). 'Serbs' figured until 1929 in the official designation of the state, and the tripartite Yugoslav coat-of-arms and national anthem continued until the end to have a Serbian component, but otherwise there was no 'Serbia'. It was not even clear any longer in people's minds what Serbia was, regionally or historically. Was it the pre- or post-1912 kingdom, or even the Serbia of November 1918?

The émigré partisans of King Nicholas of Montenegro had been amnestied, most had returned home after his death, and Montenegrins felt they were Serbs even when they were dissatisfied with the complete loss of their historical identity. Their wounded patriotic pride could make them vote 'green' for an autonomist agenda, or perceive the Communists as defenders of the oppressed, but they formed no nationalist movement. Not only did the élite of Serbia not realize how complex a state Yugoslavia was, but they were not fully conscious of the complexity of the Serbian ethnic community itself. It did not know the history, prejudices and aspirations of Serbs outside the old kingdom, any better that those of Croats, Slovenes and others.

Unification had put an end to any further development of a Serbian collective consciousness. Serbs still differed among themselves as much as in 1918; no pan-Serb feeling had been achieved within Yugoslavia. With the end of parliamentary government Serbian parties, which had been parties of individual representation, had been cut off from their life source. The process of linking Serbs from outside Serbia, let alone Macedonians, to common institutions through parliamentary parties had ceased. As the 1930s drew to a close, public opinion among Serbs was aware that in the unitary one-nation Yugoslav kingdom a Slovenian national identity had come to full expression, with its own practically homogeneous *banovina*, administered in fact by its majority party and in its own language. Croatia too had come to full maturity through its opposition to centralism. It had now finally achieved its territorial unity in the new *banovina*, run by a well-organized and all-embracing CPP, which increasingly controlled every sphere of social life.

A good measure of political relaxation had allowed parties to be reactivated, and provided all dissatisfied elements with the opportunity of increased activity. Those included outlawed Ustashas and Communists. The latter's view of Yugoslavia was imposed by the Comintern, which had decided that the satisfied Serbs were not revolutionary material, and wanted to exploit the revolutionary potential of dissatisfied non-Serbs. The Yugoslav Communists, who had started as unitarist Yugoslavs, took up the slogan that the Serbian bourgeoisie had oppressed the others.

Between the moment when the Comintern had changed its position again over Yugoslavia and the beginning of the Second World War, the Communists had managed to turn themselves into a federalist Yugoslav party, disciplined and well-organized under their new leader Josip Broz *alias* Tito (1892–1980). In Serbia they were strong among university students, but barely noticed in the villages, although they had many adherents in poorer areas such as Montenegro.

Notwithstanding the Comintern's view of satisfied Serbs, there were many dissatisfied and non-Communist ones. The Serbian Cultural Club, founded in 1937, became the most vocal expression of the Serbian intelligentsia's loss of faith in pan-Yugoslav nationalism. It had been founded as a think tank of intellectuals, professionals and businessmen, to work for the integration of Serbian culture within Yugoslavia. With the creation of the *banovina* of Croatia, it developed into an opposition pressure group to define and defend Serbian interests in Yugoslavia. If its cultural line continued under its chairman, the eminent historian and constitutionalist Slobodan Jovanović (1869–1958), younger members pushed for a reawakening of Serbian nationalism, and stressed the Serbian character of areas such as Voivodina, Bosnia, Kosovo and Macedonia. Their ambiguous motto was 'a strong Serbian identity—a strong Yugoslavia'.[13]

[13] Its first secretary was the historian Vaso Čubrilović (1897–1990), whose long life spanned a wide political spectrum, from revolutionary Young Bosnia, through the Agrarian Party with a pro-government stance, to fellow-travelling membership of the Communist government after the Second World War. He is now best known for having given a lecture and submitted a project to the Club in 1937 on how to encourage the emigration of ethnic Albanians from Kosovo through propaganda, pressure and fear. He resigned from the Club when it opposed the *sporazum* in 1939. His paper gathered dust in the archives until it was exhumed by an ethnic Albanian postgraduate for his doctoral dissertation, published in Kosovo in 1983. Immediately seized upon by Kosovo and Croatian independentists, it was serialized in the Belgrade daily *Borba* in January 1988.

A debate was started about a wholesale reorganization of the state. As far back as 1932, the Democratic Party leader Davidović had adopted a four-unit federal project, thus avoiding the difficult partition of Bosnia. The fact that the *sporazum*, achieved with no genuine representation of Serbian opinion, had given shape to a Croatian unit, but left all the rest of the country under centralized rule, gave rise to various plans, including one for a '*banovina* of the Serbian lands'.

The Comintern was right to the extent that Serbs had on the whole been satisfied with the general framework of the Yugoslav state, if not by the authoritarianism of its rulers. There had been no Serbian national or majority party, or indeed any explicitly Serbian political party. Divided into regions and parties, far from seeing themselves as a domineering element, they had rather fancied themselves to be the ultimate defenders of Yugoslavia, for which they had given up their identity. Their very identification with Yugoslavia only served to show others that they did indeed consider Yugoslavia to be theirs to rule over. Serbia had given its stamp to Yugoslavia as a result of its rôle in the Great War, but it had also been worn out by the war, and could not really lead.

Serbian parties had dominated parliamentary life, but they had not been united, and they could hardly have sustained their domination without the collaboration of Slovene and Muslim parties. The Radicals were already disintegrating by the time of King Alexander's assumption of full powers. Thereafter it was mostly ex-Radical politicians who co-operated with the royal regime, accustomed as they were to government, and what remained of the so-called 'old' Radicals were the weakest of the opposition parties. It was the Democrats who took on the lead of the Serbian opposition. They had come a long way from their centralist position, and lost much since the 1920s.

There was a Serbian over-representation in the personnel of the state, partly accounted for by the Croatian boycott. The army had expanded from Serbia's existing army, which provided uniforms, ranks, regulations and medals. Officers from the Austro-Hungarian and Montenegrin armed forces had to apply to join. Absorbing officers who had fought on the opposite side was not easy; few field officers would consider applying. Time was needed (in practice the whole interwar period) before Croats and Slovenes trained in Yugoslav military schools reached the top. Initially purged of Black Hand sympathizers, the army became a bureaucratized Yugoslav institution that stood loyally by the monarchy until the Second World War.[14] Its problem was that it was top-heavy, old fashioned, and widely believed to be stronger than it actually was.

The interior ministry's appointment of prefects and sub-prefects caused resentment against Belgrade centralism in non-Serb areas. The requirement to have ten to fifteen years previous state service again initially favoured Serbia's pre-war bureaucracy. At their disposal was a 20,000–strong gendarmerie calculated to have been 60 per cent Serbs, since they too had predominated in Habsburg Croatia. At the same time the fact that six sets of legal codes remained in force outside the old kingdom limited central control over law enforcement.

If centralized administration from Belgrade allowed Serbs (but also Slovenes) to occupy official positions in excess of their share of the population, shrinking opportunities for public employment quickly posed a problem for peasant families who educated their sons with a career as an official in view. Otherwise the government generally failed to afford Serbs the economic advantages which its non-Serb critics assumed. The exception was in the award of land for war veterans from the impoverished uplands, which created resentment among the inhabitants of the lowlands of Voivodina, Kosovo and Macedonia

Belgrade was the focus of political power. On the eve of the First World War, with 95,000 inhabitants, it was already the largest city in the lands that would become Yugoslavia. By 1929 it had grown to 226,000. Public employees accounted for a quarter, but the commercial sector had also grown to 19 per cent. The capital attracted a rich variety of newcomers and visitors, not all of them drawn by its political function, and not all wishing to be assimilated. There were professionals, business people, intellectuals and artists from all regions. Connections with the other two cultural centres, Zagreb and Ljubljana, were strong.

Most writers and artists were dependent on the state through

---

[14]Recent scholarship has shown that 2,647 Austro-Hungarian and 482 Montenegrin army officers, along with all 200 naval officers, joined Serbia's 3,555 by 1926. 300 of them were field and general (seven) officers. Of the 508 Yugoslav officers who had attained general rank between 1919 and 1941, sixty-five had started in the Austro-Hungarian and twelve in the Montenegrin army. Thirty or so more would have been promoted in the course of 1941 but for the invasion (see the several monographs and articles on the Yugoslav army by Mile Bjelajac since 1988).

In the foreign service, by 1931 fifty-one out of 215 diplomatic and consular officials were non-Serbs, including 6/20 in the minister grade (*Diplomatsko-konsularni izveštaj za 1931* [Diplomatic and Consular List for 1931]).

employment as teachers, or through commissions, purchases and subsidies, yet there was not much control of their political beliefs at the level of the cultural élite. A majority wished to be part of the European mainstream, which many had discovered through their pre-war studies in France, and many more at French universities and schools under wartime conditions. The wartime graduates from France were almost as numerous as those of Belgrade University in the 1930s. Culture in Belgrade was turning to European trends, increasing the divide between modern and traditional.

Newspapers and publishing houses flourished, creating a body of opinion impervious to control. In the 1930s there were some fifty regular periodicals, and the independent daily *Politika* had the largest circulation in the country. The prestigious literary journal *Srpski književni glasnik* published more writings of the Communist-leaning Croatian writer Miroslav Krleža (1893–1981) than appeared in Zagreb. The major and most innovative publisher and bookseller was Geca Kon (1873–1941), who had set up in business in the early years of the century, and by 1928 had published over 1,500 books (the German occupation authorities were to kill him as a Jew). Women were increasingly accepted in this cultural milieu, and were nearing a quarter of students in higher education in Belgrade by the late 1920s.

The governments had governed, in spite of political problems, obstacles, errors and failures, and they had produced relatively gratifying results in economic and diplomatic fields. At a time when there was no European labour market to absorb surplus manpower, and no IMF to provide financial help, their record in terms of reconstruction, currency stabilization, land reform, economic growth, education, intellectual and religious freedom was generally positive. Nevertheless, miserable poverty co-existed with relatively favourable peasant incomes. Regional imbalance was not a simple divide between Serb-inhabited areas and others, but its reality and, even more, its perception obscured advances.

Foreign policy made for the united state a place in the post-war European order. It managed to protect its integrity and independence by acting with and through the League of Nations and its agencies, and by seeking support from the victorious powers, until the Depression, the rise of Hitler's *Reich*, the devaluation of French power and prestige, and the Western Allies' scant sympathy for Yugoslavia's economic problems led its rulers to neutrality, with an increasing pro-Axis slant.

The Second World War began a week after the *sporazum*. The resulting uncertainties worked against the broader compromises needed to restructure the state. No elections were held, either for the new Croatian *sabor* or for the dissolved Yugoslav parliament. The regency and the government did not command the loyalty of substantial portions of the population; Croats wanted more autonomy; Serbian opposition was rising and disconnected; control had slackened of outlawed Communists and fascists, who were waiting for their chance to emerge with the help of the Soviet Union or the Axis Powers.

The regency finally gave way to Hitler. On 25 March 1941 the government adhered to the Tripartite Pact between Germany, Italy and Japan, thereby accepting the leadership of Nazi Germany and Fascist Italy in a new European order. It was the last straw for the Serbian opposition. Some Serbian ministers resigned. Patriarch Gavrilo, the head of the Serbian Orthodox church, re-animated the Kosovo ethic, which the government had betrayed by its surrender.

A bloodless military coup of officers in Belgrade overthrew the regency on 27 March. Peter II was declared of age six months before term. The vigour of anti-pact demonstrations had shown that most Serbs, but not only they, believed that the country should be on the side of its allies from the First World War. The coup was more a spontaneous emotional reaction than a prepared conspiracy. It was carried out against a weak Yugoslav government by officers who wanted to save the honour not only of Serbia but of Yugoslavia as they perceived it. They had political contacts, so that all the party leaders came together—the CPP, its Independent Democrat partners, Slovenes, Muslims and Serbian opposition parties—in the government formed under General Dušan Simović (1882–1962), who had hovered behind the plotters and who fancied himself as a national saviour. This was Yugoslavia's widest coalition since 1918, and it expressed the deep yearning for a fully representative government in an hour of need, but it could do nothing. All it could do was to keep as quiet as possible in order not to provoke Hitler, until he attacked nine days later.

7

FRAGMENTS OF SERBIA – VICTIMS, RESISTERS AND COLLABORATORS 1941–1945

After the Belgrade coup of 27 March 1941, Hitler had decided to destroy for ever the 'Versailles construct' that was Yugoslavia. He was angry that his immediate plans had been upset, and wanted to punish the Serbs, whom he saw as the main disturbers of the European order. Not only were the Slavs low on the Nazi race scale, but an anti-Serb Austrian streak erupted that went back to before the First World War. It stemmed from the Führer's own prejudices, and it ran through the many Austrian officials who dealt with Balkan affairs. It was 1914 all over again, with a vengeance—that of the Nazi *Reich* taking the place of the Habsburg monarchy.

After a violent propaganda campaign setting non-Serbs against Serbs, Germany attacked Yugoslavia on 6 April without an ultimatum or a declaration of war, and Italy followed. Code-named 'Punishment', the operation started with the merciless air bombardment of Belgrade. Eleven days later it was all over. The Yugoslav high command had to accept an unconditional surrender, and between 200,000 and 375,000 prisoners of war were taken to Germany and Italy. The government, with King Peter, had managed to fly out of the country before the surrender.[1]

The partition of Yugoslavia began even before the capitulation came into force. Slovenia was shared between Germany and Italy; Italy also annexed important strips of the coast and obtained control

---

[1] Maček had stayed behind, and so had the leader of the Yugoslav Muslim Organization. The Slovene People's Party leader and a non-party minister from Montenegro had been killed.

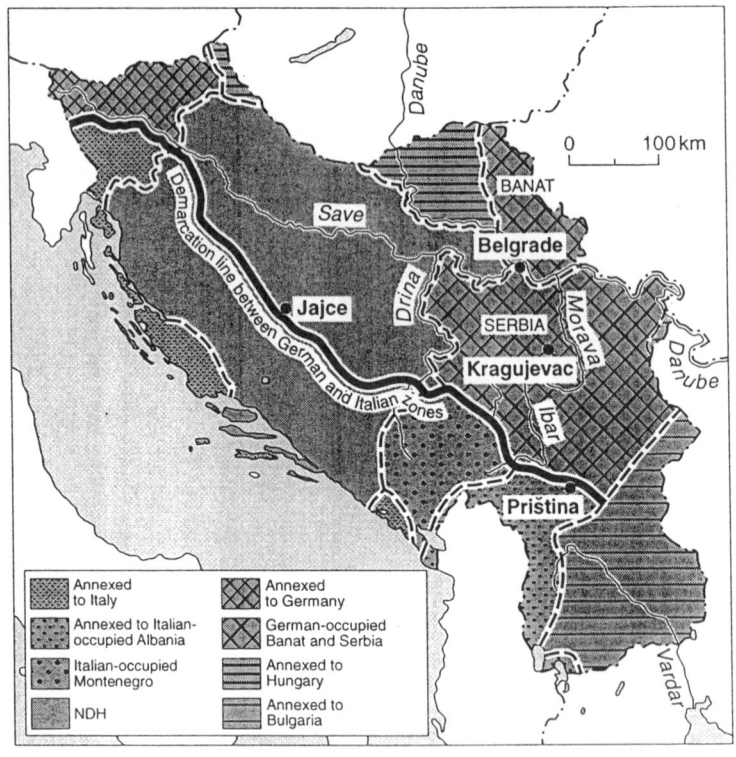

The partition of Yugoslavia during the Second World War.

of Montenegro. Albania, attached to Italy since 1939, gained Kosovo and a slice of Macedonia. The rest of Yugoslav Macedonia was entrusted to Bulgaria. Hungary took back part of what it had been made to give up at the end of the First World War. Croats were to be brought to the side of the Axis with Aryan status. Maček and the CPP withdrew into passivity. Returning from exile, Pavelić and his Ustashas were allowed to proclaim their 'Independent State of Croatia' (*Nezavisna Država Hrvatska*, usually known by its initials NDH), extending over 40 per cent of the former kingdom of Yugoslavia, across Bosnia and Herzegovina to the gates of Belgrade.

The Ustasha state was divided between a German and an Italian zone, and enjoyed only what independence it could squeeze out of the rivalry of its two Axis protectors. It contained almost as many 'aliens'—Orthodox Serbs, Muslims, Gypsies, Jews and Germans—as 'pure' Croats. The ethnic German community was given privileged minority status, and the Muslims were said to be Croats, but the new régime wanted to get rid of the others. More than half its 1.9 million Serbs lived in Bosnia and Herzegovina, with the rest in Croatia, and a concentration in the old Military Border. Since they had come to Croatia a few centuries earlier, they would have to be Croatized or go; soon it was publicly stated they would be converted to Catholicism, expelled or killed.

Immediate measures were taken against them, a state-sponsored conversion campaign began, Ustasha bands spread terror, and mass killings started. A dozen concentration camps were set up in 1941 and 1942. The biggest and most notorious was the Jasenovac complex where hundreds of thousands died—mostly Serbs, with Jews, Gypsies and Croat opponents of the régime. Those fortunate or near enough fled to German-occupied Serbia or to Italian-occupied coastal areas; the rest took to the forests and uplands. What began as panicked flight to avoid a horrible death soon turned into a disjointed revolt. A combination of ferocious racism and farce, the NDH was unable to extent its writ over the mountainous areas of Bosnia and Herzegovina.

What was left of Yugoslavia, roughly pre-1912 Serbia, was placed under direct German military rule (along with rich grain-producing Banat just north of it, controlled through its sizeable ethnic German population). It was officially called the 'Territory of the German Military Commander, Serbia'. In the defeated lands the Germans preferred to work with the subdued remains of the establishment than with mimic zealots. In the case of Serbia, Dimitrije Ljotić (1891–1945), the leader of the small Zbor (rally) movement, was the nearest to a Fascist.[2] However, rather than pick him, the commanding general settled for a low-grade administrative agency to help restore basic services, exploit the economy, and ferret out enemy agents.

There was not much left of the establishment in Belgrade; it was only in response to the outbreak of rebellion that General Milan Nedić (1877–1946) was appointed to head a 'Serbian government' in late August, with a few more generals, third-rate politicians and Ljotićists. This was the German occupiers' attempt to keep Serbia quiet by indirect means. A 24,000-strong Serbian State Guard, made up of gendarmes, was authorized for the purpose of maintaining order. However, since the followers of Ljotić's Zbor were deemed

---

[2]Briefly minister of justice in 1931, he had resigned when his constitutional proposals had not been taken up by King Alexander. He had set up and presented his Zbor at the elections of 1935, and obtained 24,000 votes, which did not entitle him to a seat.

more reliable than former Yugoslav gendarmes, they were allowed to form their own separate Serbian Volunteer Corps.

A senior commander who had not been disloyal, Nedić had believed since the fall of France in June 1940 that Germany would be the ultimate winner, and that the 27 March coup had been a crazy provocation, to be blamed on the 'English' and the Communists. He was anxious that the Serbian people should be able to survive in Hitler's New Order, but in the mean time, he wanted to provide refuge for persecuted Serbs from other regions, and to save them from Communism. All those in the Balkans who had aligned themselves with the conquerors advocated a return to native roots under German overlordship. Turning against the West, and the mistaken experiment that Yugoslavia had been, Nedić too encouraged an ideological national pastoralism that glorified simple rural life.

He faced a hugely difficult task. The tables had been turned on the Serbs, who were singled out by the conquerors as the enemy to be collectively punished. Refugees were pouring into rump Serbia from surrounding regions.[3] Soon only declared Serbs (and those few non-Serbs who chose to be 'Yugoslav') remained in prisoner-of-war camps. Nedić was in part the expression of a wide-ranging state of depression and prostration.

In the circumstances of defeat and partition, when their only concern was to survive, some people indulged in post-Yugoslav and anti-Yugoslav fantasies. Paradoxically, it was pro-German collaborators who expressed the most extreme pan-Serbian visions. No less paradoxically, the most pro-German, the most Fascist-inspired and also the most Orthodox, were Ljotić's once totally Yugoslavist followers. Memoranda were presented to the German authorities, and appeals made, to join together the disjointed fragments of the Serbian nation. They had not the slightest chance of success, since Hitler hated all Slavs, and Serbs in particular.

Far from thinking of making their rump Serbia the nucleus of an expanded one, the Germans were intent on exploiting it to the full. Several Nazi and military agencies competed for the spoils. The most active was the Office of the Plenipotentiary for the Economy, charged with provisioning troops, stepping up exports to the *Reich*, and despatching 'contract labour' to work there (more than 40,000 by 1943). It also set up a Serbian National Bank, mainly to recoup

---

[3]It is estimated that there were as many as 400,000 refugees (including 15,000 Slovenes) in Serbia by the end of the war.

occupation costs, which ended up by being six times higher *per capita* in Serbia than in the NDH. British- and French-owned mines were simply taken over. However, industry in general was not so much taken over as destroyed—by military action, by dismantling, by the manner of production for the war effort, and by turning out the labour force to work on repairing and operating railways and mines. The military were responsible for the brutality with which the population as a whole were treated. They responded to insurgency by retaliating ruthlessly with punitive expeditions, internment in concentration camps, and the execution of hostages. Unable to bring in substantial reinforcements, they demoralized society through systematic terror. The High Command formula of 50–100 hostages to be executed for every dead German was turned systematically into a 100:1 ratio, with fifty executions for every one wounded. Thus more than 25,000 Serbs were killed by October 1941.[4]

In German-occupied Serbia 8,000 Jews perished, including refugees who had fled to Yugoslavia in the hope of getting to Palestine but had been able to get no further. Notwithstanding the fact that the Nedić administration and, even more, the anti-Semitic Zbor movement adhered to these measures, the responsibility for initiating and implementing them rests firmly with the German military, who boasted in May 1942 that they had achieved a 'Jew-free' Serbia.

As part of their anti-insurgency plans, the Germans set up a large concentration camp on the site of the Belgrade Fair, to take up to 500,000 people from the rebel areas. As the rising was put down sooner than expected, the camp was used for other purposes. It first took in surviving Jews and Gypsies (mainly women and children) until May 1942, when they were all killed in mobile gas chambers to make way for new inmates. It was then turned into the main transit camp for prisoners and internees from the whole Yugoslav area, and from October 1943 from the whole Balkan area, on their way to labour locations and concentration camps in the *Reich*. Though technically in NDH territory across the river Save from Belgrade, the camp was the preserve of the German police.

The uprising in Serbia had started at the time of the invasion of

---

[4]This included the rounding up and execution of 2,778 males (including hundreds of schoolboys) in one operation alone, 19–21 October, in Kragujevac and surrounding villages, for ten soldiers killed and twenty-six wounded in an exchange of fire when attempting to free a German platoon that had been captured by insurgents. The inflated, and so even more terrifying, figure of 7,000 executions was the one widely believed in Serbia.

the Soviet Union, when the Germans had moved most of their troops out of their occupation zone. Of the many underground groups and movements two emerged which had wider designs. Dragoljub (Draža for short) Mihailović (1893–1946) was a General Staff colonel who had rejected the capitulation. He had been military attaché in Sofia and in Prague in the late 1930s, was known for his pro-British and pro-French views, and believed in the ultimate victory of the Allies. As early as May he set about trying, with débris of the regular army, to set up a clandestine military organization loyal to the king and government in exile. Beyond maintaining a symbolic continuity of the Yugoslav state, opposing the mood of defeatism, and preparing the ground for a rising against the occupying forces to take place when the tide had turned, he had no political agenda.

The only civilian personalities to have joined him were a handful of intellectuals from the Serbian Cultural Club, who immediately took charge of propaganda. They did not belong to the principal political currents, and tended to blame Croats generally and the Yugoslav state establishment for the defeat. They were now conscious of the threat posed by Communist rivalry, and determined to tackle it. They thought of restoring Serbia within the framework of a new Yugoslavia to be set up after the war, and talked of ensuring links between the territories where Serbs lived, and of punishing those responsible for '1941'—the collapse and subsequent massacres.

Mihailović was pushed into premature action by the change in popular mood and by the Communists' zeal. Remembering Lenin, Tito seized the opportunity created by the destruction of the state and the end of the German-Soviet alliance to advance the cause of revolution. He had quickly moved from Zagreb to Belgrade, where conditions were at first better under German military rule than under Ustasha police surveillance. Enjoined by the Comintern to start partisan action against the Germans, the Communist Party called on the population to come to the aid of the Soviet Union. Tito sent emissaries to various parts of Yugoslavia, but stayed in Serbia, where he expected the rapid arrival of the Red Army following on the defeat of Germany in Russia.

Meanwhile, the Communists roused the peasants against the local representatives of the old government machinery. They faced Mihailović's army officers, who were trying to set up their underground military organization. The strife that quickly developed between the two networks enabled the Germans to restore some order with less effort than expected, as they terrorized the population into submission.

There was yet a third rising in partitioned Yugoslavia in the summer of 1941. Montenegro rejected the Italians' attempt to set up a client-state with a handful of nostalgic devotees of the Petrović dynastic cause. Queen Helen of Italy was a daughter of King Nicholas, and King Victor Emmanuel even came on a visit, but Nicholas's grandson and presumed claimant would not hear of it. Montenegro had been the last bastion before capitulation; it was full of weapons, of mobilized soldiers who had walked home, and of prisoners of war freed by the Italians as a gesture of goodwill. A general uprising took place in July, in which all took part, Communists and officers alike.

The Belgrade coup of 27 March had contributed to a passing British feeling of optimism in the spring of 1941, and the risings that took place in Yugoslavia in the summer were seen as a natural sequel, the beginnings of a sustained resistance looking to Britain. The Yugoslav government and the young king were lionized when they arrived in London, to join the other exiled Allied heads of state, ministers and generals. In the dark days of 1941 it was good to believe that the plucky Serbs were doing it again, as they had in the previous war. Mihailović was precisely the kind of leader the British had hoped might emerge; they played him up, and encouraged the Yugoslav government to do the same.

The exiles had by then dropped General Simović, the difficult hero of the March coup, and replaced him as prime minister with another non-party personality, the elderly and scholarly Slobodan Jovanović. They were themselves keen to be linked to Mihailović, a loyal officer who had not turned against Yugoslavia and its establishment. He was promoted to general, formally included in the government as war minister, and made chief of staff of the supreme command of the Yugoslav armed forces. In that way they hoped to boost both their own and his prestige, but they were hopelessly paralysed by old issues magnified by events at home. They were divided by Croat-Serb issues, and by differences between 'Serbian' and 'Yugoslav' Serbs. They failed to provide leadership or even guidance for people who had risen either in self-defence, or because they believed mistakenly that powerful outside help was forthcoming.

The different Serbian communities had never been integrated into a nation, and they were now more disintegrated than ever, joined only by the fact that they were treated collectively as vanquished foes. The risings of 1941 were thus Serbian risings, and they were local risings, fragmented and diverse. They cannot even be described generally as a rebellion against the New Order, for there was not much of a new order once the *Reich* had become master of a substantial part of the European continent in the spring of 1941. It had to continue the war, while holding on to what it controlled in many different ways that, in the Yugoslav lands at least, were more like a 'new disorder'.

The insurgents were responding to local and, less frequently, outside events. They called themselves 'chetniks' (*četnik*, pl. *četnici*), meaning members of armed bands. The word had originally been used in the Dinaric uplands by marauding bands, and eventually by all irregular armed groups in the central Balkans at the beginning of the twentieth century, and by the Serbian guerrillas operating behind enemy lines during the First World War. When the Communists began to organize their own bands, they called them 'partisans'.

In the NDH the insurgents responded to the terror of Croatian sectarian fanatics. In Bosnia and Herzegovina the new authorities also enlisted Muslims, making use of the bitterness felt by landowners who had once lived in towns off the income from their land, and had been reduced to poverty since the agrarian reform. By the summer of 1941 Serbian rural settlements had regrouped and organized themselves. Heirs to a pastoral economy, they were used to going up into their mountain pastures every summer and whenever they were in danger. Bands were formed, and isolated police stations and smaller garrisons were taken over for their weapons. Unable to overcome this resistance, the Ustasha authorities had to come to terms with it. Local ceasefires were agreed which in fact put an end to Ustasha power in most of the Bosnian uplands.

The Germans had not intervened. The Italians had no overall policy in the Balkans; they had been left to keep order, a task made difficult by German occupation policies, and which they performed with increasing anti-German animosity. From their positions they did intervene—to protect the population, to check the Ustashas, and to enhance their own influence—until in September they extended their military presence to the whole of the Italian zone.

In Kosovo, however, it was under their tolerant eye that the collaborationist Albanian government encouraged the emigration of Serbs. Those who had come after 1919 were the most vulnerable. The annexation to Albania was a popular move, both in Kosovo and in 'old' Albania. From the end of 1941, as the Italians tried to broaden support for their régime through a more nationalist government in Tirana, the departure of Serbs from the annexed territories was accelerated. 23,000 found refuge in German-occupied Serbia. More ended up in concentration camps in Priština and Mitrovica, to be used as labour on fortification works or in the Trepča mines. The Germans had retained control of the Mitrovica area because of Trepča.[5]

In Montenegro the Italians restored order up to a point, with reinforcements from Albania, and with Albanian and Muslim auxiliaries. The attempt to set up a client-state was given up, and Montenegro was kept under military rule. The revolt ground to a halt once its main aim had been attained. The rest was revolution, which the Communists tried to carry on. They turned against 'traitors', and were practically chased out of most of Montenegro. Effective occupation was reduced to towns; the chetniks were left to control the rest. They felt it safer to accept the Italians than invite the Germans to lend a hand in combating insurgency. As Communists withdrew they vented their anger against 'kulaks'; partisans burned and pillaged villages that did not sympathize with them. The animosity between Communists and anti-Communists turned vicious.

When repression burst the bubble of optimism, the popular mood in Serbia also turned against insurgency and those who wanted to carry on with revolution. The Communists' difficult relations with the officer-led movement broke down. The partisans crossed over into nominally NDH territory, where they joined up with their comrades who had left Montenegro. They were eventually saved by the 'long march' to the other end of Bosnia, where the miserable Serbian peasantry had been most affected by the traumas of defeat and massacre, and who welcomed them as a 'Serbian army'.

Tito knew that Serbia was the key to victory, but he realized that there was no early prospect of restoring any influence there. At the same time he guessed that the Serbs of the western territories would eagerly welcome help and leadership from whatever quarter it came. 'This is the shortest route back to Serbia', he told his partisan commanders. 'The western Serbs were Tito's last refuge, they became the basis from which to conquer all Yugoslavia'.[6]

---

[5]Estimates of the number of Serbs who left by 1944 vary between 70,000 and 200,000; and of Albanian newcomers to Kosovo between 15,000 and 300,000. The upper limits are incompatible with Yugoslav census figures: 149,000 Serbo-Croat-speaking Orthodox and 331,000 Albanian speakers in Kosovo in 1931; 200,000 Serbs and Montenegrins, and 498,000 Albanians in 1948.
[6]Franz Borkenau, *European Communism*, London: Faber & Faber, 1953, 372.

When London adopted Mihailović as the leader of the all-Yugoslav resistance movement that did not exist, German-occupied Serbia was the only area where he had set up some sort of organization; the uprising there had been crushed, and the internecine war with the Communists had started. Mihailović went underground again; his rank and file were disbanded. He realized that there would be no second front for at least another year, so he would return to preparing for a future uprising, to be coordinated with the Allies.

Meanwhile he would try to bring together all those who could contribute to strengthening his own movement, and he would avoid further useless sacrifices. He had been gripped by fear that, caught between Ustasha massacres, German repression and all the other actions against them, the Serbs could be wiped out as a nation. In this he was influenced by collaborationist propaganda and by the horror stories told and retold by refugees.

Italian-held territory became a haven for Serbs. It was also a supply base for chetniks who, having welcomed Italian protection against Ustashas, went on to resist the spread of Communist-led partisans, and to exact vengeance on innocent Croatian and Muslim villagers. Their commanders were anxious in 1942 to acknowledge Mihailović as their nominal supreme authority in order to legitimize their position in the eyes of the population, since he represented the king and the Allies.

Mihailović accepted the risk. The chetniks kept the Communists in check, made his 'Yugoslav Home Army' appear more widespread, and he knew (as did the Italian generals) that they would not oppose the British. Mihailović geared his strategy to liberation by regular Allied forces, and he believed that, in the mean time, he would come to control the local chetniks. He gambled, and lost. Eventually he found himself dependent on armed groups whose accommodations with the Italian military he could not afford to denounce or admit. He never had any effective authority over them, and they could not fail to antagonize non-Serbs.

The various chetniks were a traditional Balkan guerrilla, local and seasonal. At a higher level in Serbia, they were also an officers' movement trying to mould their fighters into an organized fighting force. Mihailović was a father-figure who provided the symbolic authority that seemed to hold them together, but who followed events more than he could initiate them. His support was drawn from those who viewed change as a threat.

However, the occupation attempted to impose a brutal force, mainly on the Serbian population, but without the manpower to enforce it—a classic situation for the propagation of a revolutionary movement. The Communists fought a revolutionary war in a constantly shifting pattern, with clear political aims. They were interested in power—over at least the whole territory of Yugoslavia, and if possible more. Only as leaders of a patriotic movement could they hope to acquire and retain the support of their non-Communist followers, but their object was to destroy all who opposed the transformation of their war of liberation into one for the establishment of Communist rule.

The conquerors had not only destroyed the Yugoslav state; they had set its components against each other in an unprecedented way. An infernal cycle of large-scale massacres had been started by the Ustashas against the Serbs in the NDH. The latter had risen in self-defence, as chetniks and partisans, who had gone on to do their best, there and elsewhere, to eliminate each other and their supporters, while facing the brutal periodic anti-insurgent operations organized by the German army.

Bosnia became the bastion of the partisan movement, which forged there the mobile and disciplined fighting force that was the nucleus of Tito's 'People's Liberation Army'. Its development in the mixed lands of central Yugoslavia was due to a number of factors. It penetrated the desperate and leaderless struggle of the Serbs of the NDH, and prevented that struggle from turning to vengeance, thus enabling Croats and Muslims to adhere eventually. Tito used their perception of local chetniks as a propaganda weapon against Mihailović, who was anyway no more than a distant and misunderstood symbol even for the local Serbs. The Communist movement throve on the anarchy of the Ustasha state. Unobserved by the Allies, and ignored by the chetniks who believed that the partisans had definitely collapsed, Tito was able to broaden his base.

It was only from the end of 1942 that the Allies paid more attention to diversionary action in the Balkans, so as to lead the Axis astray on the location of assaults on 'Fortress Europe'. They pressed Mihailović to undertake sabotage action in Serbia, to which the Germans reacted with renewed efforts to destroy the network he had just about managed to rebuild, through incarcerations, executions and terror. The British and Americans also turned their attention to the partisans, to step up activity in other regions, and to give some satisfaction to Moscow.

With the threat of an impending landing, which Tito dreaded and Mihailović hoped for, the Germans believed that Mihailović could still link together the various chetnik formations and eventually attract the partisans as well. They wanted to eliminate all insurgents before they could be rallied and before landing took place. The badly coordinated anti-insurgent campaigns of the first half of 1943 gave rise to increasingly complicated and bloody entanglements of antagonisms and arrangements between the different sides of occupation, collaboration and resistance. Anxious to destroy each other and gain control of the Adriatic hinterland by whatever means before the presumed British landing, chetniks and partisans suffered disastrous losses, but they survived.

Mihailović came out of the ordeal very much the weaker; the chetniks' double game had broken down. Although he always stressed the legitimist Yugoslav nature of his endeavour, it was in fact almost entirely Serbian. Whatever his intentions, he held little or no attraction for non-Serbs.[7] Tito's ethnic background and his past were at the time still shrouded in mystery. Part Croat and part Slovene, a Communist who had spent most of his adult life abroad, he was a genuine internationalist, and so, on the whole, were the party leaders under him, who had managed to alter and to adapt their discourse according to time and audience.

Mostly Serbs themselves, the partisans had been greeted by the decimated Serbs, yet they also defended Croats and Muslims from retaliation by Serbs. They always appeared to be on the side of those who were fighting for their lives, unless these happened to be their political rivals. They had been able to attract non-Serbs, and to infiltrate the wider-ranging and more independent NDH administration and military, whereas Mihailović, with his base in Serbia, could only infiltrate Nedić's closely-watched government services and gendarmerie.

When Italy dropped out of the war (and of the Balkans) in September 1943, the Germans managed to hold out on their own by reducing their control to essentials and by trying locally to take a leaf or two out of their former allies' book. When Herman Neubacher was sent as special envoy for South-Eastern Europe, he attempted to make use of the anti-Communism of nationalists by presenting Germany as the only defender of Europe against Communism. He adopted a more lenient attitude, and talked of ethnic frontiers. Arrangements were made with some chetnik commanders.

---

[7]He had with him a number of able and loyal Slovenian officers, along with the odd Croat, as well as a group of officers in the southern part of Slovenia annexed to Italy.

However, pro-Allied optimism had returned to Serbia, and this again boosted Mihailović. Germany also had to satisfy Albania, which it had taken over, and it was impossible simultaneously to court Serbian anti-Communist feelings and attract Albanian anti-Serbian nationalism. Anyway Hitler always imposed strict limits on what Neubacher could do for the Serbs. More autonomy was given to an ever more nationalist government in Albania. An SS division of Albanians was formed in February 1944, mostly from the annexed territories, which took to defending Albania's borders with a new campaign against the Serbian population. The number of Serbs forced to leave was said by the Germans to have reached 40,000 by April 1944.

Mihailović and Tito both wanted to restore Yugoslavia as a federation, but as the partisans had moved across Bosnia from east to west and back from west to east, they had set up their reunification movement on totally new ideological, social and political foundations. As a power vacuum appeared and gradually expanded, they filled it up. Although it was once again a Serb-based movement, and all those who wanted to get out of the enemy camp or out of the past were turning to it, it was not based on Serbia.

Macedonia was another region which attracted Tito's attention in 1943. He saw the opportunity to benefit from the local population's alienation from both pre-war Serbian and wartime Bulgarian rule. The Communists worked from the area annexed to Albania, where enemy control was lax, Serbs were revolted by increasing Albanian excesses, and Albanians feared vengeance from the chetniks' vindictiveness. As Albanians of whatever side and ideology wanted to keep the new borders, it was all but impossible for Mihailović to establish any links with potentially anti-German Albanians. Meanwhile, Albanian Communists had to make common cause with their Yugoslav counterparts. As Tito's movement established its patronage over Albanian Communists and partisans, they hoped that they would eventually achieve the reunion of Kosovo with Albania once Communism had prevailed in both countries and all over the Balkans.

The Yugoslav Communist leadership had clarified its own concept of federation in November 1943 at the movement's congress held at Jajce in liberated Bosnian territory. This was to be a community of equal nations within a number of units set up to fit in with the Communists' conception of an ethnic equilibrium. To Serbia, Croatia and Slovenia were added a separate Macedonia as well as a separate Montenegro. Bosnia and Herzegovina were to be kept as a territory within their old colonial borders; this would prevent an impossible division of this mixed region in which no ethnic group had an absolute majority, give its Muslims a territorial base, and enhance it as a miniature model of Yugoslav integration.

Serbia would be reduced to size, without Macedonia or Montenegro; this in turn would attract Macedonian aspirations from all over the central Balkan area, deal with Montenegrin frustrations, and counter the impression of a Serbian unit that was too large compared to the others. Every nation was given its 'home' unit, but Serbs were also acknowledged as being a constituent element in both Croatia and Bosnia-Herzegovina.

Mihailović's answer was his own congress held at Ba in January 1944, in free Serbian territory. His own ideas prevailed, supported by Živko Topalović (1887–1972), leader of the small Socialist Party of Yugoslavia, whose influence on Mihailović was increasingly felt. They decided that it was high time to answer the Communist challenge with a programme compatible with, yet more positive than, mere attachment to legal continuity. The delegates included refugees speaking on behalf of the Slovenian parties, and some Croats. A resolution was passed calling for the reorganization of Yugoslavia as a federation of three units—still only Serbia, Croatia and Slovenia.

Mihailović had already been practically abandoned by the British as a hopeless cause, and was in a weak position. Yet the more homogeneously Serb-inhabited territories in eastern Yugoslavia generally still backed him. Serbia had taken little or no part in the partisan movement, but was seen by the Soviets as the pivot on which the recognition of Tito's movement at the head of a greater South Slav state would turn. Tito obtained full support from the Allies to build up the partisans' strength there, in order to impede the Germans' withdrawal—their principal line of retreat from the Balkans ran through Serbia. A new exile government team, pressed on King Peter by the Allies, stripped Mihailović of his positions, and Peter himself was made to appeal over the BBC in September 1944 to all Yugoslavs to rally to Tito.

The partisans' penetration into Mihailović's home territory in the summer of 1944 turned out to be a difficult conquest, in spite of Allied help, which included air bombardment of cities. This was civil war which did little to disrupt the Germans' ordered evacuation from the Balkans. The pace accelerated as the Red Army reached Yugoslavia's eastern borders, when all turned against the Germans. Mihailović had ordered general mobilization, so as to take over and be at hand personally to receive the Russians. Nedić's State Guard went over to him. Nedić himself, with his apparatus and some 4,000 of Ljotić's volunteers, left for Austria.[8]

The Red Army helped the partisans take Serbia from Mihailović, and install themselves in Belgrade earlier than they would have done otherwise. Even so, it was only after a week-long battle that Belgrade was liberated on 20 October 1944. Soviet troops then went on to Hungary, leaving the Yugoslav People's Liberation Army to finish off the task.

Having disbanded the mass of recently acquired recruits, Mihailović and a force of tens of thousands left Serbia and regrouped in central Bosnia. The Germans stabilized their front again, and held out till May 1945, as the three-cornered fight between Ustashas, chetniks and partisans continued. The partisans still faced much internal opposition in all communities. They used the opportunities offered by liberation to take revenge on all opponents, almost all of whom they labelled 'collaborators'. Civil war was pitiless in Montenegro as the partisans returned. They resorted to mass conscription in their now secure base of Serbia, not only to strengthen their army, but also to remove Mihailovićist sympathizers.

Establishing control over Kosovo was a full-scale reconquest, in spite of the presence of Albanian Communist partisans cooperating with the Yugoslavs. Equipped by the Germans before they left, anti-Communist Albanians rallied people frightened at the prospect of the victorious return of vindictive Serbs. A guerrilla war which turned to general revolt lasted from November 1944 to May 1945, and was crushed with difficulty by 40,000 troops who treated all Albanians as Axis collaborators.

The People's Liberation Army completed the cycle of massacres by doing away in the last days of war with more opponents who had retreated into Austria, only to be sent back by the British. Combatants of the native units armed by the occupation authorities, and their camp followers, they included Ljotić volunteers and various chetniks alongside the much more numerous NDH soldiers and Slovene paramilitaries.

The defeat of the Axis had destroyed the chances of those native movements that had thought of a solution to Yugoslavia's problems

---

[8]Nedić was returned by the Allies to the new Yugoslav authorities. He is alleged to have committed suicide in February 1946 by throwing himself out of a third-floor window of the building in Belgrade where he was incarcerated.

by withdrawing into the confines of sectional nationalism under foreign protection. The outcome of the Second World War thus led again to a united Yugoslavia, this time under Communist rule. Originally founded as a unitarist movement, the Communist Party of Yugoslavia was generally internationalist and Yugoslav-minded. It had endorsed the various about-turns of the Comintern, and ended up with the public adoption of a federal state on the principle of nationality—an imitation of the Soviet model of pseudo-federation under centralized Communist control.

The Federal Peoples' Republic of Yugoslavia was proclaimed by acclamation on 29 November 1945 by the Constituent Assembly (the latter returned in a general election where over 90 per cent of the votes had been cast for the single list of the People's Front). A constitution modelled on Stalin's Soviet constitution of 1936 was unanimously approved in January 1946, and set up the six republics (Bosnia and Herzegovina, Croatia, Macedonia, Montenegro, Serbia and Slovenia) and two autonomous regions within Serbia (Kosovo and Voivodina). Yugoslavia's Communist leaders, just like their Soviet mentors, had exploited nationalism as a tactical device. They had always denounced 'greater-Serbian hegemony', and they did not want a Serbia that dwarfed the other federated units. At the same time they utilized a structure to acquire and hold on to power that was largely manned by Serbs from Croatia and Bosnia.

As after the war of 1914–18, the scale of losses and destruction was huge. Normal economic life had ground almost to a standstill, and a large part of the population was on the verge of starvation. The real total loss of population amounted to about one million, of whom some 550,000 were Serbs. They had died in concentration camps; they had been killed by Ustasha massacres, in action against the occupiers and their auxiliaries, fighting between partisans and chetniks, and retaliation and punishment. The figures were quickly inflated, as if the real ones were not horrible enough, both at the official level—to extract better reparations—and at the popular level to make up for the suffering, and to achieve glory in greater martyrdom.[9]

The Communists had been good at enlisting in the service of their cause all the myth-making propensities of Serbian history. They

[9] For a scholarly approach to the losses, see Kočović *op. cit.* as well as his earlier *Žrtve Drugog svetskog rata u Jugoslaviji* (The Victims of the Second World War in Yugoslavia), London: Naše delo, 1985; 2nd edn Sarajevo: Svjetlost, 1990; and Vladimir Žerjavić, *Gubici stanovništva Jugoslavije u drugom svjetskom ratu* (Yugoslavia's Population Losses in the Second World War), Zagreb: Jugoslavensko viktimološko društvo, 1989.

had transformed defeats beyond all recognition by dwelling on the heroism that accompanied them. The Germans' seven successful anti-insurgent drives were turned into the seven offensives of partisan mythology. Like the contemporaries of the battle of Kosovo in 1389, those who had to knuckle under in the early 1940s knew how to embellish their defeats in order to restore morale and turn a brave face towards the future.

The survival of mentalities is a channel through which continuity flows in times of great changes. The changes of the 1940s were, as in the past, accompanied by migrations, which brought to the surface attitudes of an earlier age. The seizure of power by the Communists, just like the Ottoman conquest, did away with the visible structures of the old order, cut the territory off from Western Europe, and allowed more archaic dispositions to return, as once again populations from the highlands came down to man the new structures of power.

8

SERBIA UNDER TITO – PART OF A WIDER COMMUNIST PLAN
1945–1980

The international environment was more favourable to the 'second' Yugoslavia than it had been to the first. All the victorious powers supported it from the start. It was the successor to the first Yugoslav state, and was given international recognition in March 1945 as soon as Tito had made the necessary transitory formal concessions to satisfy the Western Allies. These were a regency (with no powers) to take over from King Peter, the addition of some selected members of the last pre-war parliament to his Anti-Fascist Council, and a provisional government under his presidency with three non-Communists added to twenty-three Communist and two fellow-travelling ministers. The whole new structure that had already been set up under the control of the Communist Party thus received formal sanction.

In the elections to the Constituent Assembly there was no need for any confrontation with non-Communist parties; all who had fled or remained abroad, all deemed to have collaborated with the enemy or to have adhered to fascist organizations, as well as all who had been condemned to the loss of political rights were disfranchised. The party leaders who had returned from abroad to Belgrade and Zagreb were unable to organize their followers.

The Serb Milan Grol (1876–1952), Davidović's successor at the head of the Democratic Party, had come home to join Tito's provisional government as deputy prime minister, but soon realized that the only part he was allowed was as a stage extra. He resigned in August, the first of the non-Communist ministers to do so. He then tried with a Radical colleague to present an opposition list and publish a

The federated units of Yugoslavia, 1945–91.

newspaper, but beset by thuggery and arson, they could do no more than decide to boycott the elections.

The whole network of the partisans' revolutionary administration was mobilized to secure an impressive result. With the reins of power already firmly in the Communists' hands, a single People's Front list headed by Tito, the opposition in trammels and shambles, and a terror-backed election campaign, no obvious intimidation was necessary to turn out the voters in November 1945. To stay at home required courage.

The constitution of 1946 enshrined Yugoslavia's new structure as a multinational federal people's republic—'a community of nations equal in rights who, on the basis of the right of self-determination, including the right of secession, have expressed their will to live together in a federative [sic] state'. Taking full advantage of the old régime's failure to weld together Yugoslavia's separate identities into a single national consciousness, the Communists had restored the country as a community of related nations. The regional units had been set up pragmatically, according to the needs of the Party, in the later stages of the war, and the establishment of their borders aroused only a minimum of disagreement at the time among the decision-makers. Even though they generally conformed to historic realities, they were considered as no more than administrative borders.

There had been no 'Serbia' since 1918. Now there was once again an entity called Serbia—the People's Republic of Serbia within the Federative Peoples' Republic of Yugoslavia. Taken over from the Soviet Union, national pluralism and federal forms were meant as lighting conductors for ethnic-national emotions until Communism had succeeded in doing away with them. Since federalism was capped with unitarism of power and ideology, ideological integration was substituted for ethnic integration.

The Communist leaders used federalism both to balance out the nationalities within the Yugoslavia they had restored, and to plan the expansion of the federation they had set up. Their Serbia fitted into a plan that looked to the peripheral groups to weaken the central ones, particularly Serbs and Croats whom it wanted to equalize in every way. These core nationalisms were repressed—that of the Croats as separatist, and that of the Serbs as hegemonist. Both were anti-Communist, hence deemed fascist. The view of Croatian nationalism as separatist satisfied Serbs; that of Serbian nationalism as hegemonist satisfied Croats.

The nationalisms of smaller or peripheral groups were, at the same time, accepted, even favoured, not to say fostered, in order to keep the Serbs and Croats in check, resolve nationalist competition over territory, and help Tito's Communist federation to expand. In time Serbia and Croatia came to feel uneasy about this situation.

The Communist movement had inserted itself into the resistance of Serbs during the war, particularly in the mixed western territories. Those western Serb fighters, and those from Montenegro, had been the nucleus of the revolutionary army with which the Communist Party had come to power. Yet the Party had also used the notion of Serbian hegemony to win support among the other groups. Serbia had to be of a size that was not too big in comparison with Croatia, and satisfaction had to be given to those who had felt dominated or humiliated by Serbia.

Montenegro recovered its historical identity, thus going against the age-old tendency for unification of these two territories, whose inhabitants had regarded themselves as belonging to one Serbian nation. Montenegro had the same flag as Serbia, but its inhabitants were henceforth, and for the first time, encouraged to think of themselves as Montenegrins rather than as Serbs. By the time of the first postwar census, in 1948, when 'nationality' replaced 'language' and 'religion', 426,000 defined themselves as Montenegrins (342,000 of them in Montenegro). Serbs amounted to 6,547,000 (41.5 per cent of the total population), only 3,811,000 of whom lived in inner Serbia, i.e. Serbia without the autonomous territories.

The Communists of Montenegro, who were over-represented in the federal power structure, had won a particularly bitter civil war in their home territory. They had also contributed substantially to winning the multi-faceted civil war throughout Yugoslavia. Backward and impoverished Montenegro had become one of Yugoslavia's most Communist areas. The status of republic was thus also something of a reward.

Macedonia was set up as a separate republic for the Macedonian nation, ending the Serbian fiction of 'Southern Serbia' for the benefit of more ambitious Balkan plans. Two autonomous territories were carved out of the republic of Serbia, in border areas with mixed Yugoslav and non-Yugoslav populations. Voivodina (shorn of its western and more Croatian part included in the republic of Croatia) was termed an autonomous *province*. Serbs were now the majority group there. Kosovo, described specifically as 'Kosovo and Metohija' (Metohija is the central area that takes its name from the Serbian *metoh*, a monastic dependency), was at first an autonomous *region*. The difference between 'province' and 'region' was not clear; the vagueness was meant to indicate a more open-ended status for the region.

Although the Communist régime was both an accomplished and a legalized fact, disorganized bands still operated, in particular the remains of General Mihailović's guerrillas. A specialized corps had been set up to deal with them, and most of its efforts were bent on capturing Mihailović, who continued to believe that all was not lost, that the Allies would intervene to enable genuinely free elections to be held, and then that they would not recognize the elections such as they had been held. This lingering hope was fairly widespread in the country at large.

Mihailović was eventually captured in March 1946, and his month-long trial in Belgrade that summer was the first and the most dramatic of a series of widely-publicized show trials meant to eliminate those individuals still considered to be potential anti-Communist poles of attraction. He was tried along with ministers and officials (*in absentia*) of the wartime government in London, some of his commanders and advisers, Radical and Democratic party personalities, and officials of the collaborationist administration and armed units in German-occupied Serbia. They were charged together for war crimes, collaboration with the enemy, opposing the resistance, and being encouraged by Britain and America. All were found guilty and ten were executed.

Mihailović's execution on 17 July marked the final defeat of the losers in the complex war fought over the partitioned and occupied territory of Yugoslavia. It removed what the leaders of the revolution considered a potentially dangerous obstacle to the re-ordering of a Communist Serbia and, even more generally, a symbol that, in spite of adverse propaganda and drawbacks, still carried prestige both in the country and abroad. It served to discredit pre-war, particularly Serb-based, political parties, not to mention the Western Allies who were alleged to have supported collaborators in order to prevent the victory of the partisans.

The trial did not discredit Mihailović in Serbia any more than the trial of Archbishop Stepinac, the head of Roman Catholic church, later that year discredited him in Croatia. What the two trials did was confirm most Croats in their belief that Mihailović and the Serbian monarchy had been planning revenge and hegemony, and provide most Serbs with proof that Croats had betrayed the state in 1941, and that the Catholic church had been instrumental in devising conversions and massacres. Political trials continued for several years, and special security forces were kept busy into the 1950s dismantling the remains of Mihailović's wartime network, by then reduced to killing local Communist bosses in rural areas.

The religious communities remained the only organizations outside complete Communist Party control. They played a large part in the traditional way of life and several forms of collective historical consciousness. They were by their very nature hostile to Communism, and therefore they had to be made harmless before they could be tolerated.

The Serbian Orthodox church was local, with no canonical links to the West. It had emerged from the war with a prestige gained at a heavy price, since persecuting it had been part of the Nazi policy of punishing the Serbs; its organization had been broken up. It had suffered most in the NDH, but elsewhere too in so far as it was an ingredient and a form of Serbian identity. Nedić had invoked it. So had Ljotić, whose movement had attracted some clerics at the same time as he accused others of being Freemasons and British agents.

Many more priests had sympathized with the resistance. Patriarch Gavrilo (1881–1950) was interned by the Germans in a monastery before being sent to Dachau concentration camp in 1944. Although a war casualty, the Serbian Orthodox church remained an implicit obstacle to the Communist order. It was the only institution that claimed to encompass all Orthodox Serbs, in the old sense of all the Orthodox of Yugoslavia considered as Serbs. The Communist government encouraged demands for local ecclesiastical units to fit the new federal structure. It also sponsored associations of clergy as a counterpart to the episcopate. Patriarch Gavrilo was able to use his great authority to reach a settlement on the separation of church and state, with the adoption of the new constitution of the Serbian Orthodox church in June 1947.

The authorities nevertheless persisted in their indirect attempts to reduce the bishops' authority, and with pressure for a separate church in the republic of Macedonia. However, these levers were considered sufficient to keep the Orthodox church in check. The government never undertook a campaign against it of the kind directed at the Catholic church, which bore the brunt of its policy of making religion harmless.

Much of the Communists' success during the war had been due to their ability to advocate the liberation and reconstruction of a Yugoslav state on the basis of ethnic and religious tolerance and equality. Party propaganda stressed the joint struggle of all nationalities against the occupying forces, and specifically attributed the greater part of their success to solving the 'national question'. One should not underestimate the legitimizing power of this myth among the first post-war generation. The slogan of 'brotherhood and unity' contained a large dose of genuine optimism, mixed with cynicism and self-interest, based on the belief that Communism would eventually make the problem redundant. Meanwhile the problem was not so much solved as paralyzed behind a façade of slogans. People did not speak of it because to do so was forbidden, but it also evoked painful wartime memories, and there were more immediate worries of everyday life. Many, inside and outside the Party, were eager to reject the sectarian exclusiveness that had killed more people than the occupiers. Yet the feeling of differences remained, destined in time to be sharpened by the impossibility of fostering anything common to all Yugoslavs other than Communism.

Embittered by the war, and then swept under the carpet without the possibility of being rationally examined and explained, the feeling of sectional nationalism was reduced to something basic and emotional. Serbs and Croats, as the two major national groups, developed their own particular allergies. The Serbs of Croatia and Bosnia were irritated by the fact that the victims of Ustasha terror were lumped together with all other casualties as 'victims of fascism' not otherwise specified, and that so many of the latter-day partisans were turncoats from the NDH army who had been accepted without much questioning. The Serbs of Serbia were embittered because they knew that the flower of their youth had been sent to their deaths by the partisans in the last stages of the war against the Germans, and because Mihailović was put on the same level as Pavelić as a traitor and enemy of the people.

The position of the Serbs in the Communist federation was complex. With Croats they shared an interdict on expressing their nationalist feelings. The Serbs of Bosnia had formed the core of Tito's partisan army along with the Serbs of Croatia, and together with the partisans of Montenegro they had gone right through the war to victory. They provided much of the executive and military personnel of the new régime. In Bosnia and Herzegovina they had accepted a separate republic, but as reliable partisans they had been left to rule over it. They were over-represented in the power structures of both Croatia and Bosnia-Herzegovina, and in the police everywhere. Serbs generally made up more than half the Party membership in the 1950s (more than 60 per cent if Montenegrins are included).

Yet Serbia too felt in part conquered and occupied by western Serbs and Montenegrins who had come to Belgrade to staff the administration, the army and the police. Serbia was the only republic to have autonomous areas within its territory. Tito did not forget that his strongest domestic opponents had been the somewhat disorganized but also anti-fascist gathering in Serbia that looked up to Mihailović. He knew that he had needed the full strength of his army of Serb partisans from the western territories, with the back-up of British and Soviet support, to overcome it. Resistance to Communism remained latently strong in Serbia, especially in Belgrade, but such political tradition as there had been was thoroughly destroyed.

Of much greater relevance was the Communist tendency of the Serbs of the western territories, who provided the core of the political, military, security and judicial apparatus. Partisan cadres, in particular those originating from the old Habsburg Military Border—Krajina— and Montenegro, long dominated the redesignated Yugoslav People's Army. Veterans from the People's Liberation War in 1960 still amounted to 44 per cent of the officer corps. Over 60 per cent of officers were

Serbs as late as the mid-1960s (half of them from outside Serbia), and up to the 1980s 57 per cent of generals were Serbs and Montenegrins (half of them from Montenegro, Bosnia and Croatia). All these figures reflected the proportions of partisan fighters.

These cadres accepted a supranational Yugoslavism as part of their Communism. They did it because it was ideologically genuine, or because they felt at home everywhere within the power superstructure that capped the formal federalism. Wartime animosities between Serbs and others, and among Serbs themselves, went largely unnoticed in the flush of revolution and reconstruction.

A new agrarian reform in August 1945 expropriated another 1.6 million hectares from non-farming owners, enemies of the people and émigrés. Most of this land had belonged to the half-million or so ethnic Germans who had left Voivodina, having either fled, been evacuated by the retreating German army, expelled or deported to the Soviet Union. About half of all that land was allocated to 300,000 land-hungry peasant families of partisan veterans, from Krajina in Croatia, and from Bosnia-Herzegovina and Montenegro, who were resettled in Voivodina. The removal of the ethnic Germans and the arrival of the new settlers increased the Serbian percentage of the province's population from 38 before the war to 52.

Aleksandar Ranković (1909–83) was the only one of Serbia's Communists in the leadership's top quadrumvirate, with the Croat Tito, the Montenegrin-Serb Milovan Djilas (1911–95) and the Slovene Edvard Kardelj (1910–79). He was in overall charge of the security police, which exercised unrestrained power to arrest, imprison and execute political opponents without public charges or trials. Yet it was also the task of Serbia's Communist leadership to combat Serbian 'counter-revolutionary' and 'hegemonist' forces.

That meant extirpating the Serbian hold on the southern regions of Yugoslavia, the better to serve the régime's expansionist plans. If Communist Yugoslavia's post-war foreign policy towards the northwest could be considered as aiming to complete the unification of its ethnic territory by bringing in the last remaining Croatian and Slovenian irredenta from Italy and Austria, its policy towards the southeast was well and truly expansionist. Federal arrangements had hardly been adopted as a first step towards reducing friction between Yugoslavia's historic regions and ethnic groups, when plans were made to expand them. Yugoslavia's leaders were so confident that their revolution would solve, or rather dissolve, national problems that they wanted to extend the federal formula. Federalism and expansionism went hand in hand.

The recognition of a Macedonian nation and republic aimed at showing the local population that its interests were best served by a Yugoslav Communist state, but also to provide a structure around which the Bulgarian and Greek portions of Macedonia could be united. Measures adopted in Macedonia to cultivate a Macedonian consciousness, language and history distinct from both Serbian and Bulgarian appealed to local feeling. They did away with the Serbian heritage, but they also parried Greek and Bulgarian claims while staking out Yugoslav claims to neighbouring regions. As part of that policy, Serbian wartime refugees and expellees were not welcomed back. The settlers who had been granted surplus land in Macedonia and Kosovo under the provisions of the pre-war agrarian reform because of war service or other services to the state, as well as all officials of the old order and émigrés, were deemed to have forfeited their holdings.

If those decrees applied to all such settlers, both in Macedonia and in Kosovo, the new régime's policy in Kosovo was otherwise very different from what it was in Macedonia. For a start, all the armed movements which had been generated in defence of the Serbian population in Kosovo had acted in retaliation. That went for partisans as well as for chetniks of one kind or another, in spite of the help and patronage given by the Yugoslav Communists to Albanian Communist partisans. At first the new Yugoslav authorities adopted towards the hostile Albanian population measures which differed little from those previously used by the wartime Albanian authorities against Serbs.

It was assumed after talks had taken place between Albanian and Yugoslav Communist leaders that Yugoslavia's Kosovo region (in whole or part) would eventually become part of Albania, which would in turn become either the seventh republic of the Yugoslav federation or a unit of the future Yugoslav-led Balkan federation. Before that, however, Tito had to drive the Germans out, destroy Mihailović and restore Kosovo to Yugoslav rule. Only after the Albanian uprising in Kosovo had been put down in the summer of 1945, and the Communist Party was safely in power in Albania and had purged itself of elements opposed to Yugoslav influence, could a more moderate approach be envisaged. The Yugoslav Communists were increasingly treating Albania as their satellite, and Stalin seemed to agree in principle that Albania ought eventually to join Yugoslavia.

Kosovo was built as a bridge for Albania to cross over into the Yugoslav federation. No separate identity or localism was fostered there as in Macedonia. Albanian was an official language along with Serbo-Croat, but it was Albania's official unified literary language rather than the Gheg dialect spoken by the ethnic Albanians of Yugoslavia. A blind eye was also turned towards the Albanian settlers who had taken over the land of departed Serbs and stayed behind. Time was needed for local Albanian cadres to be formed who could really share responsibility with Serbs. Meanwhile Serbs were still the controlling element, the Serb-manned security police remained in evidence, and the new Yugoslav Communist régime in Kosovo was no more popular than the old régime had been before the war.

The difference between Yugoslavia's Communist régime and all its East European counterparts was in the speed with which it had got off the starting-line. With its status as an Ally supported by all the powers, and with its revolutionary army, it had a substantial advance in terms of political, economic and social transformation. Proud of its achievements, it had assumed an expansionist rôle at the cutting edge of the Communist world. As such it was the only Communist régime capable of falling out with the Soviet Union. Far from wanting to do so, its first intended to follow and expand the Soviet model, but it did so with considerable naïveté. Tito and his lieutenants were still unaware of the full complexity of power relations, and of the weaknesses of a victorious Soviet Union. This is not the place to tell again the history of the schism of 1948. Suffice it to say that it was not the result of ideological differences, economic exploitation, or national pride. It was a conflict about power, and it arose out of Tito's extra-Yugoslav ambitions.[1] The result was Yugoslavia's expulsion from the Soviet bloc, which took the form of its ruling party being removed from the Cominform—the Information Bureau of Communist Parties.

The symbolism of the dates chosen by Stalin, and the historical parallels made on both sides, are worth noting. When Stalin wrote to Tito on behalf of the Central Committee of the Communist Party of the Soviet Union laying his extraordinary charges, he dated it 27 March to remind the Yugoslavs of the coup that had so easily overthrown Prince Paul in 1941. When demands were made that Soviet diplomats be allowed to attend the trial in April of two Yugoslav dissenters, who had been expelled from their own central committee, a top Serbian Communist compared them to Austria-Hungary's terms to Serbia in 1914. The expulsion resolution taken by the Cominform in Bucharest bore the date 28 June, the anniversary of the battle of Kosovo in 1389.

The break had the effect of an earthquake. Tito and his lieutenants

---

[1] Adam B. Ulam, *Titoism and Cominform* (Cambridge, MA: Harvard University Press, 1952) remains the most balanced and perceptive study of the period.

instinctively clung to power, and because the clash happened at a time when the partisans' struggle was still a live force, they were able to capitalize on the patriotism of the revolutionary war among the Communists and their sympathizers, and on the fear of the Russians in the population at large.

Rather like the Catholic faithful of England in 1535, the Communist faithful of Yugoslavia did not really know what it was all about, but the 'healthy elements', to whom the Cominform resolution had appealed to overthrow their leadership, existed in no small numbers—perhaps as many as a fifth of the Party membership.[2] They tended to come from the élite, and from all factions, regions and institutions, but they were too scattered in motivation to develop a single movement, especially once the steamroller of secret police repression got moving to crush them.

However, there was a regional concentration. Montenegrins formed over 21 per cent of all those arrested or convicted in 1948–63. Montenegro, the republic with the smallest area and population, and one of Yugoslavia's prime partisan zones, turned out to be a Cominform bastion as a result of blood and clan ties. The break with Stalin caused immense moral and psychological dilemmas among the Russophile Montenegrin Communists, and more generally among the partisans of the war-ravaged Dinaric mountains. They tended towards an uncritical emulation of Soviet models, and identified Communism with Russia. In the summer and autumn of 1948, an entire security police division was there to suppress the growing Cominformist guerrillas and prevent their flight to Albania.[3]

Montenegrins were all too conspicuous in the army and security service. To them should be added Serbian partisans, who predominated among the Cominformists of Bosnia and Herzegovina, Voivodina, Kosovo and Metohija. They also formed a significant proportion of those of Croatia. They were widespread in eastern Herzegovina, which was traditionally a virtual extension of Montenegro, and numerous

---

[2]Ivo Banac, *With Stalin against Tito: Cominformist Splits in Yugoslav Communism*, Ithaca, NY: Cornell University Press, 1998, 149–51.

[3]The only other violent reaction that necessitated such intervention was triggered off by the arrest, in the Velika Kladuša area of Bosnia at the end of 1949, of a number of Muslims for resisting the collectivization drive. An uprising developed into an intercommunal revolt in the name, not of the Cominform, but of King Peter, as Serbian and some Croatian peasants joined Muslims. Security and army units were brought in from the outside to restore order, and killed several hundred peasants.

in inner Serbia too, where many of the partisans from the western areas had come, so that Serbs in total (not counting Montenegrins) formed over 44 per cent of all those arrested or convicted.

The Cominformists' historian Ivo Banac suggests that such sympathies might have disguised many post-war dissatisfactions, latent responses to the way in which the national question had been 'solved': old-guard partisans' perceptions of policies in the western republics as being too favourable to non-Serb late-comers to the resistance, the gradual erosion of Serbian institutions in Croatia, a struggle for Serbian identity in territories distant from Serbia.[4]

The split of 1948 strengthened the Yugoslav Communists' siege mentality. They had seen themselves as being on the western frontline facing the imperialists; they were now also having to defend their revolution from misguided attacks from the Stalinist east. Security attended to Communist as well as to non-Communist subversion, and terror ensured an all-risks guarantee of loyalty. Tito personally ordered the arrest of the more important, and took the decision to send Cominformists to special camps. Some 15,000 Party members were sent without trial to barren islands in the Adriatic, to be re-educated through forced labour under a system run by repentant prisoners.

Cominformism, like collaborationism before it, was an opportunity to get rid of all potential troublemakers. As the purge widened, the wave of denunciations accelerated in a general settlement of accounts at all levels. The leadership fought back against Stalin by being even more Stalinist, by expropriating what little was left of capitalism, by accelerating the collectivization of agriculture, by strengthening the security apparatus—which increased the prestige of Ranković's police.

Western aid kept Tito afloat[5] and discouraged a Soviet-led invasion. The changes that followed the schism caused movements in several directions. Having tried to resist Stalin with a harsher Stalinist line, Yugoslavia's Communist leaders moved on to expressing the conflict in ideological terms. They sought to appear more Communist than the Soviet Union, yet more democratic than the West. The ruling party's change of name to 'League of Communists of Yugoslavia'

---

[4]In the case of Montenegrins (Banac surmises), because of their numbers, not all of them had managed to get to positions which they believed they should have occupied. They thus felt slighted to the advantage of less worthy partisans, something Stalin would probably put right (Banac, 171, 182–3).

[5]See Lorraine M.Lees, *Keeping Tito Afloat: The United States, Yugoslavia, and the Cold War*, Pittsburgh: University of Pennsylvania Press, 1997.

was meant to express its further advance towards Marxism. In January 1953 a constitutional law adapted the machinery of 1946 to the new needs. The office of President of the Republic institutionalized Tito's position, at the same time as a beginning was made to theorize socialist direct democracy. Sovereignty was said to belong to the unified Yugoslav working class, at the same time as decentralization gave added responsibilities to regional leaderships.

While outside the Party structure many felt more relaxed, within it people sank into passivity after the trauma of the schism and its sequels, or, following the lead of Djilas at the very top from March 1950, wanted to move on to more open forms of socialism. Whereas Tito merely wanted to preserve whatever could be preserved in order to see him through the storm, Djilas felt the time to be ripe for a return to revolutionary renewal. Although he represented the views of many other Yugoslav Communists, those who shared his opinions kept silent when he was disgraced in 1954 after Stalin's death.

Djilas's three trials in 1955–7 and his subsequent nine years in prison marked the limits of liberalization. After the split Yugoslavia became more open than any of the other countries of Eastern Europe. Yet the rigorously controlled breathing-space that the manipulations of Titoism permitted eventually plunged the country into a stagnation that ended in a nightmare.

The continuation of Western aid and the revival of trade with the Soviet bloc after Stalin's death provided major economic benefits from the balancing act that had become Tito's foreign policy. In terms of economic development Yugoslavia like Italy had a north-south divide, which did not translate neatly into two blocs of federated units. The 'North' was the area north of the rivers Save and Danube with the north-south Morava-Drava valleys and the more important coastal ports as southern appendices. It comprised Slovenia, the developed areas of Croatia, Voivodina and most of inner Serbia. The 'South' had poorer agricultural resources, a higher rate of population growth, extractive and basic processing industries with lower-value products, fewer skilled workers and a slower expansion rate. It was made up of Kosovo and Metohija, Montenegro, Macedonia, Bosnia and Herzegovina, and the 'have-not' (mostly Serbian) belt of otherwise 'have' Croatia.

An effort was made to invest money where it would give the best results, which meant that the advanced northern regions continued to develop more than the backward 'South'. At the same time, there were other regions which, because they had provided fighters in the war

Serbia under Tito, 1945–1980

and loyal servants since, the leadership was anxious not to antagonize. The federal government, its foreign and defence policies in particular, also cost money. With decentralization, economic differences became questions of national honour, and pent-up local feelings found new channels in which to flow. The richer republics felt that they were being exploited for the benefit of the poorer ones and the central government in Belgrade, yet their standards were higher than those of Serbia. Regional identities clashed over allocations of federal investment funds. All had grievances against the centre and against each other.

Serbia, representing Yugoslavia's average level of development, had no particular economic grievances. The dissatisfaction there was psychological. It was felt that everything which expressed Serbia's pride and tradition had been clipped back in order to satisfy the others. Such feelings fed on nostalgia and romanticism, expressed mostly in emotions and words. The local apparatus, too close to the centre on which it modelled itself, did not provide real leadership. Serbia was in the front line for possible attacks from Soviet-bloc countries, and therefore planned industrial plants were transferred to Bosnia, which became the main recipient of the funds poured into defence production. The combined effects of this relocation, together with the collectivization drive and the campaign against Cominformist sympathizers, appeared to fall on Serbia.

In 1958 renewed tension with Bulgaria over Macedonia led the government to encourage the setting up of an autonomous church organization in Macedonia. This was seen in Serbia as detrimental to the united Serbian Orthodox church. Canonical links with the patriarchate were retained for the time being, but the government had finally succeeded in dividing one of the major Christian denominations, of which it made a small section closely dependent on the state. More generally this was part of the pressure exerted on the religious communities to prevent them from capitalising on their limited but surviving influence. Even though the accelerated denial of any Serbian component in its heritage was resented in Serbia, Macedonia's self-consciousness was becoming undeniable.

Both Macedonia and Montenegro continued to be built up, to prevent them from listening to siren songs from Sofia or Moscow. Both were greedy for federal aid, yet Montenegro's national consciousness was debatable. Capital poured into military manufacture in Bosnia and Herzegovina. Macedonia, Kosovo and Montenegro had guaranteed investments to bring them nearer the Yugoslav average, and because their interests were well represented. However, their *per capita* income barely advanced, or even lost ground, in comparison with the Yugoslav average.

In spite of efforts to win over ethnic Hungarians and Albanians in Voivodina and Kosovo respectively, the latter remained a security region in fact if not in law because of renewed tension with Albania, even though the region generally appeared calm. The Cominform resolution had given Albania the chance to break free from Tito's protection, and to indulge in psychological warfare against Yugoslavia. The local Albanian population remained alienated from the Yugoslav Communists, who had earlier appealed for their support against Serbian hegemony, only to continue with high-handed treatment.

The leadership's cautious attempt in the mid-1950s to return to an overall Yugoslav consciousness through a unified working people and a common socialist culture did not last long. Slovenes and Macedonians argued that they felt handicapped by the fact that Serbo-Croatian was the language spoken by three quarters of the population, and a general medium of communication throughout the country. Croats complained that, because there were more Serbs than Croats, the Serbian aspects of the common language would dominate.

The crux was in the conjunction of economic problems and power devolution, so that by the mid-1960s the old and allegedly solved 'national question' had come to occupy a place in the domestic concerns of the Yugoslav leadership second only to 'economic reforms'. The leadership had no policy to deal with the problem of relations between nationalities except for the continued development of socialism, so that the ideology that was for ever evolving out of Yugoslavia's peculiar position became in time the only cement that held the country together. Simultaneously the pressing necessities of economic efficiency and of regional economic interests blended the overall political debate over economic reforms with the reconcentration of authority at the level of the federated units.

A third constitution in April 1963, with 259 articles after a long preamble of philosophical principles, provided the framework for one of the most complicated systems then in existence. The country was renamed the Socialist Federal People's Republic of Yugoslavia, promoted from 'people's' to 'socialist', with 'socialist' coming before 'federal'. The working people and the nations were designated as being the carriers of the supreme political power, and their sovereign rights were to be exercised through the federation and the component republics.[6] Rotation was introduced for all elective functions, except for Tito's perpetually renewable presidency. Already past seventy, mentioned by name in the constitution and with quasi-monarchical attributes, he had begun to withdraw from the day-to-day running of business. He looked after world affairs and the prestige of Communist Yugoslavia, while Kardelj and Ranković occupied second place.

By introducing at last real decentralization, the constitution of 1963 encouraged the trend towards a close association of nationality with territory. The challenges to central control by the generation of wartime revolutionaries were by then such as to require a redistribution of power. The mentality of the middle generation was still largely (subconsciously and even consciously) pre-Marxist, and not being able to satisfy it with more political freedom, the régime turned a blind eye to its indulging in nationalist emotions.

Political decentralizers and economic reformers allowed these emotions to develop in so far as they were directed against the centralist and conservative wing of the League of Communists. They were particularly strong in the two richest republics, Slovenia and Croatia, although for a long time the Party leaders in Zagreb did not dare to risk being accused of Serb-baiting or of reviving anti-Croat feelings elsewhere in Yugoslavia.

Economic reforms were half-measures incompletely carried through, with brakes applied at the first signs of difficulties. A divided and hesitant leadership saw the need for more productive competence, yet feared the political consequences of economic efficiency. Freed from a completely centralized control, the economy had been turned over to the partial control of a decentralized political structure. The more the reforms failed, the more the stage was set for regional politics to come into the open.

Many economists from Slovenia and Croatia advocated greater freedom from federal control, for the sake of market reforms and/or greater freedom from what they increasingly saw as central government in Belgrade, but liberal colleagues from Serbia also backed market reforms. The differences within the Party had crystallized. Public rumour and foreign commentators identified Kardelj and Ranković as the leaders of respectively the 'reformist' and 'anti-reformist' wings. Tito had not yet spoken *ex cathedra*.

[6]This theory of double sovereignty was no less (if not more) theological in its diphysicism than the first Yugoslav constitutional theory had been, forty years earlier, in the trinitarianism of its 'one nation with three names' theory.

In the summer of 1966, Tito came out in favour of the reformers. Inflation and foreign debts had reached a level where it was feared that outside aid would come to an end. A broad coalition of Party worthies from all the republics except Bosnia-Herzegovina wanted to bring Ranković down. Kardelj's Marxist talk of 'de-etatization' helped to win over Tito, thus leading to the fall of another of his trusted lieutenants. Ranković had to resign in disgrace. The substance of the accusations linked a struggle for power with opposition to reform and a strong hint of Serbian nationalism.

As he had always been essentially an executor of policies, there is little likelihood that he was plotting. It was more likely that the plot was to remove a colleague who could become a dangerous rival. However, Ranković did look askance at economic reforms, which he feared would create dissatisfaction in the most Party-minded areas. In so far as he stood for Serbian interests, he did so where the less developed regions were concerned. Otherwise the presence of such an eminent representative at the very top meant that the Communists of Serbia looked up to him, and that many of them were carried away by his opposition to the reforms. While the Party in Serbia was divided on the issue, with a liberal wing unable to develop, the Party conservatives everywhere looked up to him.

The fall of Ranković hit the coalition of all those who impeded economic change. He became the convenient scapegoat for all previous failures, and for all possible grievances. So anxious were Yugoslavia's leaders to blame everything on him that they made him appear, in retrospect, much stronger than he had actually been, and confused the real consequences of the changes.

In the turmoil that followed Ranković's fall, much less was heard of economic change. Tito publicly decried those who interpreted it as a victory for liberalism. Policies were applied by personnel who, except for Ranković and his police supporters, remained unchanged. Investments, prices and unemployment resumed their upward trend. Virtual free travel was allowed for people to emigrate in search of employment abroad, and for foreign tourists to help the economy. The authorities continued gradually to widen the area of permissible expression, and to foster an increased emphasis on legality. The powers of the federal government, and even of the Party's federal bodies, were for the first time reduced specifically to be of advantage to republics and provinces.

In Serbia's Party the liberals came to the fore, with the assent of Marko Nikezić (1921–90) and of Latinka Perović (b. 1933). Educated and more tolerant, they promoted meritocracy, modernization, a market economy, and cooperation with the other republics on the basis of rationally defined common interests. Nevertheless, they were not liberal enough for the non-conforming intellectuals, yet too liberal for the more conservative cadres and, eventually, for Tito himself.

The Serbian Orthodox church was well on the way to recovery. Its fabric had been restored in a rough-and-ready way under Patriarch German (1899–1991, patriarch 1958–90), and it was active in the pan-Orthodox movement and in a wider ecumenical sphere. Bridging the gap between Orthodox and Catholic created by the war was an arduous and unenviable task, yet the two churches began to lean on, and learn from, each other in order to face common difficulties. Increasing solidarity in the mid-1960s on a strictly mundane and religious level seemed to be taking the religious sting out of Serbo-Croatian relations.[7]

The 1960s were generally a golden age for literature, the arts and philosophy. Educational standards rose, exchanges with Western Europe and North America increased, and urban culture prospered. The media became significantly less restricted. Intellectual freedom was tolerated and even subsidised so long as it did not become transformed into political action. Serbia experienced a 'black wave' of novels and films which challenged socialist reality. Philosophy, hitherto the prerogative of the Party, produced a 'new left' which linked Belgrade and Zagreb. Belgrade had found its place again as a cultural centre.

There was also a nationalist strand in Serbia's intellectual dissidence, which began to criticise the Communist solution to the national question. It developed largely as a response to increased decentralization—not only of the federation as a whole, but also of the republic of Serbia, and to the revival of Albanian and Croatian nationalism.

As police pressure on Kosovo was removed, Albanian cadres were promoted, and promises were made. The autonomous region had formally become an autonomous province in 1963. Judging by what was revealed in order to relax the tension, the reforms proclaimed there at different times since the early 1950s had been so many words never put into practice. Ethnic Albanian party cadres of the Kosovo government machinery used the revelations in order to acquire

---

[7] In Banjaluka, then a city of three faiths in Bosnia, a practice of toleration and cooperation had been established. The Roman Catholic Bishop Pichler and the Serbian Orthodox Bishop Andrej had by the end of the 1960s set up, discreetly and modestly, a model Christian fellowship, which was not to everyone's liking elsewhere, about which not enough is known, and which is now forgotten.

popular support and promote the cause of their community. It had grown to 915,000 in 1961—647,000 in Kosovo, with an overspill in Macedonia, Montenegro and inner Serbia. Kosovo's Serbs (269,000 in 1961) were moving out.

The nationalist strand was also asserting itself in Croatia. In the easier political climate, it was felt that taboos over the expression of feelings discredited by the war had been lifted. Dissatisfaction was voiced with the results of the economic reforms, and it encouraged cultural complaints. Linguists demanded recognition of a separate Croatian literary language, and its public use by all officials in the republic of Croatia.[8] The nationalist strand wished to reduce the over-representation of ethnic Serbs in the republic's political and security structures, which had done nothing to redress the neglect of those areas in Croatia and Herzegovina where the Serb population had favoured the chetniks. The project for a single Serbo-Croatian dictionary was killed, and Serbs in Croatia began to demand cultural rights. There was more encouragement for a separate Montenegrin identity, while the most conspicuous and unabated nation-building continued in Macedonia. The Orthodox church there, already autocephalous, took the plunge into autocephaly, proclaimed unilaterally in 1967 after an application to the patriarchate in Belgrade had been turned down. Government intervention was blatant.

Identified with centralism, and perceived in Slovenia and Croatia as a mask for Serbia's predominance, Yugoslavism was abandoned. Communists in Serbia complained that, in its anxiety to implement economic reforms, the Party had allowed Serbs generally to be identified with anti-reformism, had given away too large a slice of the federal cake, and had ignored the consequent upsurge of anti-Serbian feelings. Serb feelings were upset too, both in and out of the Party, as it was increasingly realized that 42 per cent of Serbs and Montenegrins lived outside inner Serbia and Montenegro.[9]

★ ★ ★

[8]Croats, Serbs, Montenegrins, Slav Muslims and undifferentiated Yugoslavs all spoke Serbo-Croatian. Differences were minimal and regional. They were not ethnic, and they were certainly not linguistic barriers. The Cyrillic script, traditionally used by the Orthodox, prevailed in Serbia and Montenegro, where most people were by then equally familiar with the Latin script. Serbs in Croatia and in Bosnia-Herzegovina spoke no differently from the Croats and Muslims around them.

[9]According to the 1961 census, the total number of Serbs and Montenegrins together added up to 8,320,000 (of whom 514,000 were Montenegrins)—4,806,000 in inner Serbia, 354,000 in Montenegro.

When Warsaw Pact troops intervened in Czechoslovakia in August 1968, the flag of patriotism was waved in Yugoslavia just as it had been in 1948. The country's military traditions—those of the Second World War partisans as well as those of the Serbian army in the First World War—were extolled. The Soviet danger was used to restore the domestic position of the régime, which was challenged in that fateful year by students, intellectuals, workers, churches and local Communist groups, by nationalists, criminals and hooligans. As long as they remained separate, these challenges had been useful safety valves, but in 1968, it was feared that they would all come together.

Ever greater decentralization and regional rivalry over increasingly scarce domestic sources of investment not only prevented countrywide opposition trends from coming together, but divided the cross-republican alliance of liberal Communists. The nationalist strands of intellectual dissent took off, and reacted to one another. Without the possibility of openly discussing the important problems the country had to face, the craving for freedom was all too often reduced to a need to call oneself by the name of one's nationality.

Most local Communist leaders looked to the past for a model which would place them in a historical perspective while they worked towards the realization of a new society. In Serbia culture and religion took over the old structures left unoccupied by politics. Some in the Party, worried that the unity of the Yugoslav working class and nations was being undermined by bureaucratic nationalism, found common ground with those who feared increasing discrimination against Serbs and Montenegrins outside their own republics.

The popular writer Dobrica Ćosić (b.1921) brought out that latent alliance. A veteran Communist partisan close to the centre of power, he had voiced muted complaints about the way in which the development of a common Yugoslav culture was being hindered. In May 1968 he publicly criticized at a Party meeting the Albanian nationalism and anti-Serbian mood that prevailed in Kosovo. He warned that the situation stimulated retrograde ideas about a state for all Serbs. Having pointed to facts the political élite preferred to ignore, he was expelled from the Central Committee, and resigned his Party membership.

A more serious challenge followed in June. The student revolt at Belgrade University took everybody by surprise. Its motives were varied, contradictory and confused, but they were in no way 'Serbian', and the revolt spread to universities throughout Yugoslavia. Basically it called for the fulfilment of the proclaimed goals of the Yugoslav revolution. It attracted support from the different strands of what was by now called the 'critical intelligentsia' centred in Belgrade,[10] but offered none to the task of tackling the twin questions of power monopoly and economic inefficiency. In the short term it allowed Tito to reoccupy the high ground, and in the longer term left the field to nationalist dissent.

At the time Ćosić, like the students, was lamenting the end of Yugoslavia's revolutionary integration through the Communist Party, rather than promoting pan-Serbian nationalism, let alone regretting pre-war Yugoslav national integration. His public stand, along with the polemical exchanges between a fellow veteran partisan, Velimir Terzić, historian of the People's Liberation War, and a Croatian opposite number, the future President Franjo Tudjman, put considerable strain on Serbia's liberal leadership. Ćosić subsequently went on to rally his extensive network of friends, both former Communists and anti-Communists, around the vision of a cultural and spiritual unity of all Serbs, regardless of borders, since the government had changed the political and national equation of Yugoslavia. He would also play an active part in the human rights movement.

Later that year discontent of a different sort surfaced in Kosovo. Ethnic Albanians were more conscious of their strength. Unemployment and illiteracy in the province were the highest in Yugoslavia, and Serbs and Montenegrins still accounted for more than half of official and professional employment. Local Albanian cadres saw the solution in elevation to the status of a republic, and some kind of connection with Albania. In November there was an explosion of popular anger, with demonstrations and riots, calls for union with Albania and acclamations of its dictator Enver Hoxha, accompanied by public expressions of hatred for Serbs. The situation was hushed up, order was restored by army and security troops, prison sentences were imposed, and Party members were expelled.

Symbolic gestures were made, such as granting the right to fly the Albanian flag and establish links with Albania. Everything was done to boost Kosovo's economic and cultural development. A university was set up, and under agreements with the Tirana government the educational system was flooded with Albanian-language textbooks from Albania. With the tables turned against them, Serbian and

---

[10]See Jasna Dragović-Soso, 'Between Democracy and Nationalism: The Rise and Fall of the Belgrade Critical Intelligentsia, 1980–1991', doctoral thesis, University of Geneva, 1999, ch.1.

Montenegrin officials and professionals moved out in increasing numbers. Because of its higher birth-rate, the Albanian majority in the province had risen by 1981 to over 74 per cent of the population. After the 'Great Fear' of 1968 had been overcome, Tito once again mobilized all his energies to hold the system together. The invasion of Czechoslovakia had brought public and Party opinion closer again. The Party's self-confidence as a single unit was still strong. Growing connections to the outside world nourished a common sense of Yugoslav identity, with parallel or multiple identities. The massive movement of population to urban areas, and then to and back from Western Europe as migrant workers, played a part in creating a culture that did not fully owe its existence to the Communist régime.

Nevertheless, repairing regional imbalances at its rural roots proved difficult. Since 1953, when peasants became free to buy, sell or lease, the number of small private holdings had increased in the Yugoslav 'South' that stretched from Croatian Krajina through Bosnia to Kosovo. It was still plagued by food shortage and excessive population, in spite of increasing numbers of rural Croats and (especially) Serbs who were leaving Bosnia and Herzegovina for the towns and suburbs of Croatia and Serbia respectively, but also to work abroad. It also had the biggest pockets of illiteracy, particularly in upland rural areas, ranging from 30 to 60 per cent.

The attempt to stimulate anew some Yugoslavism—'Tito's' or 'socialist'—was counter-productive. It ensured that emotional nationalism would grow to extravagant levels, particularly in Croatia and Slovenia, where the government in Belgrade was again openly identified with Serbian influence. The situation in Croatia escalated into what came to be called the 'mass movement', uniting cultural organizations, students, younger Party activists and many industrial workers around demands for a revision of the republican constitution (to allow for a separate army and United Nations representation).

The otherwise liberal leaders of the Party in Croatia came into conflict with their liberal partners elsewhere. Feeling that his own power was threatened, Tito acted, with the Belgrade media leading the way in dramatizing the crisis. The Serbs of Croatia complained that their already war-torn areas had been neglected by a generally prosperous republic. Under the threat of military moves, the Zagreb leadership resigned in December 1971, and there followed a massive purge of the Party in Croatia. The moves were perceived in Croatia as a coup mounted by Serbian generals behind Tito.

His relations with Serbia's leaders had also been strained. They were not prepared to accept the permanent suspicions with which the republic and institutions in Belgrade were treated by others, and they told Tito so, much to his anger.[11] There were greater divisions at the time within Serbia's Party leadership than was the case in Croatia. They turned on the issue of what was generically called 'the opposition', more than on the status of Serbia and of the Serbs outside it. The latter preoccupied the nationalist strand, which expressed itself against the backdrop of the Croatian mass movement, though less virulently and widely.

Serbia's Communist liberals had seen in Ranković's fall a unique chance for the emergence of a modern Serbia, relieved of that permanent suspicion of being the guardian of the Yugoslav state. They too were in favour of less federal influence. However, having removed Croatia's 'nationalist' leaders, Tito, backed by Kardelj, took the opportunity to get rid of Serbia's 'liberals' in October 1972. They had, after all, resisted the forced resignation of their Croatian counterparts, and the balance between the republics had to be kept.

The response of the Yugoslav leadership to opposition from outside and inside the Party had been to cleanse the political élite of all those who had acquired a genuine audience, and who were accused of 'nationalism', 'liberalism' and 'technocratism'. The arguments in favour of maintaining the Party's monopoly of power still carried the day, and prevented full economic reforms.

A period of renewed censorship, trials for 'hostile propaganda' and 'verbal offences', and a purge of new-left academics somewhat muffled the flowering of a critical culture in Belgrade. Activism by dissident intellectuals nevertheless took off again in the latter half of the 1970s, mainly in the capital, with petitions and open letters on civil rights, discussion groups in private homes, and attempts at *samizdat* publications. The régime feared trans-republican cooperation between such critics, who only had a restricted audience in their own republics, and were not particularly attractive to the rising nationalism that was becoming the main rhetorical antipode to the dominant Communist ideology. They relied on personal contacts; their activities were diffused principally through the London-based Serbian monthly journal *Naša reč*.

---

[11]"The comrades from Serbia [...] made me very angry. No one has talked to me like that in the past 30 years' (quoted in Dejan Jović 'The Breakdown of Elite Ideological Consensus: The Prelude to the Disintegration of Yugoslavia, 1974–1990', doctoral thesis, University of London, 2000, 96).

The fall of the liberals did not mean any change in Serbia's position. Serbia's Communist leaders after 1972 continued to support constitutional reform, because they firmly believed that they were in Serbia's interest, but they wanted more guarantees that their republic would be equal to others. They continued to believe in the principle of non-intervention of republics in each other's affairs, whereby it was up to Croatia's Communists to oppose Croatian nationalists and protect the Serbs of Croatia. They avoided being identified with either Yugoslav centralism or Serbian nationalism, and pleased no one.

Opinion was going the other way. Since the republics were increasingly identified with ethnic groups, and Serbs were dispersed throughout Yugoslavia, Serbian opinion was not keen on giving yet more powers to the federated units at the expense of the federation. Devoid of leadership and of official channels, such feelings expressed themselves in nostalgia and empty talk.

The Serbian Orthodox church had a tradition of providing both a refuge from the world and a structure for preserving the cultural and spiritual unity of the nation. Tempted to offer, if not leadership, at least a more satisfying form of expression, it found it natural to tell its faithful to leave politics to those who wanted a reward in this world, and to unite around the church, which alone cared for their real interests. By that time as each religious denomination busied itself with its own problems again, ecumenism had come to a standstill. Popular conception associated religious and national community. The mass of the Serbian faithful and a considerable number of clergy, who identified Serbianism with Orthodoxy, wanted a framework within which to express their ethnic identity freely, and readily turned to the church for that purpose.

For some Communists and former Communists who had been ready to sacrifice their Serbian identity for the sake of socialist Yugoslavia, what they saw as the régime's capitulation to particularist aspirations was a negation of the ideal for which they had fought. Having once embraced Yugoslavism as a solution to the Serbian national question, they began confusedly to disentangle their Serbianism from their Yugoslavism.[12]

---

[12] The phenomenon whereby 1.2 million (or 5.4 per cent of the total population) registered as plain 'Yugoslavs' in the 'nationality' rubric of the 1981 census needs to be studied carefully. There were 379,000 such Yugoslavs in Croatia, 326,000 in Bosnia and Herzegovina, 272,000 in inner Serbia (163,000 of them in Belgrade) and 168,000 in Voivodina. They tended to be the better educated who had moved

The trend-setter for a new interpretation of Serbia's modern history was not a historian, but Ćosić himself. His four-volume epic of Serbia's struggle during the Great War, *A Time of Death*, which came out in the 1970s, established him as an authoritative interpreter of history for an ever wider public, unhappy with the official version. His was a view of the Serbian nation's tragic destiny to strive for liberty and greatness at the price of near extinction.

During 1967–71 a bewildering amount of constitutional amendments and laws had been passed, until the constitutional debate was brought to an end with a fourth constitution. Enacted in February 1974, it marked a new world record in length and complication: its ten-part Basic Principles were followed by 406 articles, running to 100,000 words. The ship of state was at last back on course, according to Tito's last great plan. It was yet again a Communist vision of the future, formulated by Kardelj, Tito's main ideologue and his last remaining lieutenant.

It returned to strict Party rule, but a feudalized one through the republics and the provinces, under the paramount suzerainty of the ageing dictator, whose power was once again formally absolute, and whose historic rôle and unlimited reign were enshrined in the first of the thirteen articles devoted to the President. Tito tried to reassert control by introducing into the Central Committee younger Party cadres of working-class background, and older partisan army officers, seen primarily as his men. Yugoslavia was turned into a confederation of eight party-states, with the provinces equal to the republics in all but name. Only Tito (who would have no successor) and the army were left to guarantee its unity.

More than ever, the Communists' vision of the future, guided by Kardelj, blurred their ability to view the present. 'Yugoslavia no longer exists', Tito is alleged to have complained to an old comrade, yet it was again meant to be a transitional entity, leading to a broader post-Cold War model, where the Party guided the process of the withering away of the state.

In fact the various sections of the Yugoslav political élite had reached a fragile but still viable compromise between Party control and republican autonomy, which for a time kept them and the country together.

---

away from their local roots to large cities, who were often in mixed marriages or children of such marriages. They also included Party activists, and many of the urban Serbs of Croatia and Bosnia, who preferred to appear as Yugoslavs.

Serbia under Tito, 1945–1980

The last decade of Tito's reign had a surreal air to it, as he continued with grand designs. His paternalism enabled him to discipline Party cadres without losing their support, and with his popularity at large he was able to take unpopular decisions. The state of the economy notwithstanding, the borrowing binge sustained rising standards of living through the 1970s, and thus managed to tone down regional grievances and legitimize continued Communist rule.

Yet the Serbian malaise increased, particularly as a result of developments in Kosovo. The province had been renamed the Socialist Autonomous Province of Kosovo (the name of Metohija having been removed). To keep it satisfied, special emphasis was given to its economic and cultural development. It was given priority over all other under-developed areas, with positive discrimination towards ethnic Albanians in employment. Yet it continued to lag behind relatively, despite absolute gains. Albanians had rising levels of higher education but diminished chances of graduate employment. The proportion of Serbs in official and managerial positions was still felt to be too high. The Serbs who emigrated tended to have higher levels of education, leaving behind others whose education levels fell behind those of Albanians. Social sector employment sharpened the rivalry for the remaining jobs, and distrust between the two communities deepened.

The Serbs' and Montenegrins' share of the total population of Kosovo had been stable between 1931 and 1961, at around 27 per cent but by 1981 it had fallen to 13.2 per cent. Emigration accounted for only a small element of the shift, which was mainly due to the high birth-rate of the ethnic Albanian community. There is controversy over the number of Serbs who left, and over the number of Albanian immigrants since 1948. Even greater controversy surrounds the causes of emigration: insecurity, harassment, discrimination, pressures of every kind, loss of privilege. More than two-thirds of Serbs leaving Kosovo came from areas of mixed population, and reported harassment, although rape and murder, so often stressed in the Serbian media, remained below Yugoslavia's average—at least in official figures. Clearly emigration had been a persistent phenomenon since the 1960s, but the authorities in Serbia did not wish to acknowledge the fact, afraid of a backlash and of being labelled nationalist. Clearly too, Albanians who had come to control the Party apparatus in Kosovo discriminated against Serbs.

The migrations that had moved and mixed people in the past had continued in a general way after the Second World War. Serbs had also moved to Serbia, or gone to work in Western Europe, from Bosnia and Herzegovina, without any harassment or discrimination, causing a reversal in the demographic proportions of that republic. From over 44 per cent in 1948 the proportion of Serbs and Montenegrins in Bosnia-Herzegovina had fallen to 32 per cent in 1981. The movement away from the villages that had begun in the 1950s had accelerated in the '70s, although in 1981 the overall urban share of the population was no more than 47 per cent. That is because the mass of unskilled labourers moved to semi-rural areas on the periphery of towns.

In Serbia itself there had been a deep restructuring of society after the Second World War, with immigration of Serbs from other areas. By 1948, 40 per cent of Voivodina Serbs were newcomers, as so were 11 per cent in inner Serbia. This postwar immigration was followed by industrialization. The newcomers were not just poor peasants turned into half-workers; they were also partisan veterans who felt that they were the winners in the social revolution. Serbia thus became what has been described as a great disorganized suburb. What was called the 'rurbanization' of Belgrade is the most striking instance, as the population of Yugoslavia's capital grew from 250,000 on the eve of the Second World War to almost 1.5 million in 1981. A new middle class had developed, but it was so essentially due to its standards of living, much less its culture, and even less still its political motivations. It was certainly not a *bourgeoisie*.

By 1981 a little under 2 million Serbs lived in other republics, with another 1.3 million in Serbia's two autonomous provinces, as against inner Serbia's 4.9 million Serbs. Serbs were still the most numerous national group at around 40 per cent of the total population. The territorial division of Yugoslavia had been acceptable to them as an administrative structure. The issue of borders began to arise as the republics came close to being sovereign states, and nation-states at that.

The Serbian resentment at the way in which Yugoslavism had worked for them, which had surfaced on the eve of the Second World War, had been denounced by some of the most influential intellectuals of the time. It had appeared again during the war as blatant anti-Yugoslavism, among collaborationists in Serbia and some chetniks in the NDH, but had largely disappeared by 1945. Once Yugoslavia had been reduced to an ideological vision, with its content all but evaporated, the empty ideological space enabled the nationalist strand of the Serbian intelligentsia to resort to a similar collectivist framework. To that extent it was no different from its counterparts in other republics which in many ways had shown the way, but Serbian

Serbia under Tito, 1945–1980

nationalism began to resemble an opposition to the régime, as Croatian nationalism had done in the 1930s.

Tito had known how to modulate ethnic tonality. He could get away with cutting back Serbs as a community while using them as Communist individuals. In his last years discords were still harmonised to a large extent by the great man himself, yet the country was also experiencing stagnation in government, and beginning to face the full onslaught of an economic and financial crisis. The reaffirmation of political dogmatism had produced the widespread conviction that the Yugoslav system was not reformable from within. If it still appeared to solve the country's problems in the last decade of Tito's rule, it was by a mixture of magic, pretentiousness, consumerism, corruption and foreign loans.

Kardelj died in 1979. Tito's death followed the next year.

9

SERBIA AFTER BROZ – FROM TITO'S APOTHEOSIS TO MILOŠEVIĆ'S CONSECRATION
1980–1989

In the last decade of Tito's reign, Serbia was one of the eight little party-states of the Socialist Federal Republic of Yugoslavia, glued together by ideology, under a god-like ruler. The glue was strictly for the apparatus. Beyond the apparatus, Tito was seen as the symbol and protector of the freedom of fending for oneself that characterized Yugoslavia. His death on 4 May 1980 caused grief—and consternation, as if people, out of fear of having to face reality, had wanted to believe that he would never die.

The funeral of Marshal Josip Broz Tito also marked his ultimate apotheosis, as his collective heirs pretended that his presence still ruled over the land. However, this posthumous glory did not last long. In Serbia, he was soon referred to no longer as Tito, but as plain Broz. Reality gradually intruded and revealed a crisis, which was immediately obvious to all. In the first instance the crisis appeared to be economic and financial: unemployment rose and real earnings fell. By 1985 the foreign debt was of over $20 billion, and aggregate inflation since 1979 exceeded 1,000 per cent.

In the minds of its leaders Communist Yugoslavia had always been a transitional state destined to become the core or the model of a wider integration. From 1974, more than ever before, it was based on the denial not only of the existence of a Yugoslav political nation, but of the state as well. It was supposed to be held together by its faith in Marxism-Leninism-Titoism-Kardeljism. The system had underestimated the force of present reality, and after Tito's death, his inspiring spirit notwithstanding, the federal leadership was unable to get out of a deadlocked mechanism. All it could do was prevent the organization of any pan-Yugoslav alternative, until the model itself was challenged and conflicts arose within the political élite on its correct interpretation.

The previous scapegoats—the class enemies, the capitalist West, the Stalinist East—were no longer credible. By labelling all who opposed the régime in its current version as 'nationalists', the leadership itself contributed to promoting nationalism as the main alternative. As elsewhere in Eastern Europe, the reappearance of nationalism was not just the return of an old genetic strand. It was an attempt not so much to restore links with real tradition as to erase the recent past. It was also the product of Communism, which had manipulated it for political ends.

The quasi-states that the republics and provinces had become at the expense of the federation lacked only the subjective characteristic of nationalism. Ideological anti-statism had given way to a statist obsession. Sections of the cultural élite helped in the selective recovery of a collective ethnic past, which was contrary to the principle of citizenship, but which helped to overcome the degenerative grip of atheistic Communism. As the popular mood and freer media became concerned with increasing disjunctions between model and reality, new scapegoats were found outside one's own nation. Eventually, every nation became what the others feared it to be.

Serbia's political leaders had accepted the 1974 constitution because they saw it as a step towards the preservation of a Communist Yugoslavia in which their republic would have a substantial amount of autonomy without being suspected of thwarting the free development of others. They wanted to be free to modernize Serbia's political system in the belief that they would thus increase the republic's influence on the federal decision-making process.

Serbia's position in the latest constitutional phase was an illogical one, in that its autonomous provinces could veto decisions at the level of the republic of which they were formally part, but that the republican authority in Belgrade could not do the same to Kosovo and Voivodina. Serbia had been effectively reduced to what was increasingly called 'inner Serbia' (or 'Serbia without the provinces'). For the time being its leaders objected not so much to the constitution as to its selective or incorrect interpretation. In economic terms, they also wished to reintegrate the autonomous provinces to make Serbia's industrial policy more effective, and to reunify the Yugoslav market to go along with reforms proposed by the International Monetary Fund. Their proposals met with hostility from those who argued that such change would mean deviation from 'Tito's way'. Opposition came from Slovenia, where the mood for reform stopped at the republic's borders. Croatia's conservative leadership was cautious about any political reform. Finally, the proposals were not in tune with a certain political discourse in Serbia itself that was turning to the ethnic nation rather than to the republic as the real political factor.

Blinded by Tito's legacy of a Yugoslavia that was the vanguard of a third way, the Party leadership seemed not to notice what was happening in the world at large. In spite of differences, it remained generally committed to the *status quo* in all its orthodoxy. The debates on economic management were not yet ethnic conflicts; divisions still crossed republican borders. However, by the middle of the decade Tito's way and his posthumous apotheosis came to an end without anyone saying that it had happened. Tendencies began to pull in opposite directions; Serbia tried to tighten up the federation again, and Slovenia tried to loosen it even further.

Serbia's provinces, and Kosovo in particular, were worried. In 1981 the Constitutional Court of Serbia had asked for a debate to initiate 'small changes' that would restore to Serbia some measure of control. Demands were in turn put forward in Kosovo, where ethnic Albanians wanted it to become a republic separate from Serbia; their educated minority in particular felt the economic gap widening between them and the rest of the country. As for Serbs in the province, they had become the victims of severe discrimination. Both were emigrating.

Feelings exploded in April 1981. Priština's Albanian students added ethnic and ideological dimensions to social and economic grievances. The authorities, taken by surprise, reacted brutally to the outburst of Albanian nationalism. Order was superficially restored by a show of force, stiff sentences, purges, symbolic gestures, the incantation of usual slogans, and papering over the cracks. The revolt, labelled 'counter-revolutionary', was supposed not to have affected the working people.

To reconsider the original territorial division and grant Kosovo the status of republic was not possible. Ideologically and constitutionally republics were for component 'nations' only. A republic of Kosovo would have opened Pandora's box. It would have been a pole of attraction for Yugoslavia's ethnic Albanian population in inner Serbia, Montenegro and especially Macedonia, whose loyalty to the federation would have been jeopardized. It could have led to demands from the half-million Serbs of Croatia (who differed from Croats, but also from the inhabitants of Serbia at least as much as the inhabitants of Montenegro did). It could also have led to a rapprochement between the three southern republics of Serbia, Montenegro and Macedonia. After the initial rude awakening to the reality of the situation, policy in Kosovo became more restrained, and Albanian nationalists went underground. Nothing more was done to prevent the revelation of facts hitherto kept under wraps—the extent of harassment of Serbs there, and of their emigration. Figures for the number of departing Serbs vary,[1] as do the reasons. They left because of pressure, but they also went in search of higher standards of life elsewhere.

The one certainty is that the proportion of Serbs in the province, which had remained stable at 23–27 per cent until 1961, had fallen by 1981 to 13.2. Everyone knew that it was essentially due to the birth rate of the Albanian community of Kosovo—the highest in Europe at 35 per 1,000. Nevertheless, the Serbs' departure from Kosovo was increasingly perceived by them, and in Serbia, as evidence that a process which had been associated with Turkish rule had resumed under a Yugoslav, even a Serbian, Communist government.

The leaders of Serbia used the Albanian 'counter-revolution' to bolster the need for changes in the constitutional relations between the republic and its provinces. They argued that a weak Serbia fuelled its nationalism, which was no good for Yugoslavia, and that the real danger came not from the 'statism' of the federation, but from that of its components. Their 'reformist' stance, where political reform went with economic reform, pushed them into conflict with the defenders of the *status quo*, who included the Serbs of the Voivodina Party hierarchy, the Bosnian Serb Communists, and a minority of the Party in inner Serbia itself.

The way in which the old divide between reformers and conservatives had turned into a conflict between defenders of the *status quo*, mostly outside inner Serbia, and recentralizers (or 're-federalizers'), mostly in Serbia, was made visible at the Twelfth Congress of the League of Communists of Yugoslavia in 1982. It was then also made clear that Serbia's leaders would not accept any replacement of Tito's personal arbitration in political conflicts within their republic.

---

[1] According to census data, some 65,000 Serbs had left the province since 1961. Other estimates (that took into account unregistered emigration) put the figure at over 100,000 for the decade 1971–81.

In spite of the continued imprisonment of Albanian 'irredentists', Serbian emigration from Kosovo continued, local cadres remained under strong suspicion even after the purge, and antagonism deepened between the two communities. Kosovo Serbs began to look for support in Belgrade outside government circles; clerics and intellectuals became directly involved in promoting their cause. Just as the Kosovo Albanians believed that only a republic (of Kosovo), equal to all the others, could give them what they wanted, so the Kosovo Serbs now demanded support from a republic (of Serbia), equal to all the others.

A link had been established between the Kosovo question and Serbia's status. The problem of relations between Serbs and Albanians in Kosovo was growing into one of relations between Serbs and all the other nationalities of Yugoslavia. Unease over inefficiencies led to questioning (particularly by the chattering class) of the nature of the federal framework. In the process Kosovo was again turned into a national symbol, as it had been at the time of the Balkan wars some three-quarters of a century earlier. The territory now had to be 'saved', as the battle once had to be 'avenged'. The name became an incantation that linked the present crisis to memories of past injustices, and to nostalgia for ancient glories.

By 1985 there was a widespread sense that Yugoslav Communism had failed. Belgrade was the centre of independent critical thought in Yugoslavia. The capital had benefited from the latitude accorded to non-conforming intellectuals by Serbia's political leadership in search of a broader-based legitimacy, and the 'Belgrade critical intelligentsia' was thus the vanguard of a civil rights movement. Its core was formed by the Committee for the Defence of Freedom of Thought and Expression, with a number of members of the Serbian Academy of Sciences and Arts[2] led by Dobrica Ćosić. Their first task was to defend those prosecuted for the expression of dissident views throughout Yugoslavia, without questioning the nature of such views, but they also put forward political demands that amounted to a radical critique of the Communist system.

Fusing democracy and nationalism, they gradually moved from protecting individual human rights to lamenting the fate of their nation,

[2]Heir to the old Royal Serbian Academy (founded 1886), it had been turned after the Second World War, as had its sister academies in Zagreb (founded 1866) and in Ljubljana (founded 1938), into a Soviet-type state institution operating a network of cultural and scientific centres. The three older institutions had on the whole retained a membership of genuine scholars, scientists, writers and artists. Eventually every republic came to have its academy.

and from opposing Communist myths to promoting Serbian myths. In doing so they were going along with the trend set by novels that expressed the Serbs' rising sense of disillusionment with the way in which the common state had been operated by its Communist rulers.[3]

Less read but no less talked about were the historians who set about investigating the history of the Communist Party of Yugoslavia, its rôle in the Second World War, its approach to the national question, and its treatment of the Serbian people in particular. They focused on the Comintern's anti-Yugoslav period, the campaign against 'greater-Serbian hegemony', the struggle against Mihailović's wartime movement, and the territorial division of the Yugoslav federation, so that by 1988 the betrayal of the Serbs by the Communist Party had become a current theme in Belgrade.

Another line was the continuity of an 'Austro-Catholic' anti-Serbian tendency from the statesmen, generals and prelates of the Habsburg monarchy to nationalist intellectuals and revisionist historians in modern-day Croatia, through the tragic days of the wartime NDH, and even the rule of Tito and Kardelj, seen respectively as a Croat and a Slovene. There were wild generalizations about a coalition of the two trends.

The 'White Book' produced in 1984 by the then hard-line Croatian president of the League of Communists of Yugoslavia was a veritable '*Index Expurgatorius*'—an anthology of the unacceptable writings of 120 authors (mostly Serbs) since Tito's death. It was intended to unite Yugoslavia's Communists in their fight against the whole spectrum of political opposition, but it was seen by Serbia's leadership as yet another intrusion into their domestic affairs, and one that seriously undermined their position.

Ivan Stambolić (b. 1936) had become Party leader in Serbia immediately after Tito's death in 1980. He and his team had pushed for both market reforms and a change in the status of Serbia, by agreement with the other members of the federation. Until 1984 at least, their objections were not so much to the constitution itself as to the way in which it had been interpreted to Serbia's disadvantage by other republics and by the two provinces.

---

[3]These included *The Knife* (1982) by Vuk Drašković (later founder of the Serbian Renewal Movement, at the time a Communist journalist), and the best-selling *Book about Milutin* (1985) by Danko Popović. Even the structural inventiveness of Milorad Pavić's much-translated *Dictionary of the Khazars* (1984) turned out to be an attractive post-modern gimmick to place the fate of the Serbs in the context of an impossible metanarrative.

Yet they had not been soft on nationalists. Stambolić's protégé Slobodan Milošević (b. 1941), the Party chief for the city of Belgrade, was an outright anti-nationalist and a Communist hardliner, who opposed all attempts at historical reconsideration of the recent past. When Stambolić moved to the presidency of Serbia in 1986, he backed Milošević to succeed him as the republic's Party head.

In response to official initiatives, the Serbian Academy appointed in May 1985 a working party to draft a discussion paper on the economic and political situation of Yugoslavia. As far back as 1983 the commission named by the federal League of Communists to look at constitutional reform had called for an open debate on the changes under discussion by the federal parliament. Serbia's leadership had expressed its wish that the Serbian Academy would participate, in the hope of reducing the gap between the political leadership and the intellectual opposition, and of obtaining support for its own proposals. Parallel moves were taking place in Slovenia. The working party set out, at academic pace, to produce the draft. In September 1986 an unfinished version was leaked under suspicious circumstances to a popular newspaper. It contained little that had not already been said.

More a description of a situation viewed as disastrous than a political programme for action, it called for a 'democratic' and 'integrating' federation. Serbia could not at present be a 'state' like the other republics, because of the way in which it had been fragmented. As a result of generally excessive decentralization, the Serbs were being submitted to 'genocide' in a part of their own republic, and to more subtle forms of assimilation elsewhere in Yugoslavia. Croatia and Slovenia were blamed for plotting to maintain the subordinate status of Serbia and of the Serbian nation. Serbia should now take the initiative to redress the situation—by 'integrating' again the provinces which would remain autonomous but under the republic, and by a programme aimed at the national and cultural 'integration' of the Serbian nation regardless of republican borders.

The document did not reject Yugoslavia or the Communist legacy. It did not call for a redrawing of internal borders, or even for the abolition of Serbia's autonomous provinces. However, its authors had brought together the disparate strands of the Serbian nationalist vision, and had found a conspiracy that explained the state of affairs. Few would read the document, but its message, heightened in the vulgarized form projected by the media all over Yugoslavia, was that Serbia's most prestigious group of intellectuals was calling upon Serbs to rally to the defence of a threatened nation.

An official campaign was launched against the 'memorandum', and against the Academy itself, which had to postpone its scheduled centenary celebrations. The pressure put on individual members and on the institution to condemn the document and its authors was counterproductive. Most academicians had known nothing of the draft, but they turned down the call to reject it in order to assert their independence. Public opinion felt that the Academy had confirmed the text.[4] As Serb activists from Kosovo came to Belgrade in search of support, the Ćosić committee went on to organize a petition to mobilize public opinion. This turned out to be a veritable 'who's who' of prominent intellectuals, and completed the blending of their human rights action in favour of prosecuted individual Albanians, with their spiritual vision of the Serbian nation and their critique of the régime.

Support for the Kosovo Serbs was channelled through the Writers's Association of Serbia which, even more than the Academy, had been a Soviet-type institution of the kind that every federated unit possessed. In 1986 it had elected a new board made up of prominent opposition writers, including Ćosić and several members of his committee. In the spring of 1987 it organized a series of 'literary evenings' on Kosovo, and a speech by Ćosić on one of these occasions echoed throughout Yugoslavia. Its gist was that Kosovo was a vital issue for the Serbian nation and for the future of Yugoslavia; the Yugoslav state could not survive if it allowed a minority to terrorize the majority nation in one of its republics.

Croatian and Slovenian intellectuals had not responded to their Belgrade colleagues' overtures for all-Yugoslav solidarity in any of their endeavours; least of all did they accept the 'truth' on Kosovo. The shattered expectations of cooperation from Slovenia turned into a feeling of having been betrayed. As nationalism resurfaced in Croatia, intellectuals there attempted to minimize the magnitude of wartime Ustasha massacres to remove the stigma from their own confederal projects, and their Serbian counterparts responded by magnifying Serbian losses to bolster their thesis of victimization. The Belgrade media embarked on an orgy of genocidal revelations.

All this went with a 'return to tradition' which enabled the once critical intelligentsia to link up the rhetorical defence of the Serbian

---

[4]The only two academicians to express their rejection of it publicly were the nuclear physicist Pavle Savić, Party member since before the war, and the fellow-traveller historian Vaso Čubrilović, the oldest member, whose lecture in 1937 to the Serbian Cultural Club had not yet surfaced (see p. 134, n. 13).

state and nation with deep-rooted feelings. Folk culture, which had become almost the preserve of musicology, ethnography and tourism, was revived, only to degenerate into a kitsch sub-culture. The first beneficiary of traditionalism was the Serbian Orthodox church, which since 1980 had been making a gradual comeback from the social margins to which it had been consigned. Because it had always considered itself the guardian of Serbian identity, it was the first institution to come to the defence of the Kosovo Serbs, as early as 1982. While one tendency simply aimed at returning the church to its old position in society, another was represented by a new crop of younger theologians who became actors on the Belgrade intellectual scene even before they were promoted to the bench of bishops. They linked the suffering of Serbs of different regions and times into a uniquely nationalist theology. For them the holy Prince Lazar had chosen the heavenly realm in 1389 in the name of the whole nation whose tragic history had, since then, been suspended between heaven and earth.

By 1987 the situation in Kosovo was once again explosive. This time it was the Serbs who had had enough. The critical intelligentsia had turned into a fully-fledged opposition, demanding in general terms an end to the disintegrative loosening of Yugoslavia, its democratization, the reversal of anti-Serbian policies, and reforms that would make Serbia a republic equal to all the others.

In April 1986, just before he became president of Serbia, Stambolić had gone to Kosovo. Grappling as he was with the task of obtaining support from the federal top of the Party for his republic's demand, he tried to reason with the Serbs there, and did so with the usual rhetoric of Serbian Communists opposing Serbian nationalism. Meanwhile, in Belgrade Milošević had attacked the protest meetings as nationalist. Exactly a year later Stambolić sent him to Kosovo to meet the disgruntled Serbs there.

Forced to address a crowd of militants who complained that they had been truncheoned by the (mainly Albanian) police, Milošević improvised. He turned the blame on the bureaucrats, and mixed patriotic references to the land of one's ancestors with Communist warnings against exploitation by nationalists. However, 'No one is allowed to beat you' was his one phrase that was remembered. The message that came across was that people had to take their destiny into their own hands.

On his return he continued his public attacks on the Academy. At the same time, boosted by the popularity he had just acquired, he organized his conservative Party followers to plot the removal of Stambolić, in order to seek a new legitimacy through a robust defence of Serbia's cause. Serbia's economy in the 1980s had slipped closer to that of the underdeveloped republics. Even inner Serbia had fallen below the Yugoslav average judged by all the relevant indicators. Yet its contribution to the federation was still calculated on the premise that it was a developed republic. Its leadership had not been able to identify closely enough with its grievances, or to repress the rise of ever more numerous critical voices. It had sought to deal with the crisis through the never-ending process of agreed federal constitutional and market reform, which was increasingly thought to be leading nowhere.

Milošević had realized how potentially powerful the opposition had become, and that radical steps should be taken to prevent the collapse of the régime. He moved quickly, first to re-introduce discipline in the Party; he promoted new cadres who were loyal to him. He gained the support of army conservatives and of the older generation of partisans faithful to the revolution and the defence of Yugoslavia who saw in him someone capable of using the masses rather than allowing them to be manipulated by others. He called for a return to Tito's earlier successful concept of unifying the nations of Yugoslavia, and for a restoration of Serbia's 'statehood', in reaction to the theory of decline of the state that went with the later Tito-Kardelj concept.

In September 1987 he obtained full control of Serbia's Central Committee, and moved adroitly to the nationalist side. Because the legitimating force of Titoist principles was exhausted, his call for a return to an earlier Titoism could mark him as the best leader for the task of destroying at least that part of the Titoist legacy linked since 1974 to Kardelj. The Belgrade intelligentsia had hitherto been able to combine their commitment to democracy with their commitment to the nation against the régime, which did nothing for either. Now Milošević defended the interests of Serbia: he had come out in Kosovo against the 'bureaucrats' who were responsible for the crisis, and he allowed an unprecedented degree of liberalization of Serbia's cultural scene. Most of Belgrade's 'critical intellectuals', who had once prided themselves on being at the forefront of the struggle for democracy in Yugoslavia, now put democracy on hold. They had lost their critical faculties.

His seduction of the intellectuals was one of Milošević's many ways of legitimizing his authority. He had something to offer to most people—a re-vitalization of the Party which could also be read as a step towards the advent of democracy, a defence of Serbia which could be used in the defence of Yugoslavia, a chance of promotion for younger politicians, and an alternative to open anti-Communist nationalism, namely a reformed unified socialist market.

He then proceeded to manage the removal of key media figures, so that the most powerful Belgrade papers and television channels joined his supporters in a campaign to eliminate Stambolić entirely. By December Milošević's assumption of control was completed when a retired chief of the general staff took over as president of Serbia. The other leaderships did not seem to mind. Kosovo Albanians had no reason to stand by Stambolić. Milošević had his supporters among the Communists of Montenegro; many of Serbia's Communists had come from there or, like Milošević himself, been born in Serbia of Montenegro-born parents. Elsewhere the changes were considered an internal Serbian matter. To Croats Milošević appeared less dangerous than the more sophisticated Stambolić. The federal leadership either rather liked him or did not see the need to oppose him.

He was now ready to offer a quick solution to a complex set of problems—Kosovo, the dissatisfaction of Serbs everywhere, and the economic crisis. Having absorbed most of the opposition potential of Serbia, he spoke of the need to re-centralize authority, first in Serbia and then in the federation. In 1988 he moved at high speed. In imitation of what Tito had done twenty years earlier, he put himself at the head of popular discontent by staging his 'anti-bureaucratic revolution'. He removed the carpet from under the feet of anti-Communist nationalism by allowing and encouraging public assertions of Serbian nationalism. Mass rallies, organized through the Party apparatus and the media, laid the groundwork for replacing the leaderships of the autonomous provinces and of the sister republic of Montenegro. Having solicited people directly for political support, Milošević resorted to the protection of Serbian national interests in expressing the whole variety of popular frustrations. His effective use of mass mobilization turned the grey apparatchik he had been till then into Serbia's most popular leader.[5] The cult of his personality was started.

The faceless Party hierarchies of Voivodina, Kosovo and Montenegro gave way one after another between October 1988 and January

[5]Aleksa Djilas, 'A Profile of Slobodan Milošević', *Foreign Affairs*, 72/3, New York, 1993, 33.

1989. Whereas in Kosovo Milošević supporters obtained a totally unrepresentative leadership, in Voivodina the appearance of younger faces was hailed as positive change. The assumption of leading positions in Montenegro by Milošević's young supporters Momir Bulatović (b.1956) and Milo Djukanović (b.1962) was no less popular, but it caused a strong reaction from the Slovenian leadership: Milošević's action had moved beyond Serbia's borders.

As the federal parliament passed the last of the constitutional amendments first drafted almost two years earlier, there was a mass rally of more than half a million people, at the confluence of the rivers Save and Danube in Belgrade, in November 1988. It was staged as a political spectacle, at which Milošević employed a combat rhetoric in defence of Yugoslavia—Yugoslavia had been created by a struggle, and it would be defended by the same means. The unification of Yugoslavia in 1918 had never been commemorated under Communist rule, but now for the first and last time, on the occasion of the seventieth anniversary, the formation and the history of the state of the Southern Slavs were marked by a series of television documentaries on the events of the First World War leading to 1 December 1918, and by a bulky volume of documents illustrating the themes of Yugoslavia's history since then.

For the time being the federal Central Committee had not opposed Serbia's plans for a revision of its constitution, which reduced the rights of the provinces by removing their veto in legal and administrative matters. They were enacted in March 1989, and followed by another wave of mass protests in Kosovo, direct confrontation with the security forces, and deaths ranging in number from an official twenty-four to claims of over 1,000. The federal presidency imposed a federal state of emergency in the province. Serbia had been 'reunified', and the majority of Serbs felt that Serbia's dignity had been restored. However, the provinces retained their separate representation in the federal presidency, thus giving the newly-formed Milošević camp four votes (Serbia, Kosovo, Voivodina and Montenegro) out of eight.

Since 1987 Yugoslavia had been under Western pressure to assert central control over the supply of money and credit. The presidency of the League of Communists of Yugoslavia had then presented proposals, which were a compromise to satisfy both defenders and reformers of the system. By the end of 1988 some 120 amendments had been passed by the federal parliament after long debates and compromises, but they had to be ratified by all republics and provinces before being turned into a constitutional law. In March 1989 a new federal government was formed under the reformist Croat Ante Marković, which busied itself with drawing up stabilization plans to meet IMF conditions. Milošević, who had acquired the reputation of a reformer, presented his agenda for re-federalization as a prerequisite to successful reform, and objected that Serbia would suffer from Marković's plans as they stood.

The federal government was no more than the executive arm of the federal Party leadership. Milošević's ambition to appear as a new Tito over the whole of Yugoslavia was impossible under existing arrangements. In order to achieve it he needed a complete overhaul and he attempted to do just that from the spring of 1989 by obtaining half the necessary votes in the federal presidency to support his view, and then getting it all through an extraordinary Party congress. But the legitimacy of one-party rule had already collapsed across Eastern Europe. Yugoslavia had lost its strategic importance, and was in deep economic crisis. Therefore, far from resolving anything, or saving Yugoslavia, Milošević's moves accelerated its dismemberment.

Slovenia and Croatia were not ready for any such new bargains over restructuring Yugoslavia, particularly with a new and determined strong man in Belgrade. Already homogenized into a nation-state of sorts, since its ethnicity coincided with its territory, Slovenia was ready to accept no more than the lowest-common-denominator confederation, with the right of secession for its components. Reacting to the fear of a resurgent strong Serbia under Milošević, its leaders, most of its intellectuals and its public opinion wanted to escape from Yugoslavia as if they had intimations of its impending violent collapse.

The crisis in Serbia had apparently been overcome by forging the unity of the nation, and the Communists under Milošević had acquired a new legitimacy by taking over its defence. By blaming the 1974 system rather than Yugoslavia, and by his direct appeal to public opinion, Milošević was able to link nationalist intellectuals, the people who were suffering from the economic reforms, those who wanted a return to pre-1974 Communism, and those who were simply holding on to the structures of power. At the same time, he could use and abuse the organizational network and the rhetoric of the Communist Party, thus creating an extraordinary coalition around him.

Milošević's appeals to Serbs generally implied a political threat to the power of the other republican leaderships. They perceived it as being anti-Yugoslav, or at least against the rest of Yugoslavia. However, most of the population of Serbia, and indeed most Serbs still probably favoured a Yugoslav option, seeing little difference between being a Serb and a Yugoslav; despite their many grievances, the common state still represented the best framework for the solution of their national question. This bolstered Milošević's intention of attempting to transpose the means of achieving Serbia's unity to Yugoslavia. The strategy was to achieve unity within and with the Party, bring down the bureaucrats, remove the separatists, and change the constitution, for the whole of Yugoslavia as it had been done for the whole of Serbia. In May 1989 Milošević also became formally president of Serbia.

The Voivodina party held a congress which took the initiative in requesting an extraordinary congress of the League of Communists of Yugoslavia. Delegates there were elected in proportion to the number of adherents in each republic. Through his control of the Party machineries of the whole of Serbia and of Montenegro, and with help from elsewhere, Milošević could count on a sizeable majority, and impose changes that would lead to his being able to control all Yugoslav institutions.

The reunification of Serbia, the regaining of its statehood, the national unity of all Serbs and Milošević's leadership were subsequently consecrated by the huge celebrations of the sexcentenary of the battle of Kosovo. The mood had been set by the church and by writers. The church had officially and publicly celebrated Vidovdan for the first time since the war. National romantic writers had shot off into dangerous spheres.[6]

The gigantic rally on the site of the battlefield on the anniversary, 28 June 1989, provided a splendid setting for this consecration. Milošević addressed a sea of people estimated at anything between half a million and over a million Serbs who had come from all over Yugoslavia and from all over the world, bound in one place by strong symbols and strong hopes. He blended the rhetoric of socialist development with that of national heroism, adding threats for good measure. Six hundred years after Kosovo, he said, 'we are again involved in battles ... they are

[6]The relics of the saintly Prince Lazar toured the holy shrines of Serb-populated territories before being returned to their original resting place in the ruler's monastic foundation. The poet Matija Bećković, president of the Writers' Association of Serbia since 1988, wrote of the rights of the dead, and of a land of Kosovo so steeped in Serbian blood that it would be Serbian even if not one Serb remained there. More prosaically, but no less territorially, the novelist Vuk Drašković wrote that Serbs had given and lost so much for Yugoslavia that they now wanted their freedom. However, he warned that if Yugoslavia went, so would the present borders.

not battles with arms, but these cannot be excluded ... Our main battle today is for ... the successful advance into the civilization in which people will live in the twenty-first century'.

He used the occasion to present himself not only as leader of Serbia and of the Serbs, but as the true leader of Yugoslavia, next to the pale federal presidency arraigned there at what had been billed as a Yugoslav as well as a Serbian event. The agony of Yugoslavia was about to start. Serbia entered into the purgatory of the Milošević era.

10

SERBIA IN DARKNESS – THE MILOŠEVIĆ YEARS
THE 1990s

The Fourteenth Congress of the League of Communists of Yugoslavia that assembled in Belgrade on 20 January 1990 was an extraordinary congress where the Party's constitution was concerned. It was also extraordinary in that it was the last Yugoslav Communist congress. The Slovenes' proposals for a yet looser association obtained far less than the required majority, while Serbian proposals for tightening up the federation were passed. Milošević's plan seemed to be working, until the Slovenes walked out. The Croats objected to the motion that the Congress should continue. They obtained an adjournment, and that was the end of the League of Communists of Yugoslavia.

The leaderships of Slovenia and Serbia had been fighting a proxy war over Kosovo. Slovenian rallies of solidarity with ethnic Albanians were followed by anti-Slovenian demonstrations in Serbia. Milošević even organized a rally of Kosovo Serbs in Ljubljana, scheduled for 1 December 1989 (as the anniversary of the unification of Yugoslavia in 1918 it was another symbolic date), but the Slovenian government banned it and cut its contribution to the federal budget. Serbia boycotted Slovenian goods. The animosity was the expression of two incompatible programmes, and because Yugoslavia could not accommodate them both, its end was almost certain.

Ante Marković enabled it to survive for another year and a half. As federal prime minister since the beginning of 1989, he saw the collapse of the ruling party as a chance to push for the transition to a viable federation. Serbia and Slovenia opposed his plans; a majority of the population would have to suffer initially from his shock therapy.

Yet in the spring of 1990, when economic reforms were giving hope, Marković was the most popular politician in Yugoslavia. He also enjoyed the support of Western governments and of international financial institutions. He took time to realize that the country might survive without its ruling League of Communists, but not without the backing of any countrywide movement. It was too late when he launched his Alliance of Reform Forces in July.

The impetus gained by the reforms stopped. The barriers to a market economy that Marković tried to remove were being reinforced by confrontation between the republics, which the National Bank was unable to prevent from adding to the money supply. In December Serbia's government gave the *coup de grâce* to monetary restraint by taking half of the drawing rights of the entire federation. Milošević had once called for tighter fiscal discipline to reintegrate the Yugoslav economy, but he now had to pay wages, pensions and bonuses on the eve of elections in his republic. Such was the atmosphere in which the first competitive elections were held.

The republics—Slovenia to the fore—had insisted that they should first be held at their level. Communism was collapsing; nationalism enjoyed the advantage of having a simple emotional message, and it could accommodate all shades of anti-Communism. Republican Leagues of Communists, hurriedly renamed, could hope to survive only by adopting a nationalist posture. Since the running was made by the republics, regional forces acquired legitimacy at the expense of the federation.

Slovenia started in April 1990. An opposition coalition won a safe majority, and in December a referendum produced a 95 per cent vote for independence. Elections in Croatia followed. The nationalist Croatian Democratic Union (HDZ), with less than 42 per cent of the vote, obtained an absolute majority of seats, and its leader Franjo Tudjman became president.

There were only 48,000 Serbs residing in Slovenia out of a total population of 2 million, and they were not old settlers, but there were over 580,000 Serbs in Croatia—12.51 per cent of the population. Perhaps as many as two-thirds were integrated in the towns—50,000 in Zagreb alone. The remainder were concentrated in the poorer districts of the old Border, or Krajina, settlements,[1] experiencing—along with all similar areas—the harsher economic consequences of

---

[1] Population figures are from the 1991 census. To the 581,663 registered Serbs in Croatia should be added a proportion of the 106,041 Yugoslavs and 73,376 'not declared'. There were also 9,724 registered Montenegrins.

Yugoslavia's economic crisis. In the flush of victory the HDZ also went for an independent nation-state, and behaved towards the Serbs with incompetence reinforced by much discrimination and some violence. Serbs in public employment were forced out or made to sign loyalty oaths.

The new constitution under discussion defined Croatia as the national state of the Croatian nation. Previously it had been the state of the 'people of Croatia', with an initial reference to the Croatian nation's 'brotherly unity with the Serbs of Croatia'; the latter had voted overwhelmingly for the only non-ethnic party available, the former Communists. However, the more the new government pushed for Croatization and independence, the more Serbs living in the compact settlements of Krajina moved to the new local Serbian Democratic Party (SDS).

Support for Milošević had been significantly less among Serbs outside Serbia than among those inside, and Communist Serbs in the various republican parties had stuck to the line of criticizing nationalism within their own ethnicity. However, the fanning of anti-Serbian feelings and the anti-Serbian innuendoes of political rhetoric had aroused fears among the Serbs of the mixed areas, and helped Milošević to work upon those fears.

Tudjman's controversial campaign statements about the Ustashas' wartime NDH and about non-Croats had been made to sound truly threatening by the violence mounted in various places by his party militants. The cavalier attitude of the new authorities towards the Serbian minority strengthened the hand of Serbian nationalists of all camps everywhere who believed that the Serbs of Croatia needed some form of autonomy, as well as protection from Serbia.

The SDS had originally asked for cultural autonomy, on the assumption that Croatia continued to recognize the Serbs' existence within the republic and the continuation of Yugoslavia as a federation. Serbian activists in Krajina had received encouragement from Belgrade. They had been in touch with the régime as well as with opposition personalities. At the same time as Croatia's nationalist government marched towards independence, the SDS was taken over by its radicals, backed by Milošević, and when talks with Tudjman broke down, its five elected members left the Zagreb parliament. A union of the SDS-controlled local councils in Krajina was set up.

Their territory was contiguous to the Serbian-inhabited area of western Bosnia, and they wanted to remain in Yugoslavia. At the very least, they wanted to govern themselves where they were a majority. They had requested federal protection, and the Yugoslav army prevented the Croatian government from intervening. They submitted a 'Declaration on Sovereignty' to a referendum, and in Knin proclaimed their autonomous region. By the end of the year it had become the 'Republic of Serbian Krajina', extending from northern inner Dalmatia to eastern Slavonia. All those—whether Serb or Croat—in local government as in the army or the police who had sought accommodations and tried to keep violence at bay were squeezed out.

In Macedonia no stable majority emerged from the November elections, when a nationalist coalition obtained a third of the seats. In Bosnia-Herzegovina the ballot read like a census of ethnic identities: more than 86 per cent of the electorate went for the ethnic parties in tenuous coalition—the Muslim Party of Democratic Action, the Serbian SDS and the Croatian HDZ, the latter two being offshoots of the same parties in Croatia. In Montenegro Milošević's young protégés kept two-thirds of the seats in the December elections. Bulatović was confirmed as president. That left Serbia.

The threatened dissolution of Yugoslavia posed the question of Serbs outside Serbia. What right to self-determination the 1974 constitution acknowledged ('including the right to secession') was vested in nations and not in republics. The possibility of secession by republics gave Serbian nationalists a basis for the claim to redraw borders.

Milošević had been president of Serbia under the old system since May 1989, and in November of that year, at the height of his new popularity, he was confirmed by direct election with over 80 per cent of the vote. He kept delaying the legalization of opposition movements, and because their first rallies were held in Belgrade in the wake of Communist defeats in Slovenia and Croatia, he appeared to be in trouble. His major argument was that a new constitution should be adopted before the elections in order to forestall Albanian separatism in Kosovo. A referendum in July on such a proposal was approved by 97 per cent, and not only did Albanian voters boycott it, but most Albanian members of the Kosovo Provincial Assembly gathered in Priština to declare the province 'an equal and independent entity within the framework of the federation'. The assembly was suspended and ethnic Albanians in public employment went on strike and were dismissed. Undeterred, the Kosovo parliamentarians, now gathered in the Kosovo Democratic Alliance led by Ibrahim Rugova, met secretly to adopt a constitution for the 'Republic of Kosovo'.

Albanian separatism having thus been 'forestalled', the Communists of Serbia turned themselves into the Socialist Party of Serbia, with

Milošević as its president. A new constitution was passed in September. Mindful that Serbs made up only a little more than 63 per cent of the population of Serbia, it defined the republic as the 'state of all citizens living within it', and referred to the common life of 'all the peoples and national minorities in Serbia'. Serbia was 'a single whole', however, and the autonomous provinces kept only a very limited delegated authority. A parliament of constituency 'winner-take-all' members was counterbalanced by a directly-elected president.

Elections could go ahead. The centrist challenge came from the Democratic Party, which stood for a parliamentary government, a market economy, and 'democratic federalism'. Refusing the 'Serbian' prefix, it wanted to cut across Yugoslavia in cooperation with other similar movements, and hoped that a new historical agreement could be reached between the nations. It attracted a majority of the educated urban strata. On the right was the Serbian Renewal Movement (SPO) of the one-time journalist and novelist Vuk Drašković, which favoured separate nation-states with redrawn borders, possibly linked by mutual arrangements. Drašković openly raised the national question: in strong romantic terms he envisaged a Serbian state within both historical and ethnic borders, encompassing the fully extended Serbia that had joined Yugoslavia in 1918, and all regions where Serbs were in a majority in 1941.

With the situation in Croatia worsening over the summer, both main opposition groups altered their discourse. The Milošević camp accused the SPO of fostering 'dark forces' when the cause of Serbia had already been won, and Drašković accordingly moderated his stance. He had already separated from the more hard-line nationalist 'intellectuals' with whom he had been associated in the nationalist movements that had preceded the formation of his SPO.[2]

On the other hand the Democratic Party, in fear of being isolated, came out with the view that if certain nations did secede, the Serbian nation should also try to gather as many of its own as possible into one state. The opposition parties ended up by competing to prove their patriotism among themselves and with the government, even if the shades of patriotism differed. Their divisions did not represent

---

[2]Many of these had come from Bosnia, including his close friend at the time, the maverick lecturer in international relations Vojislav Šešelj. He had been expelled from Sarajevo University and the Party after accusing local establishment intellectuals of plagiarism and of Islamism. Imprisoned in 1984 for unpublished views about the shape of Serbia, he had moved to Belgrade after his release in 1986. He was viewed with suspicion in intellectual circles because of his extremist opinions.

the interests of various sectors of society, but the ideas, personalities and marketing of their leaders.

The one-time 'critical intellectuals' were spread across the whole spectrum. Ćosić had taken up a position above parties; had he not been a belated nineteenth-century romantic nationalist, he might have fancied himself to be a Serbian version of the Enlightenment philosopher whose rôle (according to the Neapolitan Gaetano Filangeri[3]) was to direct opinion, and to facilitate the subordination of the monarch to the will of the people. For him Yugoslavia was as good as dead, and the main question in the short term was how to set up a Serbian state. He wanted to negotiate dissociation and 'realistic' new borders (including in Kosovo), and he believed that Milošević was the man for that task.

Milošević was able to ensure his own and his party's electoral victory. He controlled the institutions of power and the media. He spoke for both a 'Yugoslav' and a 'Serbian' solution. He stood for peace, security and social benefits, and offered continuity in transition. He talked of Yugoslavia, at the same time as he asserted 'Serbia's right to statehood'. The implication was that, if Yugoslavia could not be turned back to what it had been under Tito in earlier times, he would fashion another one, perhaps one shorn of those who did not want to remain in it, but one that would continue to encompass all Serbs.

Most Belgrade opposition intellectuals had evoked the 'nation' as a living and spiritual force, in opposition to the abstract and faded 'working people'. In so doing they had contributed to Milošević's ambiguous transition from power in the name of class, to power in the name of nation; 'the priority was securing the nation; democracy would come later.'[4] Milošević showed up the divided opposition as not offering much of an alternative to what he could do more successfully. He was in a better position to deal with the consequences of the victory of nationalists in other republics, who had also placed their 'statehood' and their 'national question' before democracy.

The majoritarian system gave the Socialist Party more than 46 per cent of the vote, translated into three-quarters of seats. Drašković's SPO came second, and the Democratic Party third. The results were a shock to the opposition, who had expected better. The conditions for the first multi-party elections had been set by the ruling ex-

[3]Author of *La scienza della legislazione*, first published in Naples, 1780–91.

[4]This terse quotation is from an interesting critical analysis of Belgrade intellectuals by the philosophy professor Dragoljub Mićunović (who became the first president of the Democratic Party, and president of the lower house of the Federal Assembly after the fall of Milošević) in the Belgrade weekly *NIN* as early as 7 May 1989.

Communists, but there was still hope in the confusion of the Yugoslav crisis. The Socialists represented no more than a third of the total electorate: manual workers, peasants, pensioners, the military, the police, the least educated—people who simply cast a vote but did not exercise a conscious choice.

The power apparatus had been reasserted in nationalist clothes. It had saved itself by instrumentalizing elements of tradition, taken out of context, as a way of coping with the political problems of the moment—its own crisis of legitimacy, the 'Serbian question', the conservatism of its apparatchiks and of various sections of the population. Many intellectuals shared the anti-modernism of army, police and church.

The church was the only pan-Serbian institution, and responsible for all the Orthodox faithful in the federation.[5] The hierarchy drifted leaderless and divided. Patriarch German, who had been a guide in difficult times, was gravely ill: in December 1990 the bishops declared him incapable of exercising his primacy, and in an unprecedented move, elected a new patriarch—the elderly Bishop Pavle of the diocese of the Kosovo Serbs. Monastic and ascetic, he stood above factions and was the symbol of Orthodox Kosovo. He signalled the desperate need for spiritual renewal in a largely de-Christianized society, but he was lost in the world of politics.

The issue of the nation was not illogical or illegitimate in the Yugoslav context. Nationalism had always been manipulated by Communism. Smaller nationalisms had been encouraged. Other uncontrolled nationalisms had preceded the Serbian reaction, and when the latter came, it was destructive. This was because it was not contained within one republic, and because of its hysterical character. In defending Yugoslavia as they saw it—the only state in which all Serbs were gathered—the leadership of Serbia and Serbian nationalists in fact gave the final blow to that state, and thus unwittingly destroyed it.

Its demise came as a nervous shock to all Serbs. They had tended to believe that Yugoslavia was indestructible, in spite of 1941 when it had been destroyed by Hitler. They saw in 1991 a replay of 1941— another attempt to destroy the Serbian nation. They had been praised for so long, as Titoist Yugoslavs and as heroic Serbs, that they saw only treason. They made a virtue of resistance to change.

★   ★   ★

[5]Except in Macedonia, for the Macedonian schism was real, even if not accepted by the Serbian or any other Orthodox church.

The ruling party in Serbia at first tried to maintain Yugoslavia by force. Only some extreme nationalists really wanted a 'Greater Serbia'. However, by using force Milošević was making it easier for Slovenia's and Croatia's leaders to go their separate ways, and put the blame on Serbia. The force he relied on was the Yugoslav People's Army. The constitution entrusted the armed forces—the regular army and the republics' territorial defence forces set up in 1970—with the protection of the state, its territorial integrity and its established order. The army was a constituent entity in the Party alongside the federated territories, organized politically on Party lines, and its cadres all Party members. It was also a producer of military equipment, for self-reliance and for export.

In 1989 it was the largest regular national land force in Europe after that of the Soviet Union, and it was committed to the use of force, if necessary, to preserve the system against internal and external enemies. The party-state had always relied on the use of force as the ultimate weapon, and of the threat of force as a less ultimate one. A sharp decline in applications from cities and developed areas had made recruitment more difficult in recent years. In 1985 over 57 per cent of officers, and 46 per cent of generals, were Serbs (not to mention the Montenegrins and the 'Yugoslav' Serbs), a high proportion of them from Croatia and Bosnia. They were a legacy of the partisan generation, and their morale suffered because ethnic and republican balance was required in top positions. The army was a privileged corporation, and in defending the system it defended its own position. Whatever was said about 'internal enemies', the top brass were not prepared for internal warfare. They probably did not believe that it could happen, but they were uneasy about the disappearance of supreme authority.

That was held by the federal presidency, which entered its terminal crisis in May 1991 when Serbia's representative was to give way by rotation to Croatia's in the formal post of president of the presidency. The Milošević camp tried to impede it. Croatia was holding a referendum on separation; it now offered civil and cultural rights to its minorities, but the Serbs of Krajina boycotted Zagreb's referendum as their assembly voted to join Serbia.

Direct confrontation between the Miloševićist 'centre' and the 'northern' republics had so far been avoided. The federal presidency had held a series of sessions with the presidents of individual republics; the federal prime minister Ante Marković was still trying to get agreement on minimal functions for the federation; Milošević and Tudjman had met to work out a division of Bosnia and Herzegovina.

In June Slovenia and Croatia announced that they would 'dissociate'. The army was ordered to take positions along the international borders; it withdrew from Slovenia after ten days as a result of European mediation. Was a phoney war (it left fewer than seventy dead) feigned to let Slovenia go? The units involved regrouped in Croatia and Bosnia, on Serb-inhabited territory.

Faced with a disintegrating state, loyalty among army leaders shifted towards those who could provide authority. Authority was challenged by the withdrawal of conscripts from some republics, by the unreliability of many national servicemen, by the cadres who went over to their republics, and even more by the growing number of irregulars on whom the army came to depend. The leaders of Croatia and Serbia clashed over the Serbian minority in Croatia, which was frightened by Croatian nationalism, and being urged from Serbia to secede from seceding Croatia.

In the summer of 1991, in the disputed areas of Croatia, the army vainly searched for an aim to justify its existence. It fought a war against Croatian independentists on behalf of a Serbian 'Yugoslav' leadership which had not officially entered a war that was not declared, and allowed outside gangs to do most of the dirty work. It did this allegedly to save Yugoslavia. In the process the very mixed and very Yugoslav town of Vukovar was destroyed before it fell, Dubrovnik was blockaded and shelled, and its surroundings were pillaged by military units and volunteers from Montenegro.

The West was not prepared for what happened. Ambiguous and conflicting signals were sent that encouraged all parties to the conflict to believe that their chosen course would eventually win.[6] Having first opposed secession on the ground that it would result in conflict, the powers moved to recognize it in order to end conflict. Resorting to the inviolability of internal frontiers was an attempt to impose some sort of superficial order on the chaos that had emerged. The aim was to stop the fighting, but such a basic aim ignored the principle of shared rights to national sovereignty of Yugoslavia's admired and misunderstood constitution. It ignored the claim of the Serbian inhabitants of Croatia and of Bosnia-Herzegovina to consideration of their right to self-determination. It did not establish criteria for self-determination, or enforce the inviolability of republican borders.

Stipe Mesić, Croatia's representative on the federal presidency,

---

[6]Susan L. Woodward, *Balkan Tragedy: Chaos and Dissolution after the Cold War*, Washington, DC: Brookings Institution Press, 1995, 162.

whom European pressure had eventually installed as 'the last president of the Socialist Federal Republic of Yugoslavia', resigned,[7] followed by Marković. By January 1992 all the governments of the European Union had recognized the independence not only of Slovenia, but also of Croatia whose authorities had by then lost control of a quarter of its territory to breakaway Serbs. Having negotiated the withdrawal of the Yugoslav army from its territory, Macedonia declared independence in September 1991 after a referendum. In Bosnia and Herzegovina, each one of the three ethnic parties had taken over the districts where it had won a majority. The mixed élite of Sarajevo and elsewhere were soon marginalized.

When independence was put to the Bosnian parliament in October, Serbian members walked out in protest against the fact that it went against the principle of constitutional consensus between the three communities. The SDS left the power-sharing coalition in Sarajevo. Only 63 per cent of the electorate participated in the referendum in February 1992. Independence virtually guaranteed that the Bosnian Serbs, supported by Milošević's Serbia and by the army, would follow the local SDS leader, the Montenegro-born Radovan Karadžić, and consolidate a separate entity in Serbian-controlled territory. On 6 April 1992[8], the independence of Bosnia-Herzegovina was recognized. Its Croats accepted it through lip-service only. It was rejected by its Serbs whose elected representatives had proclaimed a territorially undefined 'Serbian Republic of Bosnia and Herzegovina' (*Republika Srpska*, shortened to RS).

The Vance Plan of January 1992 ended hostilities between the Yugoslav army and Croatia. The army was withdrawn, and a United Nations 'protection force' was deployed in the contested zones. Milošević had bullied the Krajina leadership into accepting the force, which he saw as a way to save face for giving up the Serbs of Croatia. He wanted to focus, less directly, on those of Bosnia, whose leaders he was far from controlling. Right from the start they had the advantage of support from the army, although there was no real confrontation until the Bosnian government called for its withdrawal. It went, leaving

---

[7]He was elected president of Croatia after Tudjman's death. His volume of memoirs, 'How We Destroyed Yugoslavia', is subtitled 'The Political Memoirs of the Last President of the Presidency of the SFRY' (Zagreb, 1992).

[8]Another of those unfortunate dates which Western diplomats did not check in their compendiums of international history: 6 April was the anniversary of the German attack on Yugoslavia in 1941.

behind its large Bosnian Serb component—some 80,000 men, who became the army of the RS under the command of General Ratko Mladić. It also left behind equipment, supplies and control over most of the military assets located in Bosnia.

Apart from the Bosnian Serb army, the Bosnian war involved Bosnia-Herzegovina's expanded territorial defence and police forces, which now consisted predominantly of Muslims, local Croatian forces and private militias of all sorts. Initially the strongest, Serbs caused most suffering, notably in the long siege of Sarajevo that started immediately. The city defied the notion of ethnic exclusiveness, and it was required as a capital. The Serbs, whose control extended to its suburbs, went for progressive strangulation. Their settlement throughout Bosnia was discontinuous and predominantly rural, which enabled them eventually to gain control of some 70 per cent of its territory. With recognition given to Slovenia, Croatia and Bosnia-Herzegovina, the difficult aspiration of the western Serbs to continue to live in a common state was seen as aggressive, because it expressed itself by force in the territory of newly-independent states.

There were two simplified views in the West of the Bosnian war. One was that Milošević's Serbia, nationalist Serbs and the remains of the Yugoslav army were trying to create a 'Greater Serbia'. The other was that it was a revival of old tribal conflicts that Communism had managed to control. Milošević had come to accept that Yugoslavia as it had previously existed could not be preserved, that Slovenia should be allowed to go, and Croatia too—but without its compact Serbian settlements. Although it was clearly in their interest to preserve the common state, Bosnia-Herzegovina and Macedonia could not accept Milošević's concept, but their compromise proposals were likewise not acceptable to Serbia or to Slovenia and Croatia. In the end only Montenegro remained with Serbia to set up a new Yugoslavia. The smallest of old Yugoslavia's federated units had voted by a 96 per cent majority to continue to live as a sovereign republic in Yugoslavia, equal to all the other republics that wished to do so. That 'rump Yugoslavia' was seen from the outside as an old Communist state yet almost a neo-fascist one.

The intelligentsia and opposition could only look on powerless and increasingly disappointed. When the wars started in earnest, Drašković still talked of a state for all Serbs: it would take in Macedonia and Bosnia-Herzegovina, and its border with Croatia would coincide with the ethnographic map such as it had been on the eve of the Axis invasion in 1941, but it would all be done by peaceful means.

When Yugoslavia started to break up in 1991, Belgrade went through a moment of crisis. Opposition parties organized mass rallies in March to protest against the information monopoly imposed in practice through the media. The army command tried, with the moribund presidency under its then Serbian head, to impose a general state of emergency; it could do no more than order tanks to the centre of Belgrade, to back up the brutal police intervention that broke up the demonstrations. The capital for a while reverted to being a hotbed of opposition, with students in the lead, and with the support of many intellectuals.[9] Church leaders were also disappointed that the régime had not delivered what they had expected, and the Orthodox press blamed the Communists for all the ills that had befallen the nation. Patriarch Pavle held meetings with the cardinal archbishop of Zagreb, and they called for an end to the war. Soon after, however, the patriarch also said that Serbs could not remain part of Croatia, but had to be accommodated in a joint home with Serbia.

The protests in Belgrade were about the fact that the régime had retained its power structures, and that its actions had not made things any better for Serbs anywhere. Even if they opposed the war, opponents could offer no way out of the crisis. Outside Belgrade workers, the elderly and the uneducated kept quiet. With some selective repression, and a few concessions here and there, Milošević prevented the disaffection from spreading. He wanted to wield power over as much territory as he could—initially the whole of old Yugoslavia, then as much of it as he could salvage. Eventually he could only create a new state with the two remaining republics. He called it the Federal Republic of Yugoslavia (FRY), dropping the adjective 'socialist' (as well as the red star from its tricolour). Theoretically it was open to new members. More realistically, it posed as successor to the late socialist Yugoslavia, and as protector of Serbian minorities in neighbouring successor-states.

Its constitution was adopted in April 1992 by the parliaments of the two units and by what remained of the old federal legislature. The new federation was to be headed by a largely ceremonial president, elected by parliament. The church was, as ever, present yet confused; the patriarch attended the promulgation, but the bishops generally rejected the artificial borders, and supported those who

---

[9]Eighteen academicians took a stand against the war. Two of them—the eminent historians Sima Ćirković and Andrej Mitrović—pleaded for Dubrovnik.

were now called the 'diaspora Serbs'. There was a massive retirement of generals, whose ranks had to be cut to the size of the leaner army of the FRY, and whose loyalty to Milošević had to be ensured. Elections were hurriedly called in May, with a mixed majoritarian-proportional system, and were boycotted by the opposition. Only 56 per cent of the voters went to the polls (and there were 12 per cent of void ballot papers).

The Socialists won an absolute majority of seats, though not of votes, followed by the extreme nationalist Serbian Radical Party of Drašković's one-time associate Vojislav Šešelj.[10] To pre-empt criticism, Ćosić was elected federal president. Did he want to act as a bridge between the opposition, who had boycotted the elections, and Milošević, who no longer had the support of a majority of the electorate, or merely provide Milošević with an exit? He seemed willing to recognize the republics within their existing borders, but did not denounce the atrocities committed in the name of the Serbian people. For federal prime minister the strange choice was made of Milan Panić, an American citizen and successful businessman who had left Yugoslavia in his youth.

The question of borders was never officially posed. It was not possible to ask for both a reordering of some borders to satisfy Serbs in the secessionist republics, and the maintenance of other borders to keep territory inhabited by non-Serbs. Milošević placed his opponents in an awkward situation. If they denounced his nationalism, they reinforced his Socialists or, worse, Šešelj's Radicals who were Milošević's 'favourite opponents'. If they kept silent, they were his accomplices.

The aspirations of the stranded western Serbs were manipulated yet not controlled by Serbia, and expressed through irregular authorities with doubtful democratic credentials. The latter acted through military commanders and warlords whose increasingly brutal actions often took place under the eyes of foreign media. The war in Bosnia was over territories, assets and routes. The basic reason for 'ethnic cleansing' was that military control of land eventually had to be backed by the votes of those who were there. The war came to be fought by people who had little left to do but fight, led by committed radicals, often outsiders, who had to continue for fear of retribution. It gave opportunities for aspirations and acts of revenge of all sorts; it was justified as a national liberation struggle, as an anti-Communist counter-revolution,

[10]See p. 203, n. 2.

as a holy war. Proudly godless generals talked of religion, and presumably God-fearing bishops talked of war.

European mediation efforts had been reinforced by United Nations sanctions against Serbia, Montenegro and the Serbian insurgent 'statelets' in Croatia and Bosnia, followed by United States threats of military action to contain Serbian aggression. Action was in fact limited to ever-tighter sanctions against the party held most responsible for the tragic breakup of Yugoslavia. Yet conferences and mediators continued to meet, placing Tudjman and Milošević centre-stage as guardians to the Bosnian Croats and Bosnian Serbs respectively.

Sanctions and rhetoric against his FRY, against 'the Serbs' and against him personally reinforced Milošević's status as protector of, and spokesman for, Serbian interests. They facilitated his task of governing the FRY. Meanwhile relations within the opposition changed. Drašković had become a man of peace; his movement suffered from defections, but he was still a popular leader. His royalist romanticism, intent on exploiting the memory of General Mihailović, shifted to the centre as the political spectrum moved to the right. The mantle of Serbian bellicosity was taken up with a vengeance by Šešelj, whose bands had pillaged and terrorized Muslims and Croats, and whom Milošević knew how to use. The Democrats, who had shed their more right-wing adherents, notably with the secession of Vojislav Koštunica'a Democratic Party of Serbia, were now under the firm leadership of Zoran Djindjić.

Through anti-inflationary restrictions, subsidies and the rationing of necessities the government could help or punish at will institutions, enterprises and social categories. Those most capable of political action, and those who would oppose the war—urban professionals, academics and students—lost out financially and started to emigrate. The Socialists and the extreme-right nationalists favoured by Milošević increased their control of the media. Popular anger turned towards the democratic opposition when its arguments sounded like those of the powers who had imposed the hardships. A network of criminals and corrupt officials circumvented the embargo, thus acquiring an interest in its maintenance.

The unlikely Ćosić-Panić tandem assumed an unintended international rôle, and turned against Serbia's president. It was in touch with the opposition, and responded to discontent, which brought together resentment at Milošević's lack of support for the western Serbs, and at the consequences of the war in Serbia itself. When federal and republican elections were called again in December 1992,

Panić decided to stand for president of Serbia, on behalf of the opposition. Milošević realized he was at risk. Not only did he use patriotic fervour, police pressure, electoral manipulation and fraud. He actually resorted to the one-time security killer of opponents abroad and international bank-robber Želkjo Ražnatović, known as Arkan, who had set up his private militia and then his own party to mop up the Kosovo seats. The United States branded Milošević a war criminal on the eve of the ballot. Panić was denounced, and perceived by many, as a tool of the Americans.

He lost by 34 per cent to Milošević's 56. Bulatović needed a second round to be re-elected in Montenegro. However, the Socialists lost their overall majority in both the federal and the Serbian parliament; now with less than one-third of the votes, they relied on the support of the Radicals. The divided democratic opposition came third. Overall, fraud notwithstanding, the electorate had voted for the continuation of war. A no-confidence motion from the new federal parliament got rid of Panić. The following June Ćosić was also voted out, and replaced with Zoran Lilić, a Socialist nominated by Milošević.

As the powers came to accept partition within Bosnia and Herzegovina, Washington set about adjusting the military balance against the Bosnian Serbs, and forced Muslims and Croats into a federation. By the summer of 1994 mediation depended on Milošević's ability to isolate the Bosnian Serb leadership in exchange for the lifting of sanctions.

In the battle over acceptance of the Bosnian peace settlement that attributed 49 per cent of territory to Serbs, realism and pragmatism faced romanticism and myth. Romanticism had first called for a Serbian state to encompass all Serbs, then entertained the sham of four Serbian states—Serbia, Montenegro, Krajina and RS. Milošević no longer wanted to risk territorial redistribution while he grappled with Kosovo. He now wanted to appear as a peacekeeper. There were few people in Serbia willing to die for Kosovo, let alone for the Serbs of Bosnia. Milošević accused the Bosnian Serb leaders of betraying national interests by refusing the plan, he withdrew support, and launched a media campaign to destroy Karadžić. There was nevertheless sympathy in Serbia for the predicament of the Bosnian Serbs. The church had never separated the nation; it considered that Serbs, far from being aggressors, had been victims, and it condemned atrocities committed by Serbs, but considered them to be exceptions. Bishops in Bosnia gave support to the local Serbian leadership against Milošević, or tried to mediate between them.

The informal Socialist-Radical alliance broke up in the contest. Šešelj had become too big for his boots. In September 1993, he had tabled a no-confidence motion in the government, which the democratic opposition supported, but the move was pre-empted by dissolution, and the calling of new elections in Serbia for December. The Milošević-controlled media accused Šešelj of crimes committed in Croatia and in Bosnia by his men. Boosted by the eventual lifting of sanctions in return for peace, added to the division of the opposition and the usual fraud, the Socialists increased their representation, but fell short of an absolute majority. This time round, the democratic opposition parties totalled more than twice as many deputies as the Radicals.

Milošević could get away with his shifts because of his control of the power apparatus, his ability to interpret information, his manipulation of parties, and the fact that he rarely spoke in public. The army had been purged and starved of funds, and its 43,000 unwilling conscripts were considered suspect. The police were more trusted and consequently more favoured. Their strength was built up to 50,000, and in the end perhaps 100,000.

Far from the war, Belgrade was still something of a cultural oasis. Milošević had tolerated the intelligentsia's free but low-circulation press. The war and sanctions helped the government to restore control by cutting alternative sources of information, making print prohibitively expensive, and alleging that improper privatization had been permitted. Such manipulation was facilitated by the collapse into poverty. It has been calculated that between 1992 and 1993, prices in the FRY went up by 116,549,906,563,330 per cent.[11] At its highest, in January 1994, the monthly price rise had reached 313,563,558 per cent.[12] A few thousand dollar millionaires benefited from an underground economy based on sanctions-running and war profiteering. They had links, direct and indirect, with the ruling party, but also to a lesser degree with other parties, all of which needed funds, and particularly with the Yugoslav United Left. The YUL had been created as an

---

[11]Constantine P. Danopoulos and Emilia Ianeva, 'Poverty in the Balkans and the Issue of Reconstruction. Bulgaria and Yugoslavia Compared', *Journal of Southern Europe and the Balkans*, I, 1999, 190, quoting the Belgrade Economics Institute's *Human Development Report: Yugoslavia 1997*, 27. Whereas the combined gross natural product of all the republics of the one-time SFRY had fallen, in millions of 1987 US$, from 60,508 in 1990 to 34,230 in 1994, the FRY's alone that year was 10,300 (*ibid.*).

[12]Mladjan Dinkić, *Ekonomija destrukcije. Velika pljačka naroda* (The Economics of Destruction. The Great Robbery of the People), Belgrade: VIN, 1995, 328 and Table II.

Serbia in darkness—the Milošević years

alternative party of the Left, both anti-nationalist and anti-Western, and was a vehicle for the rising influence of Milošević's wife, Mira Marković, Egeria of the retired generals who dreamed of a return to old-style Yugoslav Communism.

The situation changed drastically over the summer of 1995. Strengthened by informal American help, the Croatian army wrested back most of the Serb-held territories, and ethnic Serbs fled. Croatian and Bosnian government forces, with the help of NATO bombardment, went on to reduce the territory held by the Bosnian Serbs to the 49 per cent envisaged by the peace plan. The fighting stopped, and the RS leadership mandated Milošević to negotiate the settlement. At the conference held in November 1995 at Dayton, Ohio, American mediators locked him in conclave with Bosnian President Izetbegović and Croatian President Tudjman until everything had been ironed out. Thus ended the rôle that Milošević had wanted to play as protector of the western Serbs. In exchange he had been made to appear as the man the West could do business with.

The peace formally signed in Paris on 14 December reaffirmed the existence of Bosnia and Herzegovina with a complicated central government, while acknowledging its two 'entities' of the Croat-Bosniac (the officialized term for the Muslim side) Federation, or Federation of Bosnia and Herzegovina, and the Republika Srpska. Implementation would be overseen by a NATO force of 60,000 and a UN high representative.

Milošević was keen to emphasize that a new chapter had started. Dragoslav Avramović (1920–2001), a seventy-five-year-old retired World Bank economist appointed governor of the National Bank, launched a programme of financial stabilization, based on a heavy new dinar issue, backed by the hard currency reserves and pegged to the German mark. Inflation was stopped and confidence restored, and Avramović was hailed as a superstar, but for him, this was only the first stage of a wider reform to be put into effect as soon as sanctions were lifted. He opposed the printing of more money, faced increasing criticism, and was dismissed in May 1996. With his forced departure, what credibility he had brought to the government collapsed.

Federal and local elections were due in November. Milošević set up a coalition of the Left which gave added weight to YUL, and redrew constituencies to dilute urban areas. The opposition managed a formal alliance. After a violent campaign, the government secured a comfortable majority in the federal elections. However, local elections placed the opposition ahead in all of Serbia's bigger towns.

As the electoral commission attempted to block the results, Belgraders started a series of peaceful protest rallies, mirrored in other cities. During three months there were daily sorties of 10–30,000, peaking at several hundred thousand on the old-style Christmas Eve. They had the support of a wide range of personalities, as was shown in an appeal by thirty members of the Academy and a public address by Ćosić. The church, shaken by disputes after Dayton—some bishops going so far as to attack their patriarch—condemned the falsification of the vote.

After a media blockade, the authorities launched a campaign to discredit the protests, but an organized counter-rally of the 'silent majority' failed miserably. Signs of dissension appeared within the ruling establishment and even in the officer corps. General Momčilo Perišić, chief of staff since the 1993 purge, declared cryptically that the army would not deviate from its constitutional rôle. An OSCE delegation came, and decided that the opposition had indeed won the contested elections.

The régime was shaken. The federal government first rejected the OSCE findings, but the Serbian government acknowledged that the opposition had won control of Niš, inner Serbia's second town. A 'special law' was then rushed through to accept the OSCE recommendations. Belgrade's new city council elected Djindjić mayor: The opposition had thus obtained civic power, but it had to grapple with lack of resources, government hostility and internal splits.

Having served the maximum of two terms as president of Serbia, Milošević moved to the federal presidency in July 1997, the personality cult making up for the largely ceremonial nature of his new position. The September elections in Serbia turned into a confrontation between Vuk Drašković and Zoran Djindjić. The former considered himself leader of the opposition. Although treated as such by Milošević, he was aware of the Democrats' growth in strength and of their leader's enhanced international reputation. Djindjić was reluctant to give Drašković unequivocal support; the Democrats and others decided to boycott the elections.

It was Šešelj who benefited from the damage done by the opposition to the credibility of the régime. The Left coalition lost its majority. In the presidential election Milošević's stooge Lilić, who should have swapped presidency with his boss, failed to get 50 per cent. In a second round an upbeat Šešelj obtained 49.98 to a shaken Lilić's 46.99, but it luckily turned out that participation had been just below the required 50 per cent minimum. The exercise had to be repeated. This time voting was found to be just above the limit, and Milošević's new candidate, Milutin Milutinović, became president of Serbia with 59.7.

The end of the war in Bosnia caused a political struggle in the Serbs' leadership there, between Karadžić, and a more co-operative faction whom the powers favoured. Drawing in actors from Serbia and the UN high representative, it involved television, the police, the army command and business interests. The official SDS lost its overall majority. In January 1998 Milorad Dodik, a businessman who had belonged to Marković's Reformists and led a handful of independents, eventually formed a government with support from the West, the high representative and the deputies of absentee Muslim voters. Nationalist parties remained, although adopting a more moderate tone. At the September 2000 elections, the SDS remained the largest party, still commanding 41 per cent of votes in the RS. Karadžić was not arrested, for fear of destabilizing the peace.

Montenegro had also seen an increasingly bitter struggle within its ruling Socialists. By mid-1997 President Bulatović and his prime minister Djukanović had split over control of party structures and sources of patronage. They both stood for president in October. Djukanović, one-time Milošević apparatchik who had acquired the image of a modernizer, appealed to the young, the urban dwellers and the educated; he also made gestures to Montenegrin nationalists, Muslims and Albanians. Bulatović stressed the brotherhood of Montenegro and Serbia; he appealed to the rural world and to industrial workers, denounced the new rich, and had strong support in the north of the republic

In the first round he obtained 147,609 votes to Djukanović's 145,377, but since neither had 50 per cent there was a second ballot, with inverted results. Djukanović won 174,745 to Bulatović's 169,257. Bulatović alleged fraud, the army remained neutral, and Djukanović took over in January 1998. Montenegro was no longer considered a mere adjunct to Serbia. As he had done against Slovenia in 1990, Milošević imposed a trade embargo against Montenegro, which was kept afloat by Western support.

Milošević tried to repair his battered power structure. He took over Bulatović, the defeated president of Montenegro, to be federal prime minister. He negotiated with Drašković. He brought in economic liberalizers to carry out the sale of a major share in telecommunications to Italian and Greek companies. However, Drašković's credibility was undermined when he took over control of Belgrade by turning against Djindjić with support from Socialists and Radicals.

The Socialist Party was heir to the League of Communists, and there was still no separation between state and party. It used both leftist and nationalist arguments in varying proportions. Since it determined the conditions under which elections were held, opposition parties hesitated between participation and boycott. They were divided, they had no solid institutional or ideological framework, and their resources were haphazard. They were hampered by authoritarian movements contemptuous of democracy who put down roots among the alienated and the dispossessed, and by the poor integration of ethnic minorities into public life.

Ethnic Albanians had withdrawn completely, allowing the return of pro-government Serb deputies for Kosovo. The strategy pursued there by Rugova had been to ignore the state apparatus, and to develop a parallel underground structure which the powers would eventually acknowledge. It played into the hands of the régime, who felt it could ignore its Albanian population, and made negotiation with the Serbian opposition difficult.

Dayton put an end to this delicate equilibrium as Albanian activists turned to insurrection. Early in 1998 Serbia and the world discovered that Kosovo was in a state of classic insurgency. Guerrillas of the Kosovo Liberation Army (KLA) mounted ambushes; security forces retaliated massively against villages deemed to be controlled by the insurgents. The United States had informally backed the KLA in order to destabilize Milošević. Then, fearing that the violence might spill out of Kosovo, the powers tried to mediate. They obtained truces, and sent in unarmed observers. They put pressure on Milošević to negotiate, but found difficulty in getting a team to represent the whole spectrum of Kosovo Albanian opinion.

In February 1999 the Americans got together a conference at Rambouillet, a French presidential residence, which they hoped to be a Dayton for Kosovo. A peace plan was put to the FRY and Kosovo Albanian delegations. Kosovo was to be self-governing and demilitarized within the FRY, and a NATO-led force would ensure implementation. If the Albanians failed to sign, they would be left to the mercy of Serbian retaliation; if the Serbs failed to sign, they would be bombed. Milošević, who was not at the conference, refused to accept NATO forces, and the hitherto unknown twenty-nine-year-old KLA leader

Serbia in darkness—the Milošević years

Hashim Thaçi refused to give up the principle of independence. Albanian acceptance was subsequently obtained with the promise of a review after three years.

Opinion in the FRY was exhausted and divided. In spite of strong links with Serbia, Montenegro disliked being taken for granted. The successive waves of immigrants into Serbia—from Tito's partisans in the late 1940s, through the steady trickle of newcomers since the 1970s, to the mass of refugees since 1991—looked up to Milošević, if not to Šešelj, while people with older roots in Serbia tended to regard the hierarchy and oligarchy as the main obstacles to peace. These lines cut across other divisions found all over Eastern Europe, such as town-country, young-old, educated-uneducated. The escalation of hostilities in Kosovo allowed Milošević to turn his back on Drašković, and invite the Radicals to join the Serbian government in March. Šešelj himself became deputy prime minister.

A referendum was hurried through on the question 'Will you accept the participation of foreign representatives in resolving the Kosovo issue?' Foreign mediation was rejected by 95 per cent. Did Milošević want to get rid of Kosovo, a heavy burden and a source of instability? To provoke a foreign intervention would allow him to crush the KLA, yield with honour, obtain a deal, and end a conflict that was weakening his grip on power. In the autumn more repressive measures were introduced to stifle the independent media. There was another purge of military top brass, including General Perišić, chief of the general staff. Tens of thousands of young men were mobilized, often by force. Drašković too was drafted—into the federal government as a powerless deputy prime minister, to placate opposition at home and abroad.

Milošević's obstructionism picked on a clause that gave NATO unrestricted facilities throughout the FRY to monitor implementation. The peace talks collapsed, the observers were withdrawn, and on 24 March NATO launched air bombardments of dubious legality. A state of war was declared in Belgrade, the federal government was given sweeping powers, and diplomatic relations with the participating Western powers were broken off.

As NATO raids started, so did a massive Serbian operation in Kosovo, which destroyed much of the fighting capacity of the KLA, and ejected hundreds of thousands of the local Albanian population. After army-led sealing operations, gangs of thugs moved in to destroy, pillage, kill and generally terrify. Civilians fled to escape from military operations, NATO bombs and Serbian paramilitaries. They fled to the KLA, and they fled out of the province to Albania, Montenegro and Macedonia. The army accompanied them to the borders. In May Milošević and other Yugoslav officials were indicted for war crimes and crimes against humanity.

The bombs that fell on Belgrade caused a psychological shock. They were perceived as being directed against the nation even more than against the régime. They destroyed specific official buildings, and almost destroyed the opposition. Once imprisoned and beaten as its figurehead, Drašković had been enticed into the government. The rest felt as if it had been knifed in the back. Independent figures were silenced by censorship, self-censorship, counterproductive Western appeals, and terror.[13]

The war had been brought to Serbia and to Belgrade for the first time since the break-up of Yugoslavia. Most people heard about Kosovo only what the government chose to tell them. They believed, or chose to believe, that the refugee problem was caused by KLA and NATO action. 'Some people know. Some people don't want to know. Others cannot believe the truth. Others have never heard of it'.[14] Western-leaning people in Belgrade saw NATO as having fallen into Milošević's trap; even they had their doubts about what they heard from Western sources, since NATO propaganda was almost as bad as Milošević's. A paranoid vision had been created according to which the whole world was plotting to destroy the Serbian people. Serbia had become a dark cave in which Milošević used crisis after crisis to prolong his régime.

Although Montenegro was also bombed, its government had not recognized the state of war. The war had exacerbated relations with Serbia, and Djukanović's efforts to distance himself from Milošević were dangerous. Djukanović supporters now wanted a re-negotiation of the federation, if not outright separation. The Bulatović camp increased its pro-Serb patriotism. Montenegro was divided fifty-fifty.

After a month, serious cracks began to appear in Milošević's patriotic defences. There were protests by reservists, opposition militants in provincial cities, independent economists and clerics. Drašković called

---

[13] The journalist Slavko Ćuruvija was murdered on Orthodox Easter Sunday, 14 April. Editor of an independent paper, and once close to the Milošević couple, he had openly denounced their methods.

[14] Robert Fisk in *The Independent* (London), 8 April 1999.

for peace and asked Milošević to resign, and as the result was dismissed from the government. Patriarch Pavle denounced massacres in Kosovo, and was called a traitor. Increasingly isolated, and fearing a ground war that would bring NATO troops all the way to Belgrade, Milošević gave way after seventy-three days of bombardment, and allowed NATO forces into Kosovo. On 3 June he accepted a joint Russo-Western peace plan.

With the backing of a Security Council resolution, Kosovo was confirmed as being under Yugoslav sovereignty, but under an international protectorate and NATO-led occupation. There was no longer any mention of a revision after three years, or of the whole of the FRY being made accessible to foreign troops. Yugoslav troops withdrew apparently intact, having successfully dodged attacks in a war which, paradoxically, caused many civilian casualties and very few military ones.

The war had not brought NATO any glory, and it had been a disaster for Serbia. Milošević presented it as a victory; Yugoslavia's sovereignty over Kosovo had been confirmed by the United Nations, even though his Yugoslavia had shrunk still further. Its infrastructures had been destroyed; it stood accused of endangering the peace of the region; its top officials were accused of war crimes. It was flooded with refugees, and drained of its young brains. Serbia had more refugees than any other country in Europe: 800,000 from Croatia, Bosnia-Herzegovina and Kosovo, for whom help came only from relatives, from the church, channelling aid mostly from Greece, and from Italian Catholic organizations. Over 100,000 highly educated young people had left since 1990.

As Albanian refugees returned to Kosovo, KLA activists and guerrillas inserted themselves in the power vacuum, and Serbs fled the province. They obtained no sympathy—not even in Serbia, where they were barely mentioned by the media, prevented from coming to Belgrade, dispersed, and in some cases even made to return. By mid-October UN officials estimated that of the 200,000 Kosovo Serbs there before the war, at most 40,000 remained. Humanitarian non-governmental agencies put the number at 25,000. The only significant communities left were in the capital Priština and in the divided northern town of Kosovska Mitrovica.

Milošević's surreal campaign to convince Serbia that it had won the war was a fight for political survival. His power had waned. For most people the immediate reaction at the end of the war was relief that it was over. They too wanted to survive. Prices rocketed, *per capita* income had fallen to $900, and half the population of working age were officially unemployed or only fictitiously employed. They had little energy to put up a fight; they feared that the régime would not give up without bloodshed, and they despaired of change. However much many had come to hate Milošević, they also hated NATO and the West generally. They felt betrayed and humiliated.

Dangerous tension had been created between Serbia and Montenegro. Seeing no future in a Yugoslavia that continued to be dominated by Milošević, Djukanović was proposing to redraw the terms of the federation. In October 1999 Montenegro introduced its own citizenship, as well as its own currency: the German mark. It was proud of its press freedom and of its inter-ethnic relations.[15] It provided refuge for Serbian opponents of the Milošević régime, but was reluctant to cooperate fully with them. Djukanović was backed by the West only for his opposition to Milošević. He needed to tread carefully, so as not to risk a war with Serbia, or a civil war in Montenegro. Was Milošević on the verge of giving up the pretence of a multinational FRY in favour of a minimalist Serbia, which would mean getting rid of Montenegro after having been relieved of Kosovo?

The opposition in Serbia began to reassert itself as soon as the state of war was lifted. Demands were made for Milošević's resignation, a government of national salvation, a government of experts, elections monitored by the OSCE, full co-operation with Montenegro. Ordinary people blamed Milošević and his maniac lieutenants for a series of disastrous wars that had brought shame on Serbia. Protests were voiced through a series of anti-government rallies in provincial towns, a petition to remove Milošević which collected 400,000 signatures, and an opposition rally in Belgrade on 19 August, the Feast of the Transfiguration, which 100–200,000 demonstrators attended.

But the protests limped. Both the government and Drašković warned of the dangers of civil war. As the official media lashed out at NATO-paid opponents, Drašković insisted on a compromise over transition. He too had a lot to lose: Belgrade city hall, its business opportunities, a television station—all held on sufferance. Conspiracy

---

[15]Montenegrins make up 61.86 per cent of the population (380,000/615,000), followed by 90,000 Muslims, 57,000 Serbs, 40,000 Albanians, 26,000 Yugoslavs.

theories abounded about NATO and Milošević working together. Milošević exploited the splits in the opposition, and showed his willingness to use force. People braced themselves for a winter of cuts and shortages, even of hunger and civil unrest.

Nevertheless, the opposition parties continued to negotiate a formalized election alliance, so as to be ready for the end of Milošević's mandate in July 2001. Round-table meetings had started in October 1999. By the summer the Democratic Opposition of Serbia (DOS) gathered eighteen parties around the larger Democratic Party. Drašković's SPO remained apart. In July Milošević amended the federal constitution to enable the president and the upper house to be chosen by direct election. Montenegro had not been consulted; it refused to recognize the changes, because the one-man-one-vote principle in effect reduced its equality with Serbia. The separatist tendency in the sister republic was reinforced, yet the Montenegrin parliament was sharply divided.

Milošević had decided to act quickly, while he still could, before another winter and before people woke up. Elections were called for 24 September, for the federal president, the federal parliament, the provincial assembly of Voivodina, and local councils in Serbia. Montenegro decided on a boycott, and so did Drašković.

A series of unsolved murders of various well-known figures (including shady business barons and police bosses) had culminated in January and February with the killing of Arkan and of Milošević's defence minister. They spread fear, even though they could be explained by the links between the régime and the underground economy. Even more frightening was the mysterious disappearance in August of Ivan Stambolić, Milošević's predecessor as president of Serbia. An undeclared state of emergency had been introduced, through more controls on the universities and the media, the arrest of journalists, a proposed law against terrorism, and the wild threats pronounced by Šešelj (who, in addition to his other posts, had obtained a chair at Belgrade's Law Faculty).

Since the end of the war with NATO, Milošević was increasingly enclosed in an unreal world. He spoke of Serbia defending its freedom against fascism, of standing up against the threat to humanity of American-led globalization. He received loyal delegations from Kosovo and Montenegro. He staged a war crimes trial in Belgrade of US, British, French and German presidents and ministers, and NATO personalities

The opposition parties coalesced in the DOS were working hard to overcome their divided image. Their election headquarters studied opinion surveys. As their leaders met in Montenegro to decide on a joint candidate, and nominated Koštunica, the leader of the small Democratic Party of Serbia, Drašković once again changed his mind. He would take part after all, but separately, and he nominated as the SPO's candidate the unknown person he had made mayor of Belgrade: Vojislav Mihailović, grandson of General Mihailović.

A one-time academic lawyer, Koštunica was no populist figurehead but the leader of a small secessionist fragment of the Democrats. He was 'above board' and respected. In the West he would have been a conservative. In Serbia, that meant nostalgia for a better past. Foreign journalists described him as a 'moderate nationalist', but he was hardly more so than most West European politicians, and less so than quite a number of Western conservatives. He had stood up for the interests of ethnic Serbs left outside Serbia, and had criticized Western attitudes. Surveys indicated that he could take votes from the ruling parties and from the nationalist right. Djindjić's party was the butt of accusations of being in NATO's pocket; he had sought refuge in Montenegro during the war. His stepping aside in favour of a defector from his own party was a shrewd move, even though he and his Democratic Party organization had been the backbone of the protest movement. The election to the post of federal president would signal the end of Milošević's bogus and corrupt multiparty system.

This time the opposition was well prepared. It had mustered 20,000 election monitors, and worked closely with the student movement Otpor, which spread the good word to their families and friends in the interior. Milošević ran the election as a referendum on whether the FRY would remain an independent state or become a colony of the West. The Montenegrin boycott ensured that the Montenegrin seats would go to Milošević, and the same could be said of Kosovo, and of absentee ethnic Albanian voters in southern inner Serbia. Hundreds of thousands of fake ballot papers were prepared to stuff the boxes. Lists were drawn up of opposition politicians to be assassinated if necessary. Western support for democratic non-governmental organizations, along with the promise to lift sanctions, could backfire dangerously.

The régime had not expected the extent to which, on 24 September 2000, people went out to vote an end to the years of pauperization, hopelessness, violence, corruption, shame and criminalization, and an end to the enmity of the outside world. The economic decline was such that all were convinced the country would hit rock-bottom unless Milošević went. They could bear it no longer. The Federal Electoral Commission stopped announcing results after receiving the votes of the armed forces and police, when it was realized that even they had not voted for Milošević. By that time both sides claimed victory on the basis of 30 per cent of votes. The commission eventually released final results after four days—Koštunica led with 48.96 per cent but since he had not obtained 50 per cent, there had to be a second round.

However the DOS claimed a decisive victory, and adamantly refused a second round. General Nebojša Pavković, chief of the general staff, who is alleged to have warned NATO before the bombing that he would settle accounts with the Albanians, had said on the eve of the election that the army would prevent any attempt to take power by force in the streets. This was now switched to a statement that the army would accept Koštunica if he turned out to be the winner.

Šešelj and Drašković, both of whom had suffered a terrible drubbing at the elections, hurried to congratulate Koštunica. Several leading members of the Socialist Party resigned. The DOS called for civil disobedience, and the church called on Milošević to go. Protesters went out to vent their anger against him. Miners and other industrial workers stopped work, and there were strikes in the official media. Milošević raged against an opposition that was manipulated by the West. The DOS called on people to defect before it was too late. Contacts were established—with the strikers, the police and the army. The federal prime minister, police chiefs, the army command—all defected one after the other.

Finally, on 5 October more than a million people seized central Belgrade, terrifying the police, sacking the television building and the parliament. There was no bloodshed.[16] The Constitutional Court, which had first annulled the elections, ruled in favour of Vojislav Koštunica on 6 October, and he was declared elected with 50.24

[16]There were a couple of accidental deaths, and there was vandalism at the federal parliament. A fine work of interwar architecture, it housed a collection of works of art commissioned from Yugoslav artists of the 1930s to decorate the new building. It also had a rich library of official publications dating back to the beginnings of the Serbian state, untouched by bombardments, liberations and revolutions, until over-zealous opposition bouncers reacted to the tear-gas barrage of frightened policemen, and stormed the building. An appeal has been launched in March 2001 for funds to restore the building.

per cent of the vote.[17] After General Pavković and the Russian foreign minister had been to see him, Milošević publicly admitted defeat, and congratulated Koštunica.[18] The darkness of the Milošević era was over.

[17]The final official results were: Koštunica 50.24 per cent (2,470,304 votes), Milošević 37.15 (1,826,799), the Radical candidate 5.88 (289,013), the SPO candidate 2.95 (145,019)
[18]The DOS did not obtain an absolute majority in the federal parliament, where it had to rely on support from Bulatović's Socialist National Party of Montenegro, which had obtained the votes of 25 per cent of the Montenegrin electorate. In the Serbian parliamentary elections held subsequently (23 December) the DOS won 64 per cent of the vote, giving it 176/250 seats.

CONCLUSION
A PLEA FOR SAINT GUY

The battle of Kosovo in 1389 was fought not between a Serbian and a Turkish army, but between two feudal leagues of no clear ethnic loyalty. 'States' were not 'nations' in the fourteenth century, and they were hardly states; they were identified with ruling houses. Medieval Serbia was the polity of the Nemanjić rulers, and had no fixed capital or borders. Its rulers sought to play an independent rôle; their dominions were a bridge between East and West. The realm broke up in the fourteenth century—a period of great catastrophes, seen by many throughout Europe as signs that God was looking away from His creation.

Medieval Serbia moved on to a period of transition to, and incorporation into, the Ottoman order. It entered the early modern period as part of a flexible march between Ottoman, Habsburg and Venetian dominions. Its population was on the move, accompanied by the church—the only surviving Nemanjić institution—which had made saints of its rulers.

Serbia once again became more than a memory perpetuated by church and folklore, as it entered the later modern era with the risings of the early nineteenth century. They were the result of millenarian expectations sharpened by location and circumstances, rather than the outcome of revolutionary thinking; yet they were the first of the 'national' revolutionary outbreaks against imperial rule in the Balkans. They demarcated a patch of land in which the memory of Serbia could take root. Struggling to establish its autonomy and its independence, Serbia was a territory characterized by mobility of settlement. Its inhabitants came from all sides, attracted by the prospect of a better life—available land, a more ordered government, trade, and employment.

Its rulers generally had a sense of political realities, both regional and international. They knew that they could not achieve much on their own. Their envisaged thrust of expansion varied in time, and was motivated principally by the needs of the state. Its urban élite thought of Serbia in geopolitical terms—as positioned between the Ottoman empire and the Habsburg monarchy—more than with romantic ideas of a national rebirth. Serbia's identity was imagined primarily in opposition to the interacting forces of its two external enemies—Turkey and Austria.

The idea of language-based identity tended to come from Serbian and other South Slav intellectuals outside Serbia. Serbian folk ballads were songs of love, war and death, and of man's links to God, transmitted orally from generation to generation. They perpetuated a memory that blended the real with the unreal, overflowed the banks of chronology, and connected the present to the past. In this they were not unique.

Nineteenth-century Serbia attained a high degree of ethnic homogeneity through the inflow of Serbs from neighbouring lands still under imperial rule, and the expulsion or emigration of Turks from newly-acquired territories. The élite were influenced by the pattern of a single directly-elected national representation bequeathed by the Revolution of 1789 to the French-inspired model of the political nation. With the blend of ethnic homogeneity, German ideas about the linguistic expression of the nation, and French conceptions of national representation, it was difficult for Serbia to accept that other Southern Slavs might have a different historical and political culture, hence the tendency to regard them as falling easily within Serbia's project.

Serbs understood nothing of the cherished myths that shrouded the origins of *ancien régime* 'state rights', the estates, *parlements* and sovereign courts that were meant to keep the privileges of a *pays*, realm or other entity, even if they did not challenge the ruler's right to make general policy for all his dominions. Croatia shared that tradition with many other historic lands, from Brittany and Provence to Poland and Hungary. Serbia did not grasp that on entering Yugoslavia it was entering a new and complex community.

There was no real compromise between the contrasting experiences of the state that Serbia and Croatia had known. Croats talked of federalism when their aim was to improve the 'rights' of Croatia in the new state called Yugoslavia; Serbs talked of centralism when they wanted to keep the state apparatus. But such generalizations are misleading, for not all Serbs saw eye to eye on the organization and running of the Yugoslav state.

If Croatian intellectuals invented the idea of Yugoslavia based on cultural postulates, Serbia's political leaders were instrumental in turning it into a territorial and political reality. It is often argued nowadays in post-Yugoslav Serbia that a victorious Serbia should have gone for a 'greater Serbia' at the end of the First World War, as Romania went for a greater Romania, forgetting that it could have replicated the disaster of the Greek 'Great Idea'. The fact remains that Serbia's leaders, for motives of realism and idealism (probably more realism than idealism), went for Yugoslavia.

Whatever its different postulates, Yugoslavia was the most imaginative political idea to come out of, and be implemented in, Eastern Europe. It signalled an inflection in the trend of the endless invention of ethnic states based on a strict interpretation of linguistic and religious unity, moulded by primary school, parish church and military service. But it was badly implemented by politicians whose imagination did not reach to the height of what they had created.

Serbs, who thought of themselves as the politically leading element, were willing to dissolve their identity in the broader concept of Yugoslavia. With King Alexander they even accepted an officialized and counterproductive 'integral' Yugoslav identity. Most did not, could not or would not see that the broader identity was not to the liking of all their Yugoslav compatriots. They did not even realize all that it implied for themselves.

Hitler's destruction of Yugoslavia, with his and his Ustasha imitators' anti-Serbian obsession, was a traumatic experience. The 1941 risings, however, brought new glory to the Serbs, accompanied by a civil war between Serbian insurgents. The outcome was the rise to power of the Communist Party, which restored Yugoslavia. The Communists were internationalist revolutionaries. Yugoslav-minded, they actually wanted a greater Yugoslavia. They were obviously not nationalists. Nevertheless, their utopian scheme for solving Yugoslavia's national question probably contributed more than any other factor to promoting sectarian nationalism.

Communism did not so much repress as instrumentalize nationalism. The Titoist system denied legitimacy to any alternative way of dealing with the accumulating problems of economy, society and politics. As Communism lost its magic, nationalism took over; throughout Eastern

Europe in transition it was the political idea that gathered the greatest number of supporters: most people could be made to expect something of it.

Paradoxically, the East European country that had come to experience the least repressive form of Communism went on to experience the most bloody exit from it as it disintegrated. Yugoslavs had escaped the poverty of Soviet-type socialism without having to go through the daily rigours of capitalism. They were told they were on the way to achieving a perfect society. They were—subsidized to remain on the fence between East and West. They worked little and their standards of living rose. Lulled by the relative comforts and the international fame of Titoism, most of them believed that the national problems of Yugoslavia had been solved by Marxism-Leninism-Titoism.

It was only when the Cold War came to an end, when the glamour faded and with it the relative comfort, and when regional leaderships turned from a policy of 'brotherhood and unity' to one of ethnic confrontation that Serbs noticed the anomalous structure of the republic of Serbia. No other Yugoslav republic had autonomous territories within it, even though roughly similar conditions could be found in other federated units.[1] They noticed that there had been further shifts of Serbian population—away from the south, where pre-1941 settlers had not been allowed to return, to inner Serbia, to Voivodina which had acquired a majority Serbian population as new settlers from Croatia, Bosnia, Herzegovina and elsewhere had taken the place of departed Germans.

The legitimacy of Communist rule needed a simplified and static memory of the People's Liberation Struggle, fixed exclusively on the partisans. The continued cohabitation of Serbs and Croats after the experience of the Ustashas' 'Independent State of Croatia' also required that people should not delve into the attempted genocide. It is not true that the memory of it was suppressed; there was a certain amount of academic research which produced sound monographs, but there was no public debate, and no discussion of responsibility beyond the generalized 'fascist' scapegoat.

The gaps and inconsistencies that lurked under that veil were partly filled in by secret stories, for the benefit of those who wanted

---

[1] The compactly Serbian areas of Croatia; Istria, with its transitional Slovenian-Croatian-Italian character; Dalmatia, which had a very different history from the rest of Croatia; Dubrovnik, for centuries an independent republic; and western Macedonia, with its Albanian population.

Conclusion: A plea for Saint Guy   231

to remember and those who wanted to listen. They emerged gradually as the Communist Party lost its monopoly of public discourse and its control over memory. The immediate causes of the wars that accompanied the crisis of the Yugoslav succession are to be found in the revelation by all sides of the horrors committed during the Second World War by 'them' against 'us'. Their memory was misused to ignite the Serbo-Croatian controversies of the 1980s.

Most Serbs did not believe that Yugoslavia would break up. The dominant tendency among them was still that they somehow had to be leaders in its governance, having given so much for the common Yugoslav cause. Yugoslavia was anyway vital for them because it kept all Serbs united in one state, but they still did not understand that compromise, not rhetoric or force, was the essential condition for its survival after the Cold War and the death of Communism.

As public opinion throughout Yugoslavia emerged from forty years of brainwashing, it was pounced upon by the worst remnants of Tito's power structure. This time they brainwashed their respective communities into believing that they had to get rid of others in order to survive. Some men of letters, followed by a few respected historians, adopted once again the language of romantic nineteenth-century nationalism. The fragmented and selective national memory left many gaps that could be manipulated at a time of crisis.

When all else collapses, people turn to whatever gives them a collective identity. The euphoria that followed on 1989 led many Serbs to believe that Serbia would become a 'state' on a par with all the other republics, that the battle *for* Kosovo had been won, and that the way was open for all Serbs to be unified, as they had been in a distant golden age before the battle *of* Kosovo. The outcome turned out to be the disappearance of Yugoslavia, the Serbs' dispersal in a number of successor-states, and a series of military defeats.

To cope with this conjuncture Serbia would have needed a leader with the stature and vision of Charles de Gaulle—a personality who could understand, and convince his compatriots, that in order to tackle the problems posed by the Serbs' dispersal over a disintegrated Yugoslavia, Serbia had to get rid of the burden of Kosovo. What it had was Slobodan Milošević, an offspring of Tito's regional bureaucracy, an apparatchik of the socialist feudalism that had destroyed the Yugoslav idea even before it destroyed the state. Milošević's project had no consistency beyond holding on to power. Whereas in Kosovo in 1987 he was still issuing Communist warnings against nationalists, he was in fact already wanting to turn the clock back to before the constitutional changes of 1966–74, to give Serbia more power over its provinces and to rebuild the Yugoslav federation.

After the failure of the last Party congress, and the elections in Slovenia and Croatia, Milošević wanted to get rid of the two northern republics and keep the rest, along with the Serbian districts of Croatia. He never announced it in so many words, and later turned his back on the Serbs of Croatia. When the Dayton conference ended the territorial war in Bosnia he strutted as a man of peace, convinced that he was ensconced in his Serbo-Montenegrin rump Yugoslavia, and that his party would be unbeatable in elections for the next twenty years.[2] He may later even have contemplated more contractions (Kosovo? Montenegro?).

He was able to play on confused and contradictory Serbian ideas about Yugoslavia, and about Serbia too. At one level Serbs still identified with Yugoslavia, which they thought worth fighting for. At another they had come to view the creation of Yugoslavia as a great historical mistake that had robbed them of their identity and broken their back. Between 1991 and 1995, demagogues were able to mobilize opinion around mystical conceptions of a 'Serbia' that stretched over historic sites, holy places and mass graves, while few people actually wanted to go and live in Kosovo. Milošević also moved between ethnicity, historicism and populism, backwards and forwards between Left and Right as he manipulated electoral and parliamentary alliances—but always more Left than Right.

If Serbia's leaders had done more than anyone else for the unification of Yugoslavia in 1918, so they contributed more than anyone else to its destruction in 1991. Neither lot realized how different the outcome would be from what their limited imagination had envisaged. Pašić had no vision, but he knew something about international relations. Milošević had no imagination, and no understanding of international relations either.

As the final crisis came over Kosovo, Milošević gambled. Mixed arguments were thrown around in desperation—national identity, state sovereignty, religious faith, anti-capitalism, anti-imperialism, anti-globalism. All these half-baked ideas moved around the intellectual desert that had been created by the régime. They were peddled to public opinion by Socialist Party hacks, by Milošević's extreme Left-

---

[2]Milošević is alleged to have told Borisav Jović so, in the course of his last conversation with the penultimate president of the SFRY in September 1995 (*NIN*, 19 October 2000).

and extreme Right-wing partners, by once scholarly and now deranged academicians, and by churchmen who dreamed of dragging the faithful back into an imagined past. Public opinion came to feel that its nation, its country, its culture were threatened by the combined forces of the New World Order, whatever that was.

Blaming the West was better than blaming the rulers. In that Milošević behaved like the Chinese Dowager Empress Cixi at the time of the Boxer rebellion. The feeling of victimization notwithstanding, people came to realize they were held hostage by Milošević. His rule collapsed under the weight of its own contradictions. He had come to be perceived as a greater threat than the international community. Serbia saw that it was alone and in ruins. Milošević was toppled, but resentment against the West remained.

It remained not only in the manipulated mass of the uneducated and unemployed. It also remained among the educated and among those who knew the West. They were conscious of the depth of generalized anti-Serbian feelings, of the responsibility that was placed on Serbia for all that had happened in Yugoslavia, of the wish to inflict collective punishment. Serbia had become the 'sick man of Europe', and the Serbs a faceless people with the mask of Slobodan Milošević. Many of the educated felt that after the collapse of Communist values, which had brought them nothing but misery, they were experiencing the collapse of Western values, to which they had aspired.

The elimination of one individual has removed the greatest obstacle, but it does not by itself solve Serbia's problems. The Milošević years have pulverized society, destroyed the economy, polluted the space necessary for critical thought, and almost reduced religion to a cover for xenophobia. The autism of the régime has spread to the population at large.

The Hungarian historian Jenö Szücs[3] distinguishes the fortunate Europeans, who commemorate glorious events, from the unfortunate ones, who remember catastrophes. Roughly at the same time of year as the Serbs recall Vidovdan (28 June), the French celebrate the storming of the Bastille (14 July).

In 1989 France, with the world at large, extolled the bicentenary of the French Revolution. What was praised was not the Terror, not the dictatorship of the Committee of Public Safety, not the Vendée war, but the year 1789, the end of institutionalized privilege (symbolized

---

[3]French edition, *Les Trois Europes*, Paris: L'Harmattan, 1985.

by the demolition of the Bastille), the sovereignty of the nation as a body politic expressed through its elected representatives, and the Declaration of the Rights of Man and of the Citizen, which marked the dawn of a new era. Meanwhile Serbia with the Serbs everywhere observed the sexcentenary of the battle of Kosovo, the defeat of 1389 which symbolized the threshold of a dark age.

One of the differences between the fortunate part of Europe and its unfortunate counterpart, as analysed by Szücs, is that the development of the former through cumulative changes enabled its structures to outgrow themselves to the point where nation came to coincide with state and with democracy. In Eastern Europe, there was disjunction between state and nation. Therein another Hungarian, the political philosopher István Bibó,[4] saw the causes of these nations' structural imbalances, or what he called their 'hysterias'—the collective fears following on traumatic historical experiences.

The nations of Eastern Europe have come to consciousness in a structureless environment, in transitional zones across empires, where linguistic and religious borders are blurred. They have felt the need to fortify their identities without regard to consequences, and they are weighed down by the fear of foreign powers as missionaries only marginally less than as conquerors.

Greece's disastrous attempt to extend itself across the Aegean, to the Orthodox populations of Asia Minor, ended with the catastrophe of 1922, which had a sobering effect on the perceived dignity of Greek nationalism. In attempting to spread out in the Balkans on three occasions—in 1913, 1915 and 1941, over populations perceived as kith and kin—Bulgaria found itself on the losing side, and has learned the lesson. Serbian nationalism has suffered, but psychologically it had always been victorious. It had fought in two world wars alongside winning coalitions; it had inserted itself in the search for a wider identity. Only when the wider yet misunderstood political visions collapsed did Serbia's legends, the stuff of an existence battling with itself, become dangerous drugs in the hands of manipulators, who led Serbian nationalism into a decade of disasters that culminated in the war waged by NATO against Serbia.

Serbia now wants to end its isolation, and to become a 'normal' European country. To do so it has to overcome the recent past, and the

[4]Second French edition, *Misère des petits Etats de l'Europe de l'Est*, Paris: Albin Michel, 1993.

Conclusion: A plea for Saint Guy

price for doing so will be great. The problems are huge. At the most basic level there are reconstruction, monetary reform, the settlement of refugees, legality and law enforcement. At a different level is the very question of Serbia's identity. On paper Kosovo is still part of Serbia. Serbia will come to terms with the fact that it can live without it, whatever irresponsible poets said. It may be able to negotiate a deal for the dwindling Serbian community there and a status to protect those monasteries and churches that are Serbian holy places, as well as a part of Europe's artistic heritage. Serbia will also have to negotiate the nature of its relations with the Bosnian Serb entity.

Montenegro has been linked to Serbia by history, and it is constitutionally linked to Serbia in the Federal Republic of Yugoslavia. Its historical identity started from its geography, and was strengthened through the theocracy that capped its hitherto warring clans. At a popular and mythical level, Montenegro had come to define itself as being made up of those Serbs who had never ceased to fight the Turks. Its aim had been to unite with Serbia, which it did in 1918. Now after after years of being told, within Communist Yugoslavia's complicated and ever-evolving constitutional framework, that Montenegro is a different nation, with a sovereign home base, a substantial part of the population has come to believe it. The attitude adopted by the Milošević régime after the scission within Montenegro's ruling Socialists, and the support provided to the Djukanović government from abroad to enable it to stand up to Milošević, have further widened the rift with Serbia. Does Montenegro want to go its independent way? Can it exist on its own, without becoming some power's pensioner? Can Serbia and Montenegro negotiate a new union, perhaps by going back to where they had been interrupted by the First World War?

If they do, to what extent can it still be a 'Yugoslav' union? Milošević's FRY was a simulation of Yugoslavia. A two-unit federation between a Milošević-ruled Serbia, with its population of 9 million, and a half-million-strong Montenegro, was certain to be difficult. In principle the name Yugoslavia could be kept even after Slovenia, Croatia, Bosnia-Herzegovina and Macedonia had left, as the Netherlands continued to be so called even without Belgium and Luxembourg. The trouble is that Yugoslavia is an ethnic and not a territorial name, and most of the Southern Slavs now live outside what is left of Yugoslavia.

Nationalism is no programme, and there is incompatibility between nationalism and democracy. This is beginning to be understood, both in Serbia and by the politicians of the interested powers who long equated self-determination with democracy, supporting some nationalisms against others. A new generation will have to start everything afresh, to acknowledge the harm done to others, to negotiate new links and generally to look to, and work for, the future.

In 1989, when they would have done better to look back to the 'principles of 1789' in order to find a way out of the mess of the Titoist inheritance, the Serbs marked the sixth centenary of the battle lost on the field of Kosovo. In doing so they were pushed into the darkness of the Milošević years. That period came to an end on 5 October 2000. On that day, according to the old-style calendar, the Orthodox church remembers the Holy Prophet Jonah, the one who had been swallowed by a big fish, and who spent three days and three nights in its belly.

Saint Guy—he of Vidovdan, 15/28 June, and known as Vitus in Latin, Guido in Italian, Vid in Slavonic languages—was a third-century martyr from southern Italy. He is invoked as the patron of those who suffer from epilepsy and nervous disorders, and from the bites of mad dogs and snakes. Through no fault of his own, he has been burdened for too long with the fate of Serbia. Few Serbs even knew that he could help with nervous disorders and the bites of mad dogs. And they had forgotten that they had once believed he could help them see better. It is time to release him from his bondage. The Prophet Jonah can take over. On his day Serbia emerged from the years spent in the belly of the Milošević régime. It is free to face its problems in stark daylight.

BIBLIOGRAPHY

What follows is a very personal bibliography—a catalogue of those books and articles, old and new, that the author has read or read again in the course of preparing this book, and where he has found elements that have helped him to understand what he was doing.

Alender, Branislava, (ed.), *Jugoslavija i svet 2000. Prilozi za alternativnu spoljnu politiku*, Belgrade, 2000.

Alexander, Stella, *Church and State in Yugoslavia since 1945*, Cambridge, 1979.

Allcock, John B., *Explaining Yugoslavia*, London, 2000.

Anastasijević, Dejan, with Anthony Borden, *Out of Time. Drašković, Djindjić and Serbian Opposition against Milošević*, London and Belgrade, 2000.

Banac, Ivo, *The National Question in Yugoslavia. Origins, History, Politics*, Ithaca, NY, 1984.

——, *With Stalin against Tito: Cominformist Splits in Yugoslav Communism*, Ithaca, NY, 1989.

Bariéty, Jacques, 'La France et les débuts du Royaume des Serbes, Croates et Slovènes, 1919–1920', *Bulletin de l'Institut d'histoire des relations internationales contemporaines*, 17, 1994.

Bibó, István, *Misère des petits Etats de l'Europe de l'Est*, 2nd French edn, Paris, 1993.

Bjelajac, Mile S., *Vojska Kraljevine SHS, 1918–1921*, Belgrade, 1988.

——, *Vojska Kraljevine SHS/Jugoslavije, 1922–1935*, Belgrade, 1994.

——, *Jugoslovensko iskustvo sa multietničkom armijom, 1918–1991*, Belgrade, 1999.

Bojović, Boško I., *L'Idéologie monarchique dans les hagio-biographies dynastiques du Moyen-Age Serbe*, Rome, 1995.

Bracewell, Catherine Wendy, *The Uskoks of Senj: Piracy, Banditry and Holy War in the Sixteenth-Century Adriatic*, Ithaca, NY, 1992.

Bibliography

Castellan, Georges, *La vie quotidienne en Serbie au seuil de l'indépendance, 1815–1839*, Paris, 1962.
Cioffari, Gerardo, *Gli zar di Serbia, la Puglia e San Nicola*, Bari, 1989.
Cohen, Lenard J., *Serpent in the Bosom. The Rise and Fall of Slobodan Milošević*, New York, 2000.
Ćirković, Sima, *La Serbie au Moyen Age*, Abbaye de la Pierre-qui-Vire, Yonne, 1992.
———, 'Kosovska bitka u medjunarodnom kontekstu', *Glas Srpske akademije nauka i umetnosti*, CCCLXXVIII, 1996.
———, contributions to *Istorija srpskog naroda*.
Čolović, Ivan, 'La religione della nazione serba', *Lettera internazionale*, 15/ 59–60, 1999.
Čubrilović, Vasa, (ed.), *Jugoslovenski narodi pred prvi svetski rat/Les Peuples de Yougoslavie à la veille de la première Guerre mondiale*, Belgrade, 1967.
Dedijer, Vladimir, *The Road to Sarajevo*, London, 1967.
———, *Novi prilozi za biografiju Josipa Broza Tita*, II, Rijeka, 1981.
Dinić, Mihailo, *Srpske zemlje u srednjem veku. Istorijsko-geografske studije*, Belgrade, 1978.
Dinkić, Mladjan, *Ekonomija destrukcije. Velika pljačka naroda*, 2nd edn, Belgrade, 1955.
Dogo, Marco, *Albanesi e Serbi. Le radici del conflitto*, Lungro di Cosenza, 1992.
Duijzings, Ger, et al. (ed.), *Kosovo-Kosova: Confrontation or Coexistence*, Nijmegen, 1996.
Djilas, Aleksa, *The Contested Country: Yugoslav Unity and Communist Revolution, 1919–1953*, Cambridge, MA, 1991.
———, 'A profile of Slobodan Milošević', *Foreign Affairs*, 72/3, 1993.
Djilas, Milovan, *Land without Justice*, New York, 1958.
———, *Njegoš: Poet, Prince, Bishop*, New York, 1966.
———, *Memoir of a Revolutionary*, New York, 1973.
———, *Wartime*, London, 1977.
———, *Rise and Fall*, London, 1983.
Djordjević, Dimitrije, *Milovan Milovanović*, Belgrade, 1962.
———, *Ogledi iz novije balkanske istorije*, Belgrade, 1989.
———, *Ožiljci i opomene*, 3 vols, Belgrade, 1994, 1995 and 2000.
Djukić, Slavoljub, *Slom srpskih intelektualaca*, Belgrade, 1990.
———, *Kako se dogodio vodja. Borba za vlast u Srbiji posle Josipa Broza*, Belgrade, 1992.
———, *Izmedju slave i anateme. Politička biografija Slobodana Miloševića*, Belgrade, 1994.

Emmert, Thomas A., *Serbian Golgotha: Kosovo 1389*, New York, 1990.

Gavrilović, Sima, et al. (eds), *Istorija srpskog naroda*, 6 vols, Belgrade, 1981–3.
Gervereau, Laurent, and Yves Tomic (ed.), *De l'unification à l'éclatement. L'espace yougoslave, un siècle d'histoire*, Paris, 1998.

Bibliography 239

Girault, René, et al., *La Loi des géants*, Paris, 1993.
Gligorijević, Branislav, *Demokratska stranka i politički odnosi u Kraljevini Srba, Hrvata i Slovenaca*, Belgrade, 1970.
Gordy, Eric D., *The Culture of Power in Serbia: Nationalism and the Destruction of Alternatives*, University Park, PA, 1995.
Gow, James, *Legitimacy and the Military: The Yugoslav Crisis*, London, 1991.
Guran, Petre, 'Aspects et rôle du saint dans les nouveaux Etats du Commonwealth byzantin, XIe-XVe siècles', Laurenţiu Vlad (ed.), *Pouvoirs et mentalités. Textes réunis à la mémoire du professeur Alexandru Duţu*, Bucharest, 1999.
Guskova, E.Yu. (ed.), *Yugoslavskiï krizis i Rossiya, 1990–1993*, Moscow, 1993.
Jagodić, Miloš, 'The Emigration of Muslims from the New Serbian Regions, 1871–1878', *Balkanologie*, II/2, 1998.
Jakšić, Grgur, and Vojislav J. Vučković, *Spoljna politika Srbije za vlade kneza Mihaila. Prvi balkanski savez*, Belgrade, 1963.
Janjić, Dušan (ed.), *Serbia between the Past and the Future*, Belgrade, 1995.
Jovanović, Slobodan, *Ustavobranitelji i njihova vlada*, Belgrade, 1912.
———, *Druga vlada Miloša i Mihaila*, Belgrade, 1923.
———, *Vlada Milana Obrenovića*, 2 vols, Belgrade, 1926.
———, *Vlada Aleksandra Obrenovića*, 2 vols, Belgrade, 1929.[1]
Jović, Dejan, 'The Disintegration of Yugoslavia: A Critical Review of Explanatory Approaches', *European Journal of Social Theory*, 4/1, 2001.

Kapidžić-Osmanagić, Hanifa, *Le Surréalisme serbe et ses rapports avec le surréalisme français*, Paris, 1968.
Kitromilides, Paschalis M., 'Orthodox Culture and Collective Identity in the Ottoman Balkans', *Bulletin of the Centre for Asia Minor Studies*, XII, 1998.
Kočović, Bogoljub, *Žrtve drugog svetskog rata u Jugoslaviji*, London, 1985; 2nd edn, Sarajevo, 1990.
———, *Etnički i demografski razvoj u Jugoslaviji od 1921. do 1991. godine*, 2 vols, Paris, 1998.
Koljanin, Milan, *Nemački logor na beogradskom sajmištu, 1941–1944*, Belgrade, 1990.
Kovačević, Novica, *Božićna pobuna u Crnoj Gori 1918*, Belgrade, 1991.
Krizman, Bogdan, *Hrvatska u prvom svjetskom ratu. Hrvatsko-srpski politički odnosi*, Zagreb, 1989.

Lampe, John R., *Yugoslavia as History. Twice There Was a Country*, 2nd edn, Cambridge, 2000.
Lampe, John R., and Marvin R. Jackson, *Balkan Economic History, 1550–1950. From Imperial Borderlands to Developing Nations*, Bloomington, IN, 1982.

---

[1] These have been published again in the new edition of Jovanović's complete works, Belgrade, 1990.

Ljušić, Radoš, *Tumačenje srpske revolucije u istoriografiji 19. i 20. veka*, Belgrade, 1992.
MacKenzie, David, *The Serbs and Russian Pan-Slavism, 1875–1878*, Ithaca, NY, 1967.
———, *Ilija Garašanin, Balkan Bismarck*, New York, 1985.
———, *Apis, The Congenial Conspirator*, New York, 1989.
———, *The 'Black Hand' on Trial. Salonika 1917*, New York, 1995
Manoschek, Walter, *'Serbien ist juden frei'. Militärische Besatzungspolitik und Judenverichtigung in Serbien 1941/42*, Munich, 1993.
Marković, Pedja J., *Beograd i Evropa, 1918–1941. Evropski uticaj na proces modernizacije Beograda*, Belgrade, 1992.
Mastny, Vojtech, *The Cold War and Soviet Insecurity: The Stalin Years*, 1997.
Miller, Nicholas T., *Between Nation and State: Serbian Politics in Croatia before the First World War*, Pittsburgh, PA, 1997.
Milojković-Djurić, Jelena, *Tradition and Avant-Guard. The Arts in Serbian Culture between the Two World Wars*, New York, 1984.
———, Mitrović, Andrej, *Srbija u Prvom svetskom ratu*, Belgrade, 1984.
———, 'Struktura ratnog finansiranja Srbije, 1914–1915', *Tokovi istorije*, 1–2, 2000.
———, contributions to *Istorija srpskog naroda*
Mitrović, Andrej (ed.), *Prekretnice novije srpske istorije*, Kragujevac, 1995.
Mousset, Jean, *La Serbie et son Eglise, 1830–1914*, Paris, 1938.

Nenadović, Aleksandar, *Mirko Tepavac. Sećanja i komentari*, Belgrade, 1998.
Nouzille, Jean, *Histoire de frontières. L'Autriche et l'Empire ottoman*, Paris, 1994.

Pavković, Aleksandar, *Slobodan Jovanović: An Unsentimental Approach to Politics*, New York, 1993.
———, 'From Yugoslavism to Serbism: The Serb National Idea, 1986–1996', *Nations and Nationalisms*, 4/4 1998.
———, *The Fragmentation of Yugoslavia. Nationalism and War in the Balkans*, 2nd edn, London and New York, 2000.
Petković, Ranko (ed.), *1948, Jugoslavija i Kominform. Pedeset godina kasnije*, Belgrade, 1998.
Perović, Latinka, *Srpski socijalisti 19. veka. Prilog istoriji socijalističke misli*, Belgrade, 1995.
Petranović, Branko, *Srbija u Drugom svetskom ratu, 1939–1945*, Belgrade, 1992.
Petrovich, Michael Boro, *A History of Serbia, 1804–1918*, 2 vols, New York, 1976.
Popov, Nebojša (ed.), *Serbia. The Road to War*, Budapest, 1999.
Popović, Dušan J., *Beograd pre 200 godina*, Belgrade, 1935.
Protić, Milan St., *Radikali u Srbiji, 1881–1903*, Belgrade, 1990.
Purković, Miodrag Al., *Srpski patrijarsi srednjega veka*, Düsseldorf, 1976.
———, *Knez i despot Stefan Lazarević*, Belgrade, 1978.

Bibliography

Radić, Radmila, *Verom protiv vere. Država i verske zajednice u Srbiji, 1945–1953*, Belgrade, 1995.
Roberts, Walter, *Tito, Mihailović and the Allies, 1941–1945*, 2nd edn, Durham, NC, 1987.
Roksandić, Drago, *Srbi u Hrvatskoj*, Zagreb, 1991.
Rothenburg, Gunther E., *The Austrian Military Border in Croatia, 1522–1747*, Chicago, 1960.
Rothenburg, Gunther E., *The Military Border in Croatia, 1740–1881*, Chicago, 1966.
Shoup, Paul, *Communism and the Yugoslav National Question*, New York, 1968.
Simić, Andrei, *The Peasant Urbanites: A Study of Rural-Urban Mobility in Serbia*, New York, 1973.
Soutou, Georges-Henri, *La Guerre de cinquante ans. Les relations Est-Ouest, 1943–1990*, Paris, 2001.
Stanković, Djordje Dj., *Nikola Pašić, saveznici i stvaranje Jugoslavije*, Belgrade, 1984.
Stevanović, Dragomir, *Sura grobnica*, London, 1967.
Stoianovich, Traian, *Balkan Worlds: The First and Last Europe*, Armonk, NY, 1994.
Stojkov, Todor, *Opozicija u vreme šestojanuarske diktature, 1929–1935*, Belgrade, 1969.
Szücs, Jenö, *Les Trois Europes*, Paris, 1985.

Thomas, Robert, *Serbia under Milošević: Politics in the 1990s*, London, 1999.
Tošić, Desimir, *Srpski nacionalni problemi*, Paris, 1952.
Trew, Simon, *Britain, Mihailović and the Chetniks, 1941–1942*, London and New York, 1998.
Trgovčević, Ljubinka, 'Influenze esterne nella 'inteligencija' serba nel XIX secolo', *Rivista storica italiana*, CX/II, 1998.

Vlasto, A.P., *The Entry of the Slavs into Christendom*, Cambridge, 1970.
Vucinich, Wayne S., *Serbia between East and West: The Events of 1903–1908*, Stanford, CA, 1954.
Vujačić, Veljko, 'Institutional Origins of Contemporary Serbian Nationalism', *East European Constitutional Review*, 5/4, 1996.
——, 'Historical Legacies, Nationalist Mobilization, and Political Outcomes in Russia and Serbia: A Weberian View', *Theory and Society*, 25, 1996.
Vujović, Dimitrije-Dimo, *Ujedinjenje Crne Gore i Srbije*, Titograd, 1962.
Vukosavljević, Sreten, *Organizacija dinarskih plemena*, Belgrade, 1957.
Vukotić, Manojlo-Manjo, *Srpski san Milana Panića*, Belgrade, 1994.

Wachtel, Andrew Baruch, *Making a Nation, Breaking a Nation: Literature and Cultural Politics in Yugoslavia*, Stanford, CA, 1998.
Woodford, Susan L., *Balkan Tragedy: Chaos and Dissolution after the Cold War*, Washington, DC, 1995.

INDEX

'Serbia' and 'Serbs' are not entered. Serbo-Croatian letters are listed as follows: Č and Ć after C, Dj after D, Lj after L, Š after S, and Ž after Z.

Abdülhamid II, Sultan, 77
Adriatic, 2, 4, 5, 44–5, 81, 83, 86, 96, 150, 167
Aegean, 4, 96, 234
Agrarian Party, 132, 134
Albania, 2, 8, 15, 19, 23, 45, 49, 55, 64, 83, 85, 96–7, 108, 112, 120–2, 140, 146–7, 151, 164, 166, 170, 176, 220
Albanians: medieval Serbia, 4, 10; Ottoman times, 15, 18, 20, 23– 4, 30, 48, 67–8, 77–9, 83; independent Serbia, 84–5; First World War, 97, 101; interwar Yugoslavia, 119–22, 134; Second World War, 147, 151, 153; Communist Yugoslavia, 164– 5, 170, 173–7, 181, 186–8, 194; Milošević's Serbia, 199, 202, 218, 221–2, 225
Alexander Karadjordjević, ruling prince of Serbia, *see* Karadjordjević
Alexander (Obrenović), King, ix, 71–3, 79
Alexander (Karadjordjević), Crown Prince then King, 91–2, 98, 100–1, 106–8, 115–16, 123–9, 132, 135, 141, 229
Alexius III Angel, Emperor, 2
Alliance of Reform Forces, 200, 217

Allied Powers, Second World War, 145, 148–9
Altomanović, Nikola, 8–9
America, 76, 79, 86, 88, 100–1, 149, 160, 213, 215, 218, 223
Anatolia, 122, 234
Andrej, Bishop, 173
Angora (Ankara), battle, 11, 122
Armenians, 15
Arsenije III, Patriarch, 19–20
Arsenije IV, Patriarch, 20–1
Athens, 98
Austria, 19–21, 25–6, 29–31, 34, 38–9, 42, 45–6, 49, 52–6, 61, 98, 104–6, 108, 113, 139, 153, 163, 189, 228
Austria-Hungary: 59–60, 64, 67–8, 70–6, 78, 80–3, 85–6, 88–105, 108–10, 114–15, 119, 136, 165; dualism, 56, 60, 74, 86, 127, 132; *see also* Habsburg dynasty
Avramović, Dragoslav, 215
Axis Powers, 137–40, 149, 153, 209

Ba, 152
Balkan federation, 61, 164
Balkan leagues, 50, 55–6, 59, 82–3, 90
Balkan wars, 83–4, 88, 94–5, 188
Balšić, Djuradj, 9–10

Index

Banac, Ivo, 113, 166–7
Banat, 141
Banjaluka, 16, 173
Bar, 1
Bari, 4–5
Bayezid, Sultan, 10–11
Baroque, 23
Battenberg, family, 86
Becker, Jean-Jacques, 98
Bećković, Matija, 197
Belgium, 70, 235
Belgrade: 4, 11, 14–5, 18–21, 31–4, 49, 53–5, 65, 76, 81–2, 87, 91, 94, 100, 104, 107, 117, 121, 126, 139–41, 144, 153, 182, 188–95, 199, 202, 210, 216, 218, 220–2, 225; coup of 27 March 1941, 138–9, 142, 145, 165; culture and education, 42–3, 46–7, 58, 65, 74, 80, 85, 137, 173, 175, 178, 188, 214; Belgrade Fair concentration camp, 143; government, 60–1, 93, 106, 136, 162, 169, 171, 177, 219; sanjak, 26–9, 34, 37; treaty, 21, 28
Berlin congress and treaty, 64, 66, 68, 70, 76–7
Bessarabia, 108
Bibó, István, 234
Bismarck, Prince Otto von, 70
Bitola (Monastir, Bitolj), 78, 98
Bjelajac, Mile, 136
'Black Hand', 80, 82, 84, 90–2, 95, 98–101, 127, 135
Blaznavac, Colonel, 58
Bogišić, Valtazar, 71
Bogomils, 5, 9
Bonaparte, General, 28; see also Napoleon I
Borba, 134
Borkenau, Franz, 147
Bosna river, 1
Bosnia (and Herzegovina): 16, 29, 40, 45, 74, 78, 82, 104–9, 154, 162–3, 168–9, 172–3, 177, 201–3, 206–9, 211, 215, 232; annexation, 81–2, 87; Austro-Hungarian rule, 76–9, 87–92, 94–5, 100, 113; Croats, 76–7, 89–90, 94, 149, 177, 208–9, 212–13; interwar Yugoslavia, 120, 131–2, 134–5; Muslims, 29, 33, 48, 76–7, 89–90, 94, 97, 105, 113–14, 119, 126, 130, 140, 146, 149, 152, 166, 174, 209, 213; Ottoman rule, 22, 24, 53–5, 63–4, 67–9, 82; Party of Democratic Action, 203; rebellions, ix, 49, 63–4, 79; republic, 177, 179; Second World War, 140–1, 146–53; Serbs, 46, 76–7, 89–90, 94, 105, 114, 120, 125, 140–1, 146, 152, 154, 162–3, 174, 177, 207–9, 212–13, 215
Boué, Ami, 32
Boxer rebellion, 233
Branković: Djordje, 20; Djuradj, 11, 14; Vuk, 9, 10
Britain, see Great Britain
Brittany, 228
British Broadcasting Corporation, 152
Bucharest: Cominform resolution, 165; treaties, 30, 31, 83
Budapest, 58, 74, 104
Bukovina, 108
Bulatović, Momir, 195, 202, 213, 217, 220, 226
Bulgaria, 4, 12, 16, 46, 48, 55, 64, 67–8, 70, 78–9, 81–5, 95–6, 99–100, 103–4, 120, 140, 151, 164, 169
Bulgars, 53, 62, 68, 81, 113, 234
Byzantium, 1–8, 12–13

Carinthia, 55
Carniola, 55
Catherine the Great, 24
Catholic church, Catholicism, Catholics, 3, 5, 9, 14–5, 18–20, 22, 24, 45–9, 53, 63–4, 73, 76–7, 93, 103, 113, 130, 141, 160– 1, 173, 189, 221; Catholic Serbs, 113
Central Powers, ix, 94, 96, 104, 108
Cer, battle, 94
Cetinje, 20, 86, 107
Charles, Emperor, 100, 104–5
Chetniks, 146, 148–50, 153–4, 164, 174, 182
Christianity, Christendom, Christians, 1, 8, 15, 19, 23–4, 26, 32, 37, 48–9, 62–3, 67, 78, 83, 85
Church Slavonic language, 5
Churchill, Winston, viii
Cioffari, Gerardo, 5

Index

Circassians, 67
Cixi, Empress, 233
Cluj, 61
Cominform, 165–70
Comintern, 117, 122, 124, 134–5, 144, 154, 189
Communism (and anti-Communism), viii, x, 124, 142, 150–1, 154–5, 158–61, 163, 165, 173, 178, 185, 188, 190, 194, 200, 202, 205, 209, 211, 215, 229–31, 233
Communist Party (later League of Communists) of Yugoslavia, 117–18, 122, 131, 133–4, 138, 144–52, 154, 156–62, 165–8, 171–80, 186–7, 189, 192, 194, 196–7, 199–200, 206, 229, 231
Concordats, 93, 130–1
Conservative Party, 44, 49–52, 59, 69–70
Constantine VII Porphyrogenitus, Emperor, 1
Constantine I, king of the Hellenes, 96, 98
Constantinople: 2, 7, 11, 26, 28, 33, 36–7, 40, 50, 54, 56; patriarchate, 3, 5, 8–9, 21, 24, 30, 38, 67, 78
Constitutions: Serbia 1838, 37–9, 50; 1869, 58; 1888, 71, 79; 1901, 73; 1903, 79, 117–8; 1989, 203; Yugoslavia 1921, 117–19, 122–3, 127; 1931, 128–32; 1946, 154, 157, 168; 1953, 168; 1963, 170–1; 1974, 180, 185, 202; FRY 1992, 210, 223
Constitutional Party, 36, 41–4, 49, 52, 70
Corfu: Serb exiles, 97–8, 102, 106; Declaration, 102–3, 117
Corinth, 4
Crete, 54
Crimean War, 44, 49, 54
Croatia: Croat-Serb Coalition, 87–9, 96, 99, 116; Croatia-Slavonia, 15, 61, 74–6, 85–91, 94–5, 100, 104, 113; republic, 154, 158–9, 162, 166–68, 171, 174, 177–9, 186, 189–91, 196, 200–2, 206–9, 215, 228, 232; Croatian Democratic Union, 200–2; Croatian Peasant Party, 115, 117–18, 122–31, 133, 138, 140; Illyrian movement, 20, 31, 46–7, 49, 74; interwar Yugoslavia, 123–25, 128–9, 131–5; National Party, 53, 55, 60–1; Pure Party of Rights, 74, 90, 128; Rights Party, 74; Serbs, 30, 55, 74–6, 87–8, 114, 118, 124, 132, 136, 140–1, 149, 152, 154, 162–3, 167, 174, 177, 179, 186, 200–1, 207–8, 215, 230, 232
Crusades, 2, 5
Cvetković, Dragiša, 131
Cvetković-Maček Agreement, 132–5, 138
Cvijić, Jovan, 68
Cyrillic script, 5, 103, 174
Czartoryski, Prince Adam, 45
Czechoslovakia, 113, 175, 177
Čubrilović, Vaso, 134, 191
Čuruvija, Slavko, 220
Ćirković, Sima, 210
Ćosić, Dobrica, 175–6, 180, 188, 191, 204, 211–13, 216

Dachau concentration camp, 161
Dalmatia, 13–4, 31, 40, 46–7, 61–3, 74–6, 82, 85, 87–8, 90, 95, 104–6, 109, 114, 118, 132, 202, 230
Daničić, Djuro, 48
Danilo, Prince, 59–60
Danopoulos, Constantine P., 214
Danube, 1, 4, 11, 21, 25, 94, 168, 195
Davidović, Ljubomir, 124, 129, 135, 156
Dayton conference, 215–6, 218, 232
Dečani, 7
Dedijer, Vladimir, 92
de Gaulle, General, 231
Demeter, Dimitrije, 48
Democratic Opposition of Serbia, 223–6
Democratic Party: interwar Yugoslavia, 116–19, 122–77, 136, 156, 160; post-Communist Serbia, 203–4, 212, 216, 223–4
Democratic Party of Serbia, 212, 224
Denmark, 71
Dimitrijevic ('Apis'), Colonel, 91, 101
Dinaric mountains, 1, 14, 60, 166
Dinkić, Mladjan, 214

Dobrudja, 102
Dodik, Milorad, 217
Draga, Queen, ix, 73
Dragović-Soso, Jasna, 176
Drašković, Milorad, 122–3
Draškovic, Vuk, 189, 197, 203–4, 209, 212, 216–20, 222–5
Drin river, 2
Drina river, 8
Dubrovnik (Ragusa), 2, 4, 39–40, 106, 207, 210, 230
Durrës (Durazzo), 97
Dušan, Tsar, 4–7, 9, 31, 45
Djakovo, 53
Djilas, Aleksa, 194
Djilas, Milovan, 163, 168
Djindjić, Zoran, 212, 216, 218, 224
Djordjević, Dimitrije, 73
Djukanović, Milo, 195, 217, 220, 222, 235

Eastern Crisis, ix, 63–4, 66, 77, 85
Eastern Orthodoxy, *see* Orthodoxy
Eastern Question, 54, 83
Eastern Roumelia, 70
Edward III, king of England, 5
Egypt, 28, 41
Emmert, Thomas A., 10
Enlightenment, 23, 35, 204
Entente Powers, 94, 96–100, 103
Epirus, 3, 7
Esat Pasha Toptani, 97, 101
European Union, 208, 212

Fascism, Fascists, 128, 131, 138, 141–2, 158, 162, 223, 230
Federation of Bosnia and Herzegovina, 215
Ferdinand, Emperor, 47
Finland, 72
Filangeri, Gaetano, 204
Fisk, Robert, 220
Florence: 11; Union, 18; *see also* Uniates
France: 36–7, 45, 49, 60, 94, 96–8, 107, 111, 114, 131, 137, 142; French influence, 42, 52, 54, 56, 68–71, 79–80, 144; French Revolution, 25, 29, 228, 233–4, 236
Francis Ferdinand, Archduke, 91–2

Francis Joseph, Emperor, 89, 91, 100–1
Franciscans, 45–6, 48
Freemasons, 160

Galicia, 94
Gallipoli, 7
Garašanin, Ilija, 44–8, 51, 53, 55–8, 60
Gavrilo, Patriarch, 138, 161
Geneva: 52, 79, 99, 105; Agreement, 106
Genoa, 4
German, Patriarch, 173, 205
Germany: 54, 58, 68, 94, 96, 99–100, 111, 118, 131, 137–8; occupier in Second World War, 139–44, 146–55, 161–4
German settlers, 7, 22, 40, 47, 109, 114, 119, 140, 163, 230
Gladstone, William, 64
Goldsworthy, Vesna, 59
Gračanica, 7
Great Britain, 35–7, 41, 49, 54, 69, 80, 94, 96, 111, 142, 144–5, 148–50, 152–3, 160, 162
Greece, 23, 39, 45, 55–6, 71, 83, 94–7, 112, 164, 218, 221, 229, 234
Greek War of Independence, 32
Greeks, 15, 30–1, 34, 68
Grol, Milan, 156
Guy (Vid, Vitus), Saint, 9, 72, 112, 233, 236
Gypsies, 15, 34, 68, 140–1

Habsburg: dynasty, 15–16, 18, 20, 53, 56, 60–2, 64, 67, 81, 88, 91, 95, 99–105, 110, 139, 189; dominions, 21–2, 24, 28, 31–3, 35, 38–40, 42–3, 46–7, 85, 109, 113, 227; *see also* Austria-Hungary
Heidelberg, 58
Helen, queen of Italy, 145
Henry III, king of England, 2
Herzegovina, 18–9, 29, 35, 40, 60, 63–4, 76, 82, 120, 166, 174; *see also* Bosnia and Herzegovina
Hilandar, 2; *see also* Mount Athos
Hitler, Adolf, ix, 137–9, 142, 151, 205, 229
Hobsbawn, E.J., 62
Holbein the Younger, Hans, 14

Index

Holy See, 93, 130
Hoxha, Enver, 176
Hundred Years' War, 5
Hungary: 2, 4, 7, 11–23, 46–7, 56, 60–1, 66, 74–6, 81, 86–8, 91, 94, 104–9, 113, 115, 128, 133, 140, 153, 228; nationalities, 61, 75, 87, 94

Ianeva. Emilia, 214
Ibar river, 1
Iceland, 72
Independent Democratic Party, 123, 125, 132, 138, 160
Independent Radical Party, 79–80, 94, 101, 116, 124
Independent State of Croatia, 140–1, 143, 146–7, 149–50, 153, 162, 182, 189, 201, 230
Innocent IV, Pope, 7
International Monetary Fund, 186, 196
Islam, 14–15, 21, 23–4, 26, 29, 77; *see also* Muslims
Istria, 95, 230
Italy: 54, 82–3, 85, 111–12, 121–2, 126, 128, 130–1, 163, 168, 218, 221; Risorgimento, 52, 55, 62; First World War, 96–100, 103–8; Second World War, 138–41, 145–8, 150
Izetbegović, Alija, 215

Jackson, Marvin R., 31
Jagodić, Miloš, 68
Jajce, 151
Janissaries, 21, 28–9, 34, 39
Japan, 138
Jasenovac concentration camp, 141
Jellačić, General, 47
Jerusalem, 5
Jevtić, Bogoljub, 129–31
Jews, 15, 24, 34, 63, 68, 80, 113, 137, 140–1, 143
Jihad, 29–30, 32
Jonah, Prophet, 236
Joseph II, Emperor, 24
Jovanović, Slobodan, 134, 145
Jović, Borisav, 232
Jović, Dejan, 178
Judah, Tim, 98

Kajmakčalan, battle, 98
Kállay, Benjámin, 76
Karadžić, Radovan, ix, 208, 213, 217
Karadžić, Vuk, 35, 46–8
Karadjordjević: dynasty, 41, 51, 57, 79, 101, 103; Prince Alexander, 41, 44, 49; *see also* Peter I
Karageorge, 29–33, 79
Kardelj, Edvard, 163, 171–2, 178, 180, 183–4, 189, 193
Karlowitz (Karlovci): treaty, 20; *see also* Sremski Karlovci
Knolles, Richard, 17
Kočović, Bogoljub, 84, 113–14, 154
Kolubara, battle, 94
Kon, Geca, 137
Korošec, Anton, 115, 126–7
Kosovo: 2, 8–9, 15, 19–20, 23, 31, 68, 72, 78, 83–4, 98, 114–15, 119–22, 126, 134, 136, 140, 146–7, 151, 153, 164, 191–2, 231– 2; autonomous province, 154, 156, 165–6, 168–70, 173–7, 181, 185–8, 195, 199, 202, 204, 213, 218–24, 235; battle, 9–10, 16– 17, 31, 72, 83, 92, 155, 165, 188, 197, 227, 234, 236; cult, ix, 23–4, 40, 72, 83, 85, 90, 92, 97, 99, 138, 188, 197, 231; Kosovo Democratic Alliance, 202; Kosovo Liberation Army, 218– 21; Serbs, 146–7, 151, 165, 174, 176, 181, 186–8, 191–2, 199, 205, 221
Koštunica, Vojislav, 212, 224–6
Kotor (Cattaro), 12, 104, 106
Kragujevac: execution of hostages, 143; ordnance factory, 66
Krajina: 162–3, 177, 200–1, 206, 208; Republic of Serbian Krajina, 202, 212–13; *see also* Military Border
Krivokapić-Jović, Gordana, 114
Krleža, Miroslav, 137
Kruševac, 9, 11, 72
Kukuljević-Sakcinski, Ivan, 48
Kurdistan, 49

Lampe, John R., 31, 62
Land reforms, 119–20, 163–4
Latin Monetary Union, 70
Latin script, 103, 174

248 *Index*

Lazar, Prince: 8–10, 12, 72; cult, 16–17, 19, 23, 192, 197
League of Communists, *see* Communist Party
League of Nations, 121, 137
Lederer, Ivo, 114
Lees, Lorraine M., 167
Leopold I, Emperor, 20
Liberal Party, 44, 47, 49–52, 57–9, 61, 68–71, 79, 116
Lika, 120
Lilić, Zoran, 213, 216
London: treaty, 96, 99, 103; Yugoslav exiles First World War, 98–9, Second World War, 159
Louis XIV, king of France, 19
Luxembourg, 235
Ljotić, Dimitrije, 141–2, 153, 160
Ljubljana, 115, 136, 199

Macedonia: 4, 12, 14, 16, 19, 23–4, 48, 55, 64, 67–8, 71, 78–9, 82–4, 96, 103, 140, 151–2, 169, 230; Internal Macedonian Revolutionary Organization, 82; 'Southern Serbia', 115, 117, 119–21, 134, 136; republic, 154, 159, 161, 164, 168, 174, 186–7, 202, 205, 209, 220; Macedonian Front, 96–8, 100–1, 103–4; Macedonian Orthodox Church, 161, 169, 174, 205, 208
Macedonians, 85, 95, 113–14, 119, 126, 133, 170
Maček, Vladko, 127–33, 139–40
Magyars, 109, 114, 119, 170
Makarije, Patriarch, 16
Manasija, 11
Maritsa, battle, 8
Marko, King (or *Kraljević*), 8–9, 28
Marković, Ante, 196, 199–200, 206, 208, 217
Marković, Mira, 215
Marseilles, assassination of King Alexander, 129
Mathias Corvinus, King, 14
Marxism, 168, 171–2, 184, 230
Mažuranić, Ivan, 48
Mehmed I, Sultan, 11
Mesić, Stipe, 207–8

Meštrović, Ivan, 85
Metohija, 86, 120, 159, 181
Mićunović, Dragoljub, 204
Migrations, Great, 20–1
Mihailović, General, 144–5, 148–53, 159–60, 162, 164, 189, 212, 224
Mihailović, Vojislav, 224
Milan, Prince then King, 58–9, 67–8, 70–1
Mileševo, 7–8, 18
Miletić, Svetozar, 61
Military Border (Militärgrenze, Vojna Krajina), 18, 22–3, 29, 40, 46, 49, 61–2, 74–5, 88, 114, 120, 141, 162; *see also* Krajina
Miloš Obrenović I, *see* Obrenović dynasty
Milošević, Slobodan, ix, 190, 192–206, 208–26, 231–3, 235–6
Milutinović, Milutin, 217
Mitrović, Andrej, 210
Mitrovica (Kosovska Mitrovica), 147, 221
Mladić, General, ix, 209
Mohács, battle, 14
Montenegro: 12, 16, 19–20, 24, 29, 39–40, 42, 45, 48–9, 56, 59–60, 63–4, 66–7, 71, 73–4, 78, 82–6, 91, 94, 96–7, 100, 105, 107, 112–15, 117, 119–20, 133–4, 136, 140, 145, 147, 151–3, 158–9, 162–3, 166, 169, 174, 232, 235; republic, 143, 159, 166, 168, 174, 186–7, 194–5, 197, 202, 207, 209, 212–13, 217, 219–24; Montenegrin Committee for National Unification, 100, 107
Montenegrins, 159, 162–3, 166–7, 174, 176, 200, 206, 222
Morava river, 2, 4, 99, 120, 168
Moscow: 169; Radić in, 124–5
Mount Athos, 2–3, 9
Mount Sinai, 4–5
Mrnjavčević: Uglješa and Vukašin, 8; Marko, *see* King Marko
Munich, 58
Murad I, Sultan, 9–10
Muslims: 15, 21, 23–4, 26, 28–31, 33, 48, 62–4, 67, 73–4, 76, 78, 83–5, 103, 109, 113–15, 120, 122, 147–8, 150,

Index

222; Muslim political parties in Yugoslavia, 118–20, 122, 126, 129–30, 132, 138–9; see also Islam

Napoleon I, 30, 39, 42, 46
Napoleon III, 54
Naša reč, 178
National Council of the Slovenes, Croats and Serbs, 104–8, 115, 119, 126
Nazism, Nazis, 138, 142, 160
Nedić, General, 141–3, 150, 152–3, 160
Nemanja, 2; see also Saint Simeon
Nemanjic dynasty, viii, 3–12, 16, 86, 227
Netherlands, 235
Neubacher, Herman, 150–1
Nicaea, 3
Nicholas, Saint, 5
Nicholas, Prince then King, 60, 73, 79, 85–6, 97, 100, 107, 133, 145
Nietzsche, Friedrich, 90
Nikezić, Marko, 172
Niš: 11, 19, 21, 65, 68, 94–6, 99, 216; Declaration, 95, 103
North Atlantic Treaty Organization: 215, 218–9, 222–5, 234; war against FRY, 219–24
Norway, 72, 111
Novi Pazar (Ras): 2, 21, 48, 83; sanjak, 67, 82, 85
Novi Sad, 52, 61

Obradović, Dositej, 35
Obrenović: dynasty, 41, 51, 58, 73, 70; Prince Michael Obrenović III, 41, 50–61, 78; Prince Milan Obrenović II, 41; Prince Milan Obrenović IV, see Milan, Prince then King; Prince Miloš Obrenović I, 32–9, 44, 49–50, 58, 73; see also Alexander, king of Serbia
Odessa, 102
Ohrid, archbishopric, 1, 3, 5, 16–17, 20–1
'Old Serbia', 23, 33, 82–4
Omer Pasha Latas, 49
Orbini, Mavro, 17, 23

Organization for Security and Cooperation in Europe, 216, 222
Orhan, Sultan, 7
Orient Express, 66
Orthodox church, Orthodoxy, Orthodox, viii, 1, 3, 5, 9, 14–24, 46–7, 53, 63–4, 76–7, 84, 103, 113, 121, 130, 132, 140, 142, 147, 161, 173–4, 179, 205, 234
Otpor student movement, 224
Ottoman empire and rule, Ottomans: 4, 7–33, 35, 43–6, 48–9, 52–6, 59–64, 67–8, 74, 76–8, 81–3, 85, 95, 113, 119, 155, 187, 227– 9; Porte, 15, 21, 23, 29–34, 36–7, 41, 43–4, 46, 49–50, 52, 54, 78

Paleologus dynasty, 8
Palestine, 143
Panić, Milan, 211–13
Paris: 42, 58–60, 69, 98–9, 106; congress and treaty, 49; peace conference, 111, 115; Bosnia and Herzegovina peace settlement, 215
Partisans, 146–55, 157, 162–4, 166–7, 175, 180, 193, 206, 219
Passarowitz (Požarevac), treaty, 20
Pašić, Nikola, 71, 85, 90–1, 94–5, 98–101, 106–7, 109, 111, 115, 117–18, 123–5, 127, 232
Paul, Prince, 129–32, 138, 165
Pavelić, Ante, 128, 140, 162
Pavić, Milorad, 189
Pavković, General, 225–6
Pavle, Patriarch, 205, 210, 221
Peć: 9, 11, 20; patriarchate, 16–22, 24, 86
People's Liberation Army, 149, 153
People's Front, 154, 157
Perišić, General, 216, 219
Perović, Latinka, 172
Pest, see Budapest
Peter the Great, 20
Peter I, King, 79, 86, 91, 97, 108, 123
Peter II, King, 129, 132, 138–9, 145, 152, 156, 166
Peter I, prince-bishop of Montenegro (Saint Peter of Cetinje), 40
Peter II, prince-bishop of Montenegro, 40, 47–8, 59

250　Index

Petrović-Njegoš dynasty, 40, 97, 107, 145
Philip II Augustus, king of France, 2
Philip VI, king of France, 5
Pichler, Bishop, 173
'Pig War', 81
Plašinci, 22
Plumb, J.H., viii
Podgorica, 107
Poland, 19, 45, 113, 228
Politika, 137
Popović, Danko, 189
Prague, 144
Pribićević, Svetozar, 87, 106, 116, 118, 123–4, 126
Priština (Prishtinë), 9, 147, 186, 221
Prizren, League, 77
Progressive Party, 69–72, 79, 94, 101, 116
Protić, Stojan, 106, 115, 118
Provence, 228
Prussia, 56
Purković, Miodrag Al., 11

Radical Party, 59, 69–73, 79–80, 85, 91, 100, 116–17, 119, 122–8, 130–1, 135, 156, 160
Radić, Stjepan, 117, 123–7
Rambouillet, conference, 218
Ranke, Leopold von, 29
Ranković, Aleksandar, 163, 167, 171–2, 178
Raška (Rascia), 2
Ravanica, 19
Ražnatović ('Arkan'), Željko, 213, 223
Renaissance, 11
Rijeka (Fiume), 87
Ristić, Jovan, 58
Romania, 30, 34, 49, 54, 56, 76, 95, 108, 113, 133, 229
Romanticism, 35, 40, 58
Rome, 1–2, 4, 11, 18, 53, 99
Rudnik, 8
Rugova, Ibrahim, 202, 218
Russia: 30–2, 36–41, 45–6, 49, 52, 54, 56, 58–9, 64, 67, 69, 71, 73, 80, 83, 94, 100–2, 144, 152, 166; Russian Revolution, 102, 104, 115; 'White' Russian émigrés, 121
Ruvarac, Ilarion, 72

Sabbas, Saint, 2
Sagas, 17, 72
St Petersburg, 36, 96
Salonika, 31, 78, 96, 98, 100–2
Sarajevo: 24, 90, 103, 115–16, 208–9; assassination of Archduke Francis Ferdinand, 88, 91–3, 112
Sava, Saint, 2–3, 8, 18
Save river, 4, 21, 143, 168, 195
Savić, Pavle, 191
Selim III, Sultan, 26, 28–9
Serbian Academy of Sciences and Arts, 188, 190–1, 193, 216
Serbian Bank, Zagreb, 76
Serbian Cultural Club, 134, 144, 191
Serbian Democratic Party, Croatia and Bosnia-Herzegovina, 201, 208, 217
Serbian Independent Party, Croatia-Slavonia, 87, 116
Serbian National Liberal Party, Hungary, 61
Serbian National Organization, Bosnia-Herzegovina, 89
Serbian Orthodox Church, viii, 4–5, 9–12, 16, 21, 24, 38, 61, 67, 78, 89, 113, 130, 138, 160–1, 169, 173, 179, 192, 197, 205, 210, 213, 216, 225, 227; *see also* patriarchate of Peć
Serbian People's Radical Party, Hungary, 75, 87
Serbian Radical Party (Šešelj), 211, 213–14, 218, 225
Serbian Renewal Movement, 203–4, 219, 223–5
Serbian Republic, Bosnia-Herzegovina, 208–9, 212–13, 215, 217, 235
Serbian State Guard, 141, 152
Serbian Volunteer Corps, 142, 153
Serbo-Croat (Serbian) language, viii, 5, 17, 31, 35, 46–8, 58, 78, 80, 84, 113, 147, 164, 170, 174
Serbo-Croatian Progressive Organization, Bosnia-Herzegovina, 90
Servia, Cunard liner, 69
Sharp, Alan, 93
Shköder (Scutari, Skadar), 2, 97
Sigismund of Luxemburg, 9, 11
Simeon, Saint (Nemanja), 3
Simeon, Tsar Dušan's brother, 7

Index 251

Simović, General, 138, 145
Sipahis, 13, 21, 28–9, 32, 34
Skopje (Üsküb, Skoplje), 5, 78, 83, 99
Slavonia, 14, 18, 46–7, 53, 82, 87, 105, 132, 203
Slavo-Serbian language, 23
Slovenes, 62, 85, 95, 100, 102, 107, 109–10, 113, 119, 133, 135–6, 138, 142, 150, 152–3, 170, 199
Slovenia: 74, 89, 95, 104, 130, 139, 150–2, 154, 163, 168, 171, 174–5, 186, 190–1, 195–6, 199–200, 202, 206–9, 232; Slovene People's Party, 116, 118, 126–7, 130, 132, 139; Slovenian Liberal Party, 116
Smederevo, 11–12
Sobat, Stojan, 23
Social-Democratic Party of Serbia, 79–80, 84, 117, 122
Socialist Party (formerly League of Communists) of Serbia, 203–6, 211–14, 218, 225, 232
Socialist Party of Yugoslavia, 152
Sofia, 144, 169
Sokolović (Sokollu): Ferhad Pasha, 16; Mehmet Pasha, 15–16
Sopoćani, 7
Southern Slavs, viii, 1, 17, 19, 29, 39, 44–8, 52–3, 55, 59, 66, 71, 73–4, 76, 81, 85, 88, 95, 99, 105, 108, 113–14, 117, 152, 195, 228, 235
Soviet Union; 126, 131, 138, 144, 152–4, 158, 162–3, 165–7, 175, 206, 230; Soviet (Red) Army, 152–3
Split, 115
Srebrnica, 11
Srem, 82
Sremski Karlovci: archbishopric of Karlovci, 22, 38, 47, 61; *see also* Karlowitz
Srpski književni glasnik, 80, 137
Stalin, 154, 164–8
Stambolić, Ivan, 189–90, 192–4, 223
Starčević, Ante, 74
State of the Slovenes, Croats and Serbs, 105–8, 115
Stephen the First-Crowned, 2–4, 31
Stephen Lazarević, Despot, 10–11, 17

Stepinac, Archbishop, 160
Stoianovich, Traian, 28, 42
Stojadinović, Milan, 130–1
Strossmayer, Bishop, 53, 55
Studenica, 2, 7, 31
Styria, 55
Suleyman II, Sultan, 15
Switzerland, 69, 79, 103
Syria, 49
Szücs, Jenö, 233–4
Šešelj, Vojislav, 203, 211–12, 214, 216, 219, 223, 225

Tamerlane, 10
Tennyson, Alfred, Lord, 64
Terzić, Velimir, 176
Thaçi, Hashim, 219
Thirty Years' War, 18
Thrace, 55
Tibet, 59
Timars, 13, 34
Timok rebellion, 70
Tirana, 121–2, 146
Tito, Josip Broz, 134, 144, 147, 149–52, 156–8, 162–8, 170–3, 176–8, 180–1, 183–4, 186–7, 189, 193–4, 196, 204, 229–31, 236
Topalović, Živko, 152
Transylvania, 108
Trgovčević, Ljubinka, 101
Trepča, 147
Tripartite Pact, 138
Tripoli, 82
Trumbić, Ante, 99, 106, 111, 115
Tucović, Dimitrije, 84
Tudjman, Franjo, 176, 200–1, 206, 212, 215
Turkey, 94, 98, 100, 120, 122, 228
Turks, 15, 29–34, 43, 49–50, 54, 58, 63, 67–8, 72, 84, 119–20, 228
Turnovo, 4
Tvrtko I, king of Bosnia, 8–10

Ulam, Adam B., 165
Uniates, 18, 21
United Nations, 177, 208, 212, 215, 217, 221
United States, *see* America
Uroš, Tsar, 7–8

252   Index

Ustasha (Ustaša) movement, 128–9, 134, 140–1, 144, 146, 148–9, 153–4, 162, 191, 201, 229–30

Vance Plan, 218
Vardar river, 2, 4, 8, 99, 120, 168
Varnava, Patriarch, 130
Velika Kladuša, 166
Venice, 2, 4, 7, 18–20, 23–4, 39, 227
Venizelos, Eleutherios, 96, 98
Versailles, peace treaty with Germany, 111–12, 139
Vesnić, Milenko, 111
Victor Emmanuel III, king of Italy, 86, 145
Vidovdan: see Constitution of 1921, battle of Kosovo and Saint Guy
Vienna, 15, 19, 34–5, 46–8, 56, 58, 60, 67, 74, 81, 93, 100, 104–5
Višegrad. 15
Vitezović, Pavle (Paulo Ritter), 31
Vlachs, 7, 34, 80
Voivodina: 20, 46–7, 52, 61, 75, 82, 87, 107, 109, 114, 121, 134, 136, 163; autonomous province, 154, 159, 166, 168, 170, 179, 182, 185, 194–5, 197, 223, 230; United Serbian Youth, 61
Vukovar, 207

Wallachia, 20, 34
Warsaw Pact, 175
'White Hand', 98
Wilson, Woodrow, 100, 103
Woodward, Susan L., 207
World Bank, 215
Wrangel, General, 121
Writers' Association of Serbia, 197

'Young Bosnia', 90–2, 134
'Young Turks', 81–3

Yugoslav Committee, 96, 98–9, 102–3, 105, 111, 115
Yugoslavia: 118, 131, 134–5, 139, 142, 144–5, 147, 151–4, 156–7, 164–5, 168–71, 175–6, 180, 186, 189–99, 201, 204–7, 209–10, 212, 228–9, 231–2, 235; Kingdom, viii, 128–9, 133, 139–40, 144, 149; Federative Peoples' later Socialist Federal Republic, viii–ix, 151, 154, 158, 170, 180, 184, 208; Federal Republic (Serbia-Montenegro), 210, 212, 218–22, 224, 232, 235; interwar Yugoslav armed forces, 115, 135–6; Yugoslav People's Army, 162, 193, 206–9
Yugoslav Division, First World War, 102, 107
Yugoslav Home Army, 148
Yugoslav National Party, 128, 130
Yugoslav Radical Union, 130–2
Yugoslav United Left, 214
Yugoslavism, Yugoslav movement, 40, 50, 53, 55, 58, 60, 62, 64, 74, 80–1, 85–91, 94–6, 98–9, 102–10, 127–30, 163, 170, 174, 177, 179, 229;
Yugoslavs, 179, 200, 205, 222

Zadar (Zara), 87
Zagreb, 46, 53, 55, 61, 63, 74, 87, 89, 100, 103, 106–7, 114–15, 125–8, 136–7, 144, 156, 171, 173, 177, 200
Zbor movement, 141–3
Zeta, 2, 9–10, 12–13
Zogu, Ahmet, 122
Zurich, 58
Žerjavić, Vladimir, 154
Žiča, 7, 11
Živković, General, 127
Žolger, Ivan, 111